"In a turbulent and tumultuous world, cha..g. ... . can bring fear, insecurity, even pain. Navigating these rough waters requires leaders who have identified their own convictions and commitments around God's unique purpose for them individually, and have summoned the courage to shift thinking and actions to experience deeper missional impact through the life of the local church. *Learning Change* shares the journey of a group of influential leaders who have grown through collaborative learning that is both personal and purposeful and catalyzes change internally and externally. Reading this book is your first courageous step toward personal and congregational transformation!"

—Tom De Vries, General Secretary, Reformed Church in America

"This is a biblical, hope-filled, and practical guide for Christian leaders who are ready to move past efforts to be heroic rescuers or organizational managers in order to experience life-giving transformation. *Learning Change* describes what authentic personal and congregational transformation looks like from the front-line experience of faithful Christian pastors. It's a biblically and theologically sound approach to personal transformation and congregational leadership expressed in practical, realistic ways. The format blends foundational concepts, stories, and resources with reflective questions that guide personal and corporate response. Leaders who allow God to transform their mental models, values, and practices will discover a powerful guide for experiencing and catalyzing deep change."

—Dr. James H. Furr, President and Professor, Houston Graduate
School of Theology; Coauthor, *Leading Congregational Change*

"For the past decade, Jim Herrington and Trisha Taylor, working with a cohort of pastors in the Ridder Church Renewal process, have sown seeds of change and cultivated transformational learning in the hearts and lives of church leaders. They have now gone into the field, gathered the fruit of their labors, and shared it with us. *Learning Change* is a beautiful and helpful resource, conserving of all that has been learned and of all that has been accomplished in the lives of pastors who have given themselves to the Holy Spirit, to one another, and to the process of transformation. This book invites readers to join in the feast and celebration, not simply by reading, but by engaging the process on their own. Each chapter offers compelling stories, inviting questions, and thoughtful exercises to help the truth about personal and congregational transformation become reality in the lives of pastors and those they serve. This inductive study of pastors' lives and growth will inspire and instruct those willing to engage the demanding, but rewarding, journey of personal transformation."

—R. Robert Creech, Hubert H. and Gladys S. Raborn Professor of
Pastoral Leadership and Director of Pastoral Ministries,
George W. Truett Theological Seminary, Baylor University

"A careful reading of the book of Acts, the Epistles, and especially the letters from John reveal that a key ingredient for the growth of the Christian community, both in number and in service, was the life of the community together. People in the first century witnessed something so powerful in the way that members of the church served God, loved each other, and cared for their neighbor that they were willing to risk their own life to join the Christian community. This is the power of discipleship. In an age when we falsely put too much hope in the power of leadership to drive the church forward, Jim Herrington, Trisha Taylor, and their team of pastors have rightly reached back to the origins of the church to discover the power of discipleship. They are hitting the center of the target when they examine the key problems of our post-Christian age and propose that the answer to problems of declining congregations, apathy, and spiritual despair will be found in radical obedience to Christ Mission through discipleship. Their book will help us get to the answers for our age and for ages to come."

—The Rev. Tony Campbell,
Assistant General Secretary for the Reformed Church in America

"Jim, Trisha, and their team don't just talk transformation. Anchored in the gospel of Jesus Christ, nurtured in relational community, and sharpened by good thinking, they walk individuals and congregations through change. I'm excited to see how this resource can bring further transformation to the church."

Dr. Chuck DeGroat, Professor of Pastoral Care and Counseling,
Western Theological Seminary

"The authors of *Learning Change* understand that profound change must root in individuals before it transfuses systems. Having observed the cycle in themselves as well as in others, they shepherd us into the remissioning work of the Holy Spirit. Their penetrating wisdom confronts the hard places and speaks peace to the unsettled. Transformation becomes a verb as we journey with them toward the authentic hope of God's church as the stunning bride of Christ.

I have witnessed the impact of the *Learning Change* principles on dozens of pastors from all over world. A team of professors and I stepped deeper into integrity and authenticity at one of Jim's and Trisha's Faithwalking retreats. If you will do the work, this poignant book will be God's evocative grace gift for the next chapter of your ministry."

—Thomas F. Tumblin,
Associate Provost for Global Initiatives & Academic Affairs,
Professor of Leadership, Asbury Theological Seminary

Jim Herrington & Trisha Taylor

LEARNING CHANGE

Congregational
Transformation Fueled
by Personal Renewal

Kregel
Ministry

*We dedicate this book to the courageous
community of leaders who helped create
the most challenging, loving, and life-giving
community that we have ever engaged.*

*Learning together with you has been one of the
greatest privileges of our lives.*

Contents

**Part 4 — Additional Tools for the Journey: Equipping Ourselves
for More Effective Leadership**

Preface

I told God that I wanted to run. I said that I felt like I had gotten stuck again in a congregation that I didn't fit or that didn't fit me. I was bitter. I said to God, "I am done. I'm leaving. This is not working."
—Michael DeRuyter, Pastor

*T*his is the story of a community of pastors who came together to learn whether real change was possible in their personal lives and in the lives of their congregations. This is the story of real people who were willing to engage in transformational learning with no quick fixes. These are our stories of hope that we want to share with you. Real change is possible. We know it. We've seen it. We're living it!

Key Players

Trisha Taylor and Jim Herrington

Jim and Trisha live and work in Houston. From 1989 to 1998, Jim served as the Executive Director of Union Baptist Association in Houston, and from 1997 to 2009, Trisha served as a therapist in the UBA Center for Counseling. Early in Jim's tenure, his leadership team conducted a study that confirmed what we all know today: Congregations are in rapid decline numerically, and they have increasingly lost their capacity to impact their communities and the culture. In 1990, eighty percent of Houston-area Southern Baptist congregations were plateaued or declining despite the rapid and long-term growth of the city. Even growing congregations were not growing at a pace that kept up with the city's growth.

Jim Herrington

Seeking solutions to these challenges, Jim and Trisha and many others partnered for over a decade, serving pastors and congregations in an effort to help them reconnect to their intended calling. They conducted a series of pilot projects, did a lot of pastoral coaching, and participated in ongoing reflection on their own experience with personal and congregational transformation. In addition, Jim coauthored with Mike Bonem and James H. Furr *Lead-*

Trisha Taylor

ing Congregational Change: A Practical Guide for the Transformational Journey; and along with R. Robert Creech, Jim and Trisha co-authored *The Leaders' Journey: Accepting the Call to Personal and Congregational Transformation.*

The Ridder Planning Team

Jim and Trisha's story intersected with a pastoral leadership initiative in the Reformed Church of America (RCA), generously underwritten by former Western Theological Seminary President Hermann J. (Bud) Ridder and his wife Lenora. The Ridder Leadership Initiative (now known as Ridder Church Renewal) began as a series of invitation-only annual events, with Lyle Schaller (1997), Max DePree (1998) and Bill Hybels (1999) as keynote speakers.

Jim was invited to speak in 2002, and he reframed the conference's format to allow participants to reflect on and interact with the content in real time. Jim's experiential model led the Ridder planning team (Keith Derrick, George Brown, Vicki Menning, Ken Eriks, Dan Gillette, and Lenora Ridder) to begin asking questions about the value of the one-time event model. While the annual conferences were attracting a great response, these leaders were wondering, "Was real change in congregations actually taking place?" In 2007, recognizing that transformational learning takes time, the planning team decided to move from an episodic format to a more intensive long-term process that engaged pastors of "reasonably healthy" congregations along with key leaders. Directed by a partnership that included Western Seminary, the RCA and regional synod, as well as Christian Reformed Church in North America (CRCNA) congregations, Jim and Trisha were invited to provide the leadership for this newly imagined process.

The Pastors and Their Leadership Teams

Seventeen churches accepted the invitation to participate in the first round of the Ridder Church Renewal process, and 128 leaders (pastors plus six to eight key lay leaders from each congregation) began to engage in a two-year process of learning. The format included five multi-day retreats, and guidance and support for practicing and reflecting upon their learning in their congregational contexts. Of the 128 people who began the process, 126 completed it—an astounding completion rate. Something different was happening in this process. The original seventeen teams were invited to participate in a second two-year module of learning, and twelve teams said yes. The typical cynicism and resignation experienced after church leadership events had given way to stories of hope and possibility.

The following pastors agreed to join a team that would take responsibility for working with Jim and Trisha to continue developing the Ridder content and resources:

Michael DeRuyter
Pastor, Midland Reformed Church
in Midland, Michigan

Drew Poppleton
Former Pastor, Heartland Community Church
in Lafayette, Indiana; currently, PhD student
at Fuller Theological Seminary

Nate Pyle
Pastor, Christ Community Church,
Indianapolis, Indiana and author of
Man Enough: How Jesus Redefines Manhood

Chip Sauer
Pastor, Community Reformed Church
of Charlevoix, Michigan

Jessica Shults
Pastor, Standale Reformed Church,
Grand Rapids, Michigan

John Sparks
Formerly Co-Pastor, Haven Church,
Kalamazoo, Michigan

Brian Stone
Formerly Co-Pastor, Haven Church,
Kalamazoo, Michigan

Hopeful Stories

These pastors also became the coauthors of this book, and it is their stories of real change in their personal lives and in the lives of their congregations that inspired its creation. We see *Learning Change: Congregational*

Transformation Fueled by Personal Renewal as the third in a trilogy, complementing *Leading Congregational Change* and *The Leader's Journey*, by taking the content of the first two texts and showing it lived out in practice, in community, and over time, in a wide variety of congregational contexts.

And there are more hopeful stories on the way. In February 2012, Western Seminary, through the diligent work of Keith Derrick, Ken Eriks, and Lee Ann Sotok, applied for and received a generous grant from the Lilly Foundation. These funds allow us to continue to share our learning with RCA and CRC communities across North America.

It is our great desire that every pastor and congregational leader who reads *Learning Change* will experience hope that real change is possible. Hope that, over time, congregations can be revitalized and restored to become centers of reconciliation and *shalom*, where fruitful and faithful missional living is central to their identity. Hope like Pastor Mike DeRuyter discovered as he engaged in this new way of learning:

> As I began to connect the dots, I could see that often my running was about my sense that things were not working and would never change. I felt stuck. As I began to see myself as part of a system, I was able to see that staying didn't mean that I was helpless or stuck. I could change. There was something I could do to get a different outcome.

In January 2009 we (Jim and Trisha) sat waiting for the first group of pastors to arrive from "up north" to begin the Ridder process. With some nervous laughter, I (Trisha) said to Jim. "I must be crazy to be taking this on. I mean, my life really works right now, you know? The kids are doing well and they'll be leaving home soon; we'll have an empty nest. Our marriage is as good as it's ever been. Professionally, I'm having a lot of success and I love my work. We live in the most comfortable house we've ever had. Really, why would I want to do this?"

I glanced over at Jim and saw that he had tears in his eyes. Quietly but intensely, he said, "Because, Trisha . . . you could have an epic life."

The silence gave me the space to consider the impact of Jim's words. I knew what he meant by an epic life. He didn't mean fame and fortune. Jim meant that I could have the life God created uniquely for me, so that I could live the dreams God has for me. In that moment, I knew that I didn't want to settle for anything else.

We invite you enter into these stories of hope, into these stories that demonstrate that you don't need to settle for anything less than the epic life God is dreaming for you and your congregations. There are no quick fixes, but when we are willing to commit to a different way of learning, real change is possible.

Introduction

*T*he enthusiasm was palpable when we decided to write *Learning Change: Congregational Transformation Fueled by Personal Renewal.* We were eager to share our stories of personal and congregational transformation in our own voices. We wanted to share (1) the core content of the Ridder Church Renewal process—the information we have learned about deepening our core values, recognizing and shifting our mental models, and the end game of faithful and fruitful missional living; (2) the new tools we have developed to become more effective leaders; and (3) our experiences of learning to learn in community. And most of all, we wanted to share with you, pastors and congregational leaders, our stories of real change that have taken place over time, as we committed to a new way of learning.

Our deepest hope is that you will say "yes, this is possible for me too"; that you will become inspired to form your own learning community inside your congregation; and that you will journey towards the "end game" we all desire—faithful and fruitful missional living expressed personally and corporately.

How This Book Is Organized

Learning Change is divided into four parts. The chapters in *Part One: The Keys to Real Change* are foundational to understanding the rest of the text. Chapter 1 invites us to dream big again and casts the vision for missional living. In Chapter 2, we define key concepts used throughout the book, and in Chapter 3, we convey our deep conviction that personal transformation must precede congregational transformation.

In *Part Two: Core Values: Reconnecting to Our Intended Design*, we dig deep into the values of integrity, authenticity, courage and love. These core values are central to our identity as children of God, yet without focused efforts at renewing our commitment to these values, we drift away from this identity. Each chapter shares stories about reconnecting to our intended design, the way we were created to be by God.

In *Part Three: Mental Models: Shifting the Way We Think*, we explore how the way we think affects how we manage ourselves and others in our personal and congregational contexts. Chapters 8–12 contain information and stories of hope about discipleship, creative tension, appropriate emotional boundaries, congregations as systems, and high performance teams.

In *Part Four: Additional Tools for the Journey: Equipping Ourselves for More Effective Leadership*, we include information and stories about practices we believe are critical to effective leadership: recognizing the vows that block us from responding thoughtfully; finding the courage to have crucial conversations; and committing to processes that help us become more accountable. We conclude with the vision of where we started: faithful and fruitful missional living expressed personally and corporately. It is our deep conviction that this "end game" is possible when a church becomes a learning community, engaged in practical and reflective learning over time, in and out of its congregational context.

Within each chapter, we've included:

- *Information:* Content, both biblical and theoretical, learned in the Ridder retreats and then practiced and reflected on in the congregational context
- *Stories:* Stories about our experiences with the content—what we learned and how we've been changed by our learning
- *Practice and Reflect:* Questions and suggestions for taking this information into your own congregational context, and then practicing and reflecting upon what you've learned
- *Going Deeper:* Each chapter includes resources to encourage further exploration of the subject matter

How to Use This Book Effectively

Learning Change is best read:

- In community, with a small group
- With an active stance, committed to working through the exercises and reflecting upon what you've learned
- With a journal in hand for personal reflection
- Over time—this is not a book to be raced through or read on a strict schedule
- With an open mind—see where the Spirit leads you
- In conjunction with the online resources available at http://www.westernsem.edu/journey/ridder

Let's begin the journey together!

Acknowledgments

R idder Church Renewal was born when a small group of people began to wonder, "What kind of system could support and equip congregations and pastors as they grapple with the kinds of challenges that face the church today?" Those early conversations included George Brown, Keith Derrick, Ken Eriks, Dan Gillette, and Vicki Menning. Later, Ben Becksvoort, George Hunsberger, Rodger Price, Steve VanderMolen, Wayne Van Regenmorter, Angie Mabry-Nauta, Rick Veenstra, and Art Wiers joined the conversation.

Over the years, others have joined the Ridder Sustaining Team, including Tim Rotman, Michael Kooy, Sherri Meyer-Veen, Lee Ann Vandyke, Jill Ver Steeg and Tim Brown.

About half-way through our journey, Kyle Small and Megan Mullen conducted a massive research project among participants in Ridder Church Renewal that catapulted our learning.

This book exists because of the hard work, commitment to excellence and spirit of adventure of the contributing authors. They embody the learning with integrity. They have captured that learning in their writing and share it here with authenticity and vulnerability. Their example inspires us daily.

The contributing authors are part of a larger community of pastors that also include Ridder Church Renewal faculty Scott Lokers, Andy Bossardet, Edie Lenz, Chad Schuitema, Scott Stephan and Marijke Strong. Others in the Ridder learning community are Heidi DeJonge, Kevin DeRaaf, Vance Elzinga, Bill Flavin, Tom Grabill, Taylor Holbrook, Dave Kingma, Mike Meyer-Veen, Sherri Meyer-Veen, Greg Town, Jeff Vandermeer, and Andrew Vis. These pastors have made learning an adventure of friendship.

As Ridder Church Renewal has expanded into 6 regions in two countries, we have been joined by strong advocate Martin Contant, Rick Droog, Chris Godfredson, John Kapteyn Abby Norton-Levering, Amy Nyland, Tom Smith, and Lyle Zumdahl.

This book is also dedicated to the memory of Adrian Van Giessen and Ben Becksvoort who helped to make Ridder a reality before they could even know what it would be. They left us too soon and their supportive presence is deeply missed.

Suzette Mullen Harrell read the first draft of this book and offered invaluable feedback that made it a much better resource.

Shawn Vander Lugt and the team at Kregel Publications were gener-ous, thorough, and deeply encouraging. They made everything about the book better.

Lee Ann Sotok has consistently made Ridder a place of welcome and hospitality, while also making all the details work. We're forever grateful for her.

Chris DeVos started as a participant and eventually joined the staff at Western Seminary where he gave faithful, effective oversight that helped this function as a true collaborative partnership between denominations, seminary, synods and local congregations.

Before Ridder Church Renewal even existed, Herman "Bud" and Lenora Ridder were working to equip pastors for the work of the Church, sharing their resources and dreaming dreams that in large measure gave birth to this community of practice that now exists across the United States and in Canada.

Finally, the work that we do is supported and deeply encouraged by our spouses, Betty Herrington and Craig Taylor. They are our most avid fans and our first and most important learning community.

To all of these and many more, we are deeply grateful!

Part 1
The Keys to Real Change

When we began this journey together, we had no idea where our learning would take us. We knew that our congregations needed to change, but we didn't realize how much we would change along the way. We knew that we needed to learn some new things, but we didn't know that first we would have to learn *how* to learn.

In Part One, we share what we learned and how we learned it, and what we still have left to learn. We invite you to learn along with us.

Chapter 1
Fully Alive: God's Dream For Us

Brian Stone

> *I dream of a community that will not settle for good enough, or for the kingdoms of our hands, but will tirelessly fight for the kingdom of God in our neighborhoods, our city, our country and to the ends of the world.*
>
> —Nate Pyle

> *I dream of missional life—a life where fear, doubts, masks, and surface relationships are no longer necessary—a life where I live what I believe, that my child, my family, and others who meet me might learn not by preaching but by example.*
>
> —Edie Pekich Lenz

I was born with a dream inside me. So were you. We were designed to dream of the epic life God created us for—the abundant life, the fully human, fully alive life that Jesus lived.

Along the way, we exchanged that dream for a seriously compromised version, characterized by the pursuit of comfort and convenience—the pursuit of the American Dream. We wanted to learn to dream again, to hear the call to join God in bringing *shalom* to our broken world.

*E*very person is born with a God-sized dream inside them. We were designed to dream of the epic life God created us for—the abundant, fully human, and fully alive life that Jesus lived. This is the life we were created to live, and when we are living in this way, our congregations and communities are being transformed into places of mission, and fruitful and faithful living.

As church leaders, it's easy to forget our dreams and move away from our true calling. Do you remember your dreams? When I was little, I pinned a towel around my neck like a cape and dreamed of being Superman. As a teenager, I dreamed of being a rock star. As a college student, I dreamed of being the kind of English teacher with whom students would clamor to study. Reconnecting with our childhood dreams helps us ignite our imaginations and allow ourselves to go to the "what ifs" and "could it bes" we all possess. Connecting to our childhood dreams helps us set aside the tyranny of congregational maintenance and opens up a spiritual space where we allow God to show us once again the full life he is calling us to. God created you full of potential and to dream big dreams for the Kingdom!

Practice and Reflect

So, I invite you to stop and set aside some time (an hour would be ideal) to get away and remember with God the dreams you had as a child and adolescent. It might feel hard to find the time. You might need to cancel a meeting. You'll definitely need to turn off your computer and your smartphone. Take your journal, your Bible, and go someplace where you won't be disturbed or distracted. You can pray this prayer, or one like it, and then quietly sit with God and remember. Journal whatever God brings to you.

Holy Spirit, I invite you into this space with me. It has been _____ years since I have allowed myself to remember the dreams you planted in my heart long ago. Would you remind me of those dreams? Give me the courage to imagine them again.

When I did this exercise and remembered my dreams to be a superhero, a rock star, and the world's best teacher. I was struck that I had a deep desire to have an impact in the world and to influence others—even when I was young! In that moment, God again stirred up in me a dream to make a significant impact for the Kingdom.

Dreaming Differently

Somewhere along the way, we stopped dreaming. We went from having big dreams about how we would have influence and change the world to settling and buying into the lie that we couldn't make a difference.

Some of us got hurt along the way. We were told, taught, or otherwise bought into the lie that we weren't good enough, smart enough, bold enough, or creative enough. We believed these lies and began to form a life around this diminished view of ourselves. And we settled.

We gave up on our dreams of making a difference and settled for dreams that were small and safe. We decided to find a job, make a living, and play it safe. We began to seek our significance in the accumulation of things. We learned to dream what the world around us supported and encouraged. In Romans, Paul tells us that we "exchanged the truth of God for a lie, and worshiped and served created things rather than the Creator" (Romans 1:25).

Many of us settled or accepted someone else's dream for us. In either case we got something less than God's intention for our lives. What makes a lie so powerful is that it seems so right. Making more money to buy a better car, a bigger TV, a nicer house, and a smart phone with unlimited texting—we dreamed of these things hoping that they would satisfy us.

This lie permeates every area of our lives in ways we are not even aware. It even impacts the church. In the church tribe I am part of, it was often said in jest that some of the best reasons for being in ministry were the tax breaks, pastoral perks, a great health plan, and one of the best denominational pension plans in the United States. Really?

But the lie doesn't impact pastoral leaders alone; it impacts entire congregations as well. The church I serve is fifty-eight years old as I write this. It was started out of a dream to bring the gospel to a community in desperate need for transformation. Along the way, however, the dream lost to the power of the lie that success for the local church was found in the world's definition of success—increasing membership and financial stability along with the comfortable consumption of religious goods and services. As a church we learned to make great church members, but had no plan to make disciples who would impact their homes, neighborhoods, or workplaces with the gospel. We exchanged the dream of God for the American Dream of increasing ease and comfort.

Practice and Reflect

I invite you to stop reading again. A significant part of the learning journey is developing the capacity to tell yourself the truth. Please open your journal and spend a few moments in quiet. What does this last section stir up in you? Have you given up on your dreams? When did that happen? What hurt caused you to settle? Is there evidence that you have substituted God's dream for your life for the American Dream? Be courageous and write down what you hear.

I'm inviting you to relearn that the fully human, abundant life that Jesus calls us to is a life driven by a God-given dream. I'm inviting you to dream dreams that move you toward the calling that was yours from your creation. Are you ready to dream the kinds of dreams for which you are designed? Are you ready for dreams that propel you into aligning your life with God's mission in the world?

Dreaming Is Rooted in God's Creation

In the beginning of Genesis we read about God creating, out of nothing, all there is. Why? Why did God create? Why did God create You?

I have a deep conviction that God created the world because God is love and because God is on mission. In the beginning, God created the perfect environment for all to live and thrive. The restoration of this perfect environment is what we call the *shalom* of God, a Hebrew term for deep peace and wholeness.

With all the brokenness in the world, we can still experience this deep peace, this shalom, when we are fully alive, living into our intended design, and functioning as God intended. When a community—a family, a school, a business, or a congregation—lives into its God-given design, shalom is experienced. Wherever God's love is fully expressed and experienced, God's shalom is at work.

Created in the image of God, we were entrusted with responsibility for the land (Genesis 1:28–30), and we are called to be a blessing to the world (Genesis 12:1–3). Though sin marred God's shalom, God chose us to partner with him in recreating and restoring shalom in our own families, our communities, and ultimately in the world. How can we reconnect to this central purpose, this central calling to be God's partners in restoring *shalom*?

Practice and Reflect

Stop here and spend some time journaling. Where is your world marred by sin and brokenness? What part of the brokenness stirs your heart, your passion? What wrong do you feel passionate about righting? What brokenness calls to something deep in you? What would your family or community or workplace look like if there were movement toward the full shalom of God being expressed?

Challenges in This Book

As you read through *Learning Change*, you will be asked to take an honest look at yourself. The journey of living into your dreams is fueled by a growing capacity to tell the truth about what is actually happening in your life, what we call "saying what is so." We will challenge you to be courageously authentic about your life, your work, your family, and your community.

When I get challenged like that, all my defenses go on high alert, and I find myself stiff arming the Holy Spirit and others. I stop listening to understand, and I begin to disagree, argue, or feel shameful with a desire to hide who I really am.

We will challenge you to find time in solitude to reflect on what you are reading. This work will have more impact if you are aware of experiences that you have of shame, of not being right, of not being enough. With awareness and persistence, you can quiet those voices more effectively.

God does not reveal our brokenness or integrity gaps to shame us. Remember, "There is now no condemnation for those who are in Christ Jesus" (Rom. 8:1).

Integrity gaps are those places in our lives where we don't do what we said we would do, or where we don't live into the design for which we were created. God reveals those gaps to help us grow. It's as if God is saying, "I love you and I have a calling that I want to entrust to you, and if you are going to own that calling, this wound needs to be healed. Or, that integrity gap needs to be closed."

Finally, it is in the practice and reflection—the places in this book where we ask you to stop and write a journal entry or have a conversation or say a more authentic prayer than you've ever said—where your dreams increasingly come true. So in order to get the most benefit from this book, please make the time to do this important work.

Dreams Rooted in Who We Are in Christ

St. Irenaeus, who lived in the second century, made this observation: "The glory of God is a human being fully alive." In Jesus Christ, God has given us an example of such a fully alive person. I am operating with a classical, orthodox understanding of the person of Jesus Christ—that he was both fully human and fully divine. Jesus, as a human being, lived fully into the design of what it meant for him to be human. He is our example and model for who we are to be.

As a human being, Jesus had to do the work of hearing God's calling, just like we do. In the baptism experience, God speaks and Jesus's calling as the Messiah is fully imparted. Jesus immediately goes to the wilderness for forty days to hear from God and to clarify his calling. And as disciples, we follow the example of Jesus. He heard the Father's plan for his life and he followed it. We are called to do the same. When you realize that God has an intention for your life and you begin to live into it, you will experience God's shalom.

Central to every person's call is a sense of mission. You don't just have a job. You are not just pursuing a career. You have a calling to be on mission in the places where you spend most of your day. There you pray for and work for the coming of God's Kingdom—the full shalom of God. God's call for you will be expressed in your work in the world.

When you find that calling, you will know the full, abundant life that Jesus promises in John 10:10 where Jesus says, "I came that they may have life, and have it abundantly." Jesus intends for you to have a big life, an epic life. Jesus didn't come so that he could be the means to a life of greater ease and comfort or to help us get the next promotion or bigger church. He came to give us a full life. A full life is a missional life. Don't substitute his calling by taking on the American Dream.

The full life Jesus came to give us is expressed powerfully in John 15. We cannot live this abundant life unless like a vine, we are deeply connected to Jesus, the branch. When we are connected to Jesus, we bear fruit. We have the life for which he designed us. We become truly like him, fully human and fully alive.

Jesus says that those who follow him and become like him, will do "greater works that these" (John 14:12). Wait! Did Jesus really mean that? I believe he did. When you look around at your life you might say, "I don't know anyone who is doing all the things Jesus did, let alone greater things?" That's true for most of us. In unprecedented numbers, followers of Jesus have substituted his call to a fully human, fully alive missional life for a very small life driven by consumerism. What would happen if we began to recapture Jesus's vision for what it means to be human and began to live into that?

I'm challenging you to take on the possibility that by learning to dream again—learning to hear God's calling for your life—the promise of John 14:12 could begin to be realized in you.

The full life we were created for is found in Jesus. It is found in our becoming so much like Jesus that we begin to do the kinds of things that Jesus did. Your calling and my calling is not to be the Messiah. But like the Messiah, if I am connected to God, God will show me what my calling is. God will fill my heart with the dream of a missional life that contributes to God's shalom coming into the world where I live.

So what kind of dreams are you dreaming? Are your dreams guided by consumerism? Are they thwarted and made small by some experience of wounding from your childhood? Or are they dreams about living the abundant life that Jesus models for you; the abundant life to which Jesus calls us all?

Heal Our Land

When we settle and live small lives that pursue greater ease and comfort, and when our dreams become about making ourselves feel good, we stop becoming like Jesus, and the world suffers. So, in this opening chapter we have called you back to dream again. We've rooted that call to dream in the biblical narrative of God's mission to establish shalom over all the earth. We've rooted it in the biblical narrative regarding God's design of human beings.

In 2 Chronicles 7 we have a picture of what happens when God's people stop pursuing the things of God. It is a picture of famine. Look at our world today: high unemployment, skyrocketing divorce, unprecedented numbers of children living in poverty, a pervasive sex culture, failing schools, declining cities, homelessness and despair. There is famine in the land. In 2 Chronicles 14, God promises that if we, God's people, will repent and turn from our wicked ways, God will come and heal our land.

We have a deep conviction that when we live into the design and purpose for which we are created, God brings healing to the land. When we begin to live into the full life to which Christ calls us, God brings healing to the land. When we abide in Christ in such a way as to produce fruit, God brings healing to the land.

Created in the image of God, we are called to be a blessing. We are given authority to declare the shalom of God and demonstrate it through love. We are invited to abide in Christ so we might do even greater things. We are commissioned with a ministry of reconciliation and reminded that God's people will feed the hungry, clothe the naked, visit the imprisoned and care for the single mother and her family.

That is the full life Jesus offers us. It is this epic life that we are created to live as we step into the good works that God has already prepared for us.

Dream Big

How we see our future determines how we live today. If you know you will be going on vacation in a week, you begin to live toward that vacation. You begin laying out clothes to pack. You arrange for your mail to be held. You get your yard ready for when you will be gone. You get things lined up at work. You buy tickets for flights or program your GPS.

Begin to dream again. Begin to dream with God, through God's Word, and through prayer. Begin to invite God to shape your dreams. Begin to dream about your life of mission in the world. Not about what you will do, but who you can become. Not about the things you will accomplish, but about becoming so much like Jesus that those things happen naturally.

Begin to dream about your church on mission in the world. It's not about the buildings, your budget, the number of small groups, or a new sound system and lights. Dream with God about the people in your congregation and who they can be as they abandon themselves to the work of the Kingdom.

Begin to dream about your neighborhood, community and cities. Dream about what it would be like if everything worked according to God's design. Dream about the shalom of God taking over the broken places, the parts of your community that aren't working as they should. Dream about children learning to read, about caring for single mothers, families staying together, or eradicating homelessness. And dream about your part in bringing that larger dream to pass.

Dream big. It will shape the way you live now. Big dreams will increase your capacity for more of the best that God has for you.

Practice and Reflect

It's not enough to have big dreams. We must share our dreams so they can grow. Are there encouraging people in your life with whom you can share your dreams?

Don't rush. This isn't a test. It is about learning and growing and becoming fully human and fully alive in the pattern of Jesus Christ. In solitude, ask the Holy Spirit to speak to you about God's dreams for you in your context today. Some questions you might find helpful:

- God, what is your dream for the kind of person you want me to be?
- What gifts or passions have you given me, that when expressed, cause me to experience being fully alive?
- What wrong exists in the world that angers or disturbs me so much that I want to do something about it?
- What have I always wanted to do to make a difference but have been too afraid to try?

Questions like these can help you begin to reconnect to God's dreams for you.

I Have a Dream

As part of the Ridder Church Renewal process, we spent time reflecting and reconnecting to God's dreams, and then we shared our dreams with each other.

My dream is deeply personal and is birthed out of the redemptive work God has consistently worked out in my life. I remember the flood of feelings I experienced when I put my dream on paper for the first time—when I completed the assignment to write my "I have a dream" speech. I remember the anxiety I felt as I began to share it with others and eventually made it public to my congregation. Here are the three parts to my dream for my family, congregation, and the larger community:

I have a dream that with authenticity I will be able to lead my family into full-out radical obedience, that I will love, honor, and cherish my wife so deeply that she has the safety necessary to be the woman God calls her to be. Although I meant it when I described that dream, I didn't love, honor, and cherish my wife in the way I had hoped and promised and brought deep hurt and brokenness into my family. Today, however, Cathy is an amazing story of God's ministry of reconciliation and forgiveness. Not only have I been blessed to be by her side as she courageously brings reconciliation into the lives of others and ministers tirelessly to disadvantaged children, but I have experienced God's grace through her first hand, as God restores our marriage. Because many in our congregation embraced the concepts in this book, Cathy and I are part of a small community that walks with us and continues to encourage us to dream and live missionally.

I believe God is calling us to become the kind of missional disciples that make disciples; that we are being shaped to no longer be able to look at our community and context while ignoring the reality of what is taking place; that we are becoming the kind of faithful community that looks at the needs of this place to which we are called and says, "We can't live with that!" and actively partners with God in the re-creation of our schools, workplaces, and neighborhoods. Since sharing this dream with the congregation, we have launched three missional communities! One in a local elementary school, one serves children at a local mobile home community, and one serves adults, and their families, with developmental disabilities.

I have a deepening conviction for, and dream of, catalyzing a movement where the Church of Kalamazoo will become unified and mobilized around seeking the transformation of our city; that this is part of God's call on my life. Keeping this dream in front of me has allowed me to experience a ministry called *"Jesus Loves Kzoo"* grow from a handful of churches one year, to more than a dozen the next, to more than fifty ministries uniting together to transform the city of Kalamazoo! Can you imagine? Churches who normally compete against one another are coming together for one purpose—to love our community in Jesus's name.

Be willing to dream! It's what you were designed to do!

Going Deeper

We were designed to dream God-sized dreams and when we settle for anything less, we live small lives and abdicate our responsibility to be God's partners in restoring shalom to the world. To hear more of our personal and corporate dreams, go to http://www.westernsem.edu/journey/ridder.

References and Additional Resources

Eriks, Ken. 2003. *Purposeful Living.* Grand Rapids: Reformed Church Press. To view online, see: www.rca.org/purposefulliving.

Furtick, Steven. 2012. *Greater: Dream Bigger. Start Smaller. Ignite God's Vision for Your Life.* Colorado Springs: Multnomah Books.

Lutzer, Erwin. 2003. *Keep Your Dream Alive: Finding and Holding God's Vision for Your Life.* Ann Arbor, MI: Servant Publications.

Stanley, Andy. 1999. *Visioneering: God's Blueprint for Developing and Maintaining Vision.* Colorado Springs: Multnomah Books.

Daring to Dream: Another Story

The Ridder process has challenged and empowered me to dream a bigger dream for my life by crystallizing a picture of missional living as the church functioning and alive in all the places that people gather.

In one of the early retreats, we were asked to spend some time in solitude. We had heard a presentation that envisioned the possibility of all the churches in our city working collaboratively to impact the city for good. It was in that time of solitude that I really began to consider what it might look like for me to participate in leading that kind of a movement in Midland.

From that time of solitude, fast-forward several months when we were sent home to work on describing God's emerging future for our congregation. We were encouraged to change the question from, "How will our church be different in five years?" to "How will our city be different in five years if we are effective at our work as a church?"

The vision from that time of solitude and the work we did to envision our changes in our city changed the trajectory of my life.

Now, fast-forward five years—at a recent board meeting, we had a conversation that indicates the lasting impact of this work. Our elders were asking if I was focusing my time and energy on the most important things. It wasn't a punitive question. It was one that emerged from a vision of impacting the city. In that meeting we formulated a clear sentence about my role: "The elders of Midland Reformed Church want me to be a pastor to the city through the church." There is this growing vision within the life of board members and leadership that they can have an impact on their city, and that accelerates my vision because it's a shared vision.

So, the clear and direct challenge to live the life Jesus calls us to live inspired me deeply. I was also impacted by the amazing gift of the authentic community that has emerged with the Ridder pastors and team leaders in my learning community. I remember the night that Jim [Herrington] said to me, "You are designed for so much more." I was able to hear those words as words of love rather than words of judgment because we had shared so much together. I understood his heart, and my heart was moved by his love for and belief in me.

Then there was this magical moment with the group. As my cohort was concluding our time with Ridder Church Renewal, we had a time of solitude where each of us was assigned to write an "I Have a Dream" speech. Then we came to those gathered on the sixth floor of the library at Western Theological Seminary, and we read these speeches out loud. It was one of life's most memorable moments. None of us were famous. No megachurch or celebrity pastors in the room. Just me and my friends willing to take the real, personal, and public risk of dreaming about a big life that would influence our family, our communities, and our cities for and with the love of God.

That story is powerful to me as an inspiring stand-alone moment. It has even more power because I am—and I also see my friends—living into those dreams in very real and tangible ways.

—*Mike DeRuyter, Pastor, Midland Reformed Church*

Chapter 2
Defining Key Concepts

Drew Poppleton and Jim Herrington

Dreaming God-sized dreams and connecting to our calling as God's partners in reestablishing shalom required a different way of learning. This different way, "transformational learning," was about learning content through practice and reflection.

This chapter introduces you to concepts that were key to *how* we learned *what* we learned. We are also sharing some of the language and terms that we commonly used in our process and that you will find referenced throughout the chapters of this book.

*T*ransformational learning model. Learning community. Transformational learning disciplines. Mastery. Mental models. Saying what is so. Getting into the action. Current reality. God's emerging future. Faithwalking. To better understand our stories of real change, we provide here an introduction to some of the key concepts and terms that have shaped these stories.

Transformational Learning Model

To be a disciple is by definition to be a learner, and we knew that pursuing the work of discipleship would put us on a steep learning curve. The first thing that we had to learn was how to learn. Before we entered into the Ridder Church Renewal process, our primary way of learning was through acquiring information. We read books. We went to conferences. We filled in blanks. We put workbook after workbook on the bottom shelves of our bookcases. We often remained basically unchanged.

We needed a different way to learn, so we looked at research about adult learning and we looked at how Jesus facilitated the learning of his disciples. Both led us to a model of learning that included acquiring information, but also led us to rigorous practice and purposeful reflection. When we learned by doing and by sharing, something in us started to change.

The transformational learning model is not a new concept. Our understanding of the model draws from many sources, including the work of Chris Argyris (1992) and Peter Senge (1990). The transformational learning model *put into practice* is one of the central stories in *Learning Change*. The Ridder Church Renewal process was developed on the conviction that transformational learning happens best in an information-practice-reflection model with four key components:

1. *High expectations*—A clear covenant is entered into and honored, with all participants expected to "play full out" and take responsibility for their learning.
2. *In community*—Pastor and congregational leaders learn, practice, reflect, and engage further learning together.
3. *In and out of context*—New material is learned in a location outside of the congregational context, and the practice and reflection is done in the congregational context.
4. *Over time*—There are no quick fixes. In the Ridder process, a two-year transformational learning module is offered and second module of two years is also available, for a total of four years.

In Parts Two, Three, and Four of this book we share information and our stories about deepening core values, shifting mental models and acquiring tools that can help in the journey towards personal and congregational transformation. We've engaged with this content using a different type of learning model that has become a new way of life for us.

In traditional learning models, a student receives information from an "expert." The student passively receives the information into her brain with the expectation that she will call up that information in particular ways, especially when tested. We see this traditional model at work when we think that we can pick up a book like this, read it, and then act on what we have "learned."

We are convinced that is not the way adults learn. That way of learning may have worked in high school when you took a history class, read a book, and then aced the test. But it does not work for our purposes because in that kind of learning there is no transformation involved. Nobody reads a book about bicycling and then knows how to ride a bike. Instead, they actually need to straddle the bike, sit on the seat, and put their hands on the handlebars, and their feet on the pedals. They need to attempt that first ride, making adjustments in balance and speed. They need to listen to instructions and perhaps feel a guiding hand on the seat behind them. When they fall off, which they'll inevitably do, they'll need to reflect on what happened and receive encouragement to get back on the bike.

Similarly, if we are seeking to be transformed, we will need to practice a different model of learning. We call this the Transformational Learning Model (see Figure 2.1). The discussion that follows is a refinement of the learning process originally explained in *The Leader's Journey* (Herrington et al., 2003):

Figure 2.1—The Transformational Learning Model

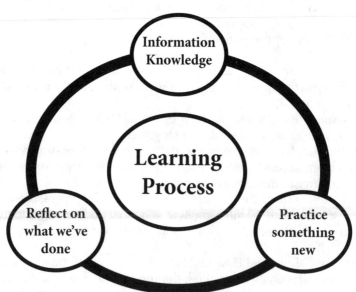

Information	We get information about a concept that we want to master. Our heart and mind (primarily our mind) absorbs theory associated with the concept.
Practice	We try to apply the theory to our relationships and our work in the world. Out of obedience, we "get into action" by practicing what we are learning, even if we're not perfectly prepared to get it right. Practice makes us teachable because it exposes those areas where we are deficient and need more theory/information.
Reflection	We reflect by engaging in spiritual disciplines that put us in a posture of listening—prayer, solitude, meditation—and by participating in authentic dialogue in a learning community. We listen to the guidance of a coach. We inquire into the experience of our peers. The learning community makes it safe to be authentic, because it is full of grace in the face of breakdowns and full of love in the presentation of the truth.
Repeat	Once we have "gotten into action" and reflected, we begin to see two things more clearly: (1) the information we need to learn in a deeper manner and (2) what we did not know that we did not know. This creates urgency that primes the pump for more learning in the "information" stage ... and the cycle repeats.

This way of learning is transformational because we don't fruitlessly spin around and around in a circle. Instead, as we circle around the material, we experience a spiral that drills deeper and deeper into the core of the material. The core of the material meets and impacts the very core of our being—it transforms us.

For instance, the first time I (Drew) heard the content in the Ridder process relating to "Family Systems and Emotionally Mature Leadership," I immediately recognized that my emotional *immaturity* was affecting key relationships. As I sought to put some of this information into practice and came back to reflect, I not only saw my need to grow, but also realized that I did not truly grasp the concepts. After revisiting the material, I felt more confident in my understanding, but putting it into practice only more sharply revealed my immaturity. As I reflected, I saw how deep wounds from my past were shaping my present and my future. Upon revisiting the theory, it became obvious that I needed to invite Jesus into some formative experiences in my childhood. It also became clear that I needed to "practice" being different with my family of origin. This led to further reflection and further engagement of the information and so on and so on. At this point, I not only have a cognitive understanding of the material, but I have also experienced transformation that allows me to live more as Jesus intended.

The traditional model of learning might be called "informational learning" because it involves the transfer of information or the reception of knowledge. But neither information nor knowledge transform. Experience transforms. That is why transformational learning involves practice and purposeful reflection through dialogue. *We have to actively experience the information, rather than passively receive it.*

The transformational model of learning is consistent with the way Jesus taught his disciples. He sent them out to practice (before they were actually ready!) and then they came back and reflected on what they discovered. In Luke 9, Jesus sends out the twelve disciples to proclaim the kingdom of God and to heal, and "on their return the apostles told Jesus all they had done. He took them with him and withdrew privately." Jesus's own life reflects this rhythm of engagement and solitude (Luke 6; John 6).

Learning Community

Throughout this book, we are going to ask you to experience what you are learning. Each chapter will suggest ways to get into the *action* of learning. We will also suggest ways to reflect on your progress in a *learning community*. If you do not presently have a learning community, your first task is to gather a group of peers with whom you can take this journey. This small group of peers will become a true learning community as you embrace the transformational learning model together.

For the authors of this book, the formation of a learning community has been one of the most powerful components of this process. Our learning community grew as we engaged this learning model during retreats. The content presented numerous opportunities to share authentically. As we shared, our trust grew, and we increasingly found that we could not learn apart from "saying what is so" in community. Since we could not be physically present on a regular basis, we subsequently expanded our interaction to private social media groups, video conferencing, and one-on-one peer coaching calls. In each case, we make every effort to process our experience authentically and share our learning proactively.

Transformational Learning Disciplines

With your learning community, you will engage in disciplines essential to transformational learning: new ways of listening and speaking, a posture of responsibility, courage, and accountability. These disciplines cannot be effectively practiced without a learning community.

Different Way of Listening

Transformational learning requires a different way of listening when we receive the information. Usually, adults listen out of a right/wrong, agree/disagree framework. This type of listening creates zero space for the Holy Spirit to create change. Transformational listening is a listening where we ask of everything, "What if this was so?" We "try on" new material. We are open to being changed.

Different Way of Speaking

Transformational learning also requires a different way of speaking. This manifests itself in three ways. First, we say out loud what we are "getting." This is a tremendous act of vulnerability because it puts our imperfection on display for others as we invariably share what we do not understand. Second, we seek to courageously make meaning from the results of our practice that empowers us. Unlike other animals, God made us meaning makers. For every event, we get to choose the meaning and the meaning helps determine our future behavior. If our initial attempts to practice are not fruitful, we can make that mean "I'm a failure," or we can make that mean "This is challenging and I have a lot more to learn." Notice how the second meaning is so much more empowering. Third, as we speak, we begin to teach others, which helps us recognize the shortfalls in our own mastery and then moves us one step closer.

Posture of Responsibility

In transformational learning, we take on a posture of responsibility. This means the learner owns the idea that it is entirely his or her responsibility to master the information. The learner is not passive in the process, but is active or more accurately, proactive. This is important because we live in a culture where we expect a teacher, coach, or mentor to tell us what to do next. But in this model, it is the learner's job to figure out the next step through a posture of responsibility. The learner actively creates from what they learn rather than waiting for a leader to tell them what comes next.

Courage

We need tremendous courage in order to see the fruit of transformational learning. Transformation assumes we are stepping into uncharted territory and thus, most transformational learning leads people through a "tunnel of chaos." This is a place of darkness and ambiguity much like the Israelites' trek through the wilderness in Exodus 14–18 where things feel uncomfortable and we desire the old ways. We need to persevere through this phase in order to achieve breakthrough and end up in a new and better place. Often, this courage comes as we lean heavily on God and our learning community.

Accountability

Transformational learning requires accountability because (1) we are only transformed when we are held accountable to the mastery of the material, and (2) our reflection becomes dramatically more fruitful when a coach or accountability partner asks us hard questions and holds up a mirror to our lives. If we do the "Reflection" piece of the learning cycle by ourselves, our potential for growth will be slighted since alone we can only see a fraction of our full selves.

Mastery

You will notice that we use the terms "mastery" and "master" through-out this book. Mastery is a natural byproduct of the type of content we're sharing here. We're less interested in having you learn information about core values, mental models and leadership skills; we're more interested in you developing a new way of being. If we primarily cared about learning information, we might seek to be "experts." But since our learning is about a series of habits, behaviors, and a very way of being, we seek to become "masters" who have a high level of "mastery." You might be deemed an expert in calculus by getting an "A" in certain coursework, but you cannot get an "A" in love or courage or authenticity or generating and sustain-ing creative tension or discipleship. You can only develop those qualities within you. By mastery, we do not mean perfection. We mean a level of proficiency that has been intentionally cultivated over time and has re-sulted in a high level of skill or character.

Also, mastery is the naturally occurring result of the transformational learning model. The very goal of the learning model is transformation, not expertise. As we circle around the material, we grow in our mastery. The very way we learn helps us internalize the content such that we come to "own" it, and it comes to "own" us. Returning to the example of bike riding:

> Learning any new behavior is like learning to ride a bicycle. Un-til we see someone riding one, we are *unconsciously incompetent*; we do not know how to ride one and we do know that we cannot. Once we see someone cruising effortlessly down the road on a ten-speed, however, things change. We become *consciously incompetent*. We now know two things: there is such a thing as a bicycle, and we do not know how to ride one. At the next stage of learning we become *consciously competent*. We have to focus hard on balancing, steering, and pedaling. We give all our atten-tion to the task, and although we do not present an elegant ex-ample, we are doing it. Over time, our muscles and brains learn the new skills. Eventually, we cruise effortlessly down the road, *unconsciously competent*, doing without thinking the thing we once could not do at all (Herrington et al., 2003, p. 147).

We're calling this level of unconscious competence "mastery." This is not just the acquisition of a new behavior, but an entirely new way of being. Actions that once required keen awareness and artless mechanics, no longer require conscious attention, but become automatic. While "expertise" may be the end result of learning information, "mastery" is the natural end-result of learning new skill sets and values. We have a level of transformational learning that is so full of integrity that we actually become who God created us to be.

Over and over again, we have experienced this phenomenon. Every pastor in our learning community could tell a story about developing a different way of being in the face of resistance and anxiety. At first, we only saw ourselves in the rear-view mirror and had to go back and clean up the messes created by our anxious reactions. Later, we saw ourselves in the present moment and had to consciously take a deep breath and choose to be different. And finally, we experienced someone else's anxiety, and without consciously thinking much at all, we found ourselves responding calmly, according to our deepest held values.

Mastery Requires Practice

In sports, music, art, and science, we practice, practice, practice. Yet, in our effort to master the art of living in the way of Jesus, we somehow lose sight of the need for practice.

Practice, by definition, assumes we will mess up. Practice assumes that mistakes *will* happen and that we will learn from those mistakes. Yet, there are so few places in our lives where we leave room for mistakes—for our own mistakes and for the mistakes of others. This is tragic because the process of becoming fully human, of mastering the art of living like Jesus, the Fully Human One, first requires us to acknowledge that we are *not* fully human at the present time. It requires us to be okay with not being competent even though "always being competent" is an image that so very many of us try to project.

"Always being competent" cannot be an expectation when trying to master the art of living in the way of Jesus. And quite frankly, that's a lot to give up for most of us. We are sons and daughters of Adam and Eve. We like to hide our full nakedness (Genesis 3:8–10). We don't like being fully exposed, imperfections and all.

Ironically, it's in that exposure that we become whole, or at least stand the best chance of becoming whole. It's as we take on our lack of wholeness that we learn to be more fully alive as God intended. Practice is the process of taking that on. Practice assumes it is safe to fail because practice assumes we're not perfect, but we want to get better. We want to grow.

Practice and Reflect

If we want God to transform us, we will need safe places to practice. We will have to examine ourselves through questions like these:

- Do I create an environment for myself where it is safe for me to make mistakes?
- Do I create environments for others where it is safe for them to make mistakes, and they are actively encouraged, even in their failing?

The truth is I (Drew) am inspired by people who make it safe for me to make mistakes. My life is greatly enriched by those who realize that my relational skills are not polished because I am still practicing. They help me see that I am maturing, not fully mature, or entirely immature. They love me so much that they coach me through my mistake rather than condemn me, judge me, or write me off because of the relational letdown. Through them, I become more fully human as Jesus intended . . . and I love them for it.

Mental Models

The final key concept we introduce here is the idea of mental models, the focus of Part Three. A mental model is just what the two words convey. It's a model of how the world works that you carry around in your head. We are designed by God to have mental models. They help us generalize about the data we are experiencing.

A friend comes to your office and says, "I've got a headache." You respond, "Take an aspirin." That brief exchange illustrates the power of mental models. Both parties are able to use common terms about the situation and a possible response because of their shared premises (or models) about how the world works and how to take effective action in it.

A more complete definition comes from *Leading Congregational Change:* "Mental models are the images, assumptions, and stories we use to interpret our world and guide our actions" (Herrington et al., 2000, p. 111). Each of us has a long list of mental models—images, assumptions, and stories that we unconsciously carry around in our heads that inform our actions. You have a mental model of what it means to be a good parent or a good child and you act out of that model without thinking. You have a mental model about how to act when you are in a new place or when you are trying to win an argument. We have scores of mental models, and what makes them really powerful is that they often operate below the conscious level of our thinking.

We have mental models that inform us about church. Some people believe that a pastor should act like a chaplain. Others see her as a corporate CEO. Yet others see the pastor as the prophet who proclaims the word of the Lord. Each of these mental models leads to a different set of expectations about how to take effective action in the world. A church with a chaplaincy mental model of pastor would see his primary role as visiting those in the hospital and the homebound, conducting marriages and funerals and baptisms. A church with a CEO mental model would be focused on church growth and staff management. A church with a pastor-as-prophet mental model would expect the pastor to spend hours in her study because preaching is the most important thing she does.

Acts 1:6 provides an illuminating illustration of the power of mental models: "Then they gathered around him and asked him, "Lord, is this the time when you will restore the kingdom to Israel?" For three years Jesus had been teaching and demonstrating that his Kingdom would not be an earthly Kingdom driven by political and military power. Despite this, the disciples—who lived in a culture that held a deep expectation of a coming earthly King who would restore Israel to political prominence—filtered what Jesus said to fit their mental models.

When our mental models are aligned with our world in a way that our actions produce the results we desire, they are very powerful. When we do not align our mental models with our world in a way that our actions produce the results we desire, these models become like millstones around our collective necks.

A fundamental assumption that we make in our learning community is that our congregations have a set of mental models that no longer work. There has been a massive shift in our context. We were once a churched nation. We are now an explosively growing mission field. This shift has challenged many assumptions that we make about how to take effective action as a church.

When your mental models are producing the results that you want, you simply live into them. When they don't produce the results you want, the first temptation is to work harder. For decades, congregations in the United States have been in slow, steady decline. In the past two decades the rate of that decline has accelerated. (David Olson [2008] provides a detailed analysis of the decline.) In many of our congregations, the response to this decline has been to change the type of music or to look for the newest program or relocate to a community that is growing. None of these actions have changed the overall trends.

We must adopt a new set of mental models if we are going to reach this new missional context. That is easy to say but as the disciples demonstrated in Acts 1:6, monumentally challenging to do. Throughout the book, you will be asked to consider some new mental models for what it means to be a disciple and what it means to be church. Considering new mental models in the context of information, practice, and reflection with a learning community will make this challenging task more feasible.

Additional Key Terms

Saying what is so: Shorthand for being authentic. It means you express your experience as clearly and transparently as you can. This includes saying that you don't understand, that you are feeling resistant, or that you hold a different point of view.

Getting into the action: Because we believe that experience is what ultimately transforms, we frequently end every coaching conversation with a question: "What are you going to do about what you have learned and to whom will you be accountable for taking the action and reflection on the outcome?"

Current reality: A key component of the skill of generating and sustaining creative tension is developing a clear, shared and compelling narrative about the current context in which you find yourself. For the church, that includes both internal measures of success (attendance, baptisms, giving) and external measures of the community (demographics and psychographics). The congregation completes a process of analysis and reflection that gets the narrative about current reality clear and shared. This is an ongoing process that must be revisited over time because the context changes.

God's emerging future: A second key component of the skill of generating and sustaining creative tension is developing a clear, shared, and compelling narrative about God's emerging future for the congregation. Based on the analysis done in getting clear about current reality and based on prayerful dialogue about the mission of God in your context, you describe how the community will be different five years from now if the mission of God is achieved in this context.

Faithwalking: This is a spiritual formation process that incorporates the information, practice, reflection process described earlier in the chapter. It includes a three-day weekend retreat, a twenty-four-week small group process, and a leadership course. When a congregation joins the Ridder learning community, the pastor completes the Faithwalking work; and then parallel to the learning being done in Ridder Church Renewal, the pastor introduces Faithwalking to the congregation. The ultimate goal of Faithwalking is to equip individuals to live missionally in their neighborhoods or workplaces.

Practice and Reflect

1. Take thirty minutes to journal about the Transformational Learning Model we presented in the beginning of this chapter. What do you believe about how adults learn? What is your current model for learning? How does this learning model differ? What will it take for you to implement this model in your life, both in your learning and in your teaching?

2. Have a conversation with someone about your learning in this chapter. This exercise will force you to "own" the material and it will bring to the surface any places of resistance or doubt. Most of us did not really "get" this the first time. We had to learn to learn this way of learning and unlearn the old way!

3. Who will be part of your learning community? Who will take this journey with you? Prayerfully reflect on this and seek to gather a group of people before reading any further.

Going Deeper

In this chapter, we've introduced you to key concepts that have shaped our stories. To learn more about these concepts, we invite you to check out our online resources at http://www.westernsem.edu/journey/ridder.

References and Additional Resources

Argyris, Chris. *On Organizational Learning.* Oxford: Blackwell Publishers, 1992.

Herrington, Jim, Mike Bonem, and James H. Furr. *Leading Congregational Change: A Practical Guide for the Transformational Journey.* San Francisco: Jossey-Bass, 2000.

Herrington, Jim, R. Robert Creech, and Trisha Taylor. *The Leader's Journey: Accepting the Call to Personal and Congregational Transformation.* San Francisco: Jossey-Bass, 2003.

Herrington, Jim, Steve Capper, and Trisha Taylor. *Faithwalking Notebook 201.* 2013.

Kolb, David. *Experiential Learning: Experience as the Source of Learning and Development.* Englewood Cliffs, NJ: Prentice Hall, 1984.

Olson, David T. *The American Church in Crisis: Groundbreaking Research Based on a National Database of over 200,000 Churches.* Grand Rapids: Zondervan, 2008.

Senge, Peter. *The Fifth Discipline: The Art and Practice of the Learning Organization.* New York: Doubleday, 1990.

Chapter 3
Personal Transformation First: What Must Change in You?

Drew Poppleton

> *Why do you see the speck in your neighbor's eye, but do not notice the log in your own eye? Or how can you say to your neighbor, "Let me take the speck out of your eye," while the log is in your own eye? You hypocrite, first take the log out of your own eye, and then you will see clearly to take the speck out of your neighbor's eye.*
> —Jesus (Matt. 7:3–5)

Many of us started this process with the goal of getting our congregations (and certain people in particular) to change. What we learned is that personal transformation always precedes congregational transformation. That means that we have to focus on changing ourselves and let go of the fantasy that we can change others.

When we stop trying to change other people, we free up vast amounts of energy to focus on cooperating with God's efforts to change us. We may even see others begin to change in response to God's work in us. However, when we begin with the idea that we can change others, our efforts are doomed before we even get started.

*W*hen my wife and I came to First Reformed Church in Lafayette, Indiana in the fall of 2005, the church was in a paradoxical position. Five years earlier, the congregation had purchased thirty-six acres of land in an up-and-coming section of town. They had God-inspired dreams of being a beacon of light to all the families that would move into this area.

A sign on the property declared: "Future Home of Heartland Community Church," the new church name reflecting its future location adjacent to the Hoosier Heartland Highway. There was a palpable sense of hope. Yet, reality belied the hope. The current church building was listed for sale for the second time, with no legitimate offers. Only a year before we arrived to pastor the church, only sixty to seventy people gathered to worship together on any given Sunday.

For almost its entire history, the church had sustained itself through marriage and birth. Dutch immigrants helped plant it in 1888, and it was still mostly Dutch in heritage.[1] We rarely had guests on Sunday mornings, volunteers for the nursery often sat in the worship service for lack of children, one of our current deacons confessed he did not even believe in God, and any vital ministries tied to the community had long since run their course.

My wife and I were called as the new pastors of this church with the express purpose of leading the congregation to the new location. Our first decision may have seemed like a step backward to those who were looking on, but we thought it was imperative: We took the building off the market and focused on revitalizing the congregation. We adopted a mantra we repeated often: "Let's be the church before we build the church."

Notice the implication: We were telling our congregation they were not currently "being" the church. That is quite an indictment for new twenty-something pastors to levy on a congregation in its 117th year of existence. Yet, it very much reflected our thinking. We never said it out loud, but we doubted that we would ever build a new church building. How could we move forward with people who were labeled by one outsider as "stubborn old Dutch people who say they want change, but don't really mean it?"

How could we reach out when every Sunday was a family reunion? How could we make this move if some of the current leadership doubted God's existence?

Changing the Focus

I wonder if you notice the assumption behind all those questions? Or perhaps you noticed the number of times I used the words "they" and "the

---

1. In fact, in 2008, one extended family had a celebration of the two immigrants who started their American lineage in 1908. We were the only non-family members invited to this one-hundred-year anniversary. While there, I counted the number of attendees that went to our church: *thirty-eight.*

congregation" in the preceding paragraphs? I was operating under the assumption that *they* were the reason the church was not moving forward into God's dream. I bought into the thinking that said, in essence, "traditional, inward-focused churches have no clue and you're going to need to give them one." I believed the one who labeled the people as "stubborn" and "old" and "resistant to change." All the while, I began to subconsciously think, "If only I could fix them, then God would use us."

What I discovered, over time with the help of the Ridder Church Renewal process, is the futility of that way of thinking. While it may be true that the people of First Reformed needed to change in order to live into God's dream for our church, I could not change them. I could only change myself. If I always focused on other people, I never had to get my own house in order. Then, if the whole endeavor failed, I could continue to blame the failure on those who would not change.

When we were a year or two into our ministry and yet in the same paradoxical predicament, I came to see something very important: Instead of focusing so much energy on "fixing" these people, I had to take a long, hard look in the mirror. I had to own the reality that I was now an ingrained part of the congregational system and as such, an avid contributor to any dysfunction in the system. If I wanted God's dream for this congregation, I was going to have to change, not just this way of thinking, but my very way of being.

Personal before Corporate

We believe it is God's design that personal transformation always precedes corporate transformation. Moreover, we believe this corollary to be true: Corporate transformation is impossible without personal transformation. This is distressing news for many of us. We tend to see problems in the institutions as "out there" and think, "If I could just fix that mentality or that person or that way of doing things, then everything would be as it should be. Then we would see the Kingdom come." The assertion we will make over and over again in this book is that corporate transformation is impossible without personal transformation. Personal transformation must come first.

We will consistently ask you to stop looking "out there" and with God's help, start looking inside yourself. It may be painful at times. It may seem counterintuitive to you. And perhaps, as a good Christian, you may feel uncomfortable with the notion of so much time and energy focused on yourself. Try to hold those feelings in tension as you engage this book because we are convinced that we need to focus more on ourselves. Why? Because when we increase our own emotional and spiritual maturity, it has a direct impact on everyone around us. It is our own emotional and spiritual immaturity that is preventing our congregations and communities from reflecting God's design. Paraphrasing the second greatest commandment, we are to love others to the extent that we love ourselves.

Practice and Reflect

Please take out your journal and write the following sentence:

I am the number-one obstacle to the deep change that God desires in my family, in my congregation, and in my community.

Our temptation is to see all the other obstacles external to ourselves. "If my wife weren't so protective of our kids, we could use our house for more missional activities." "If the young people in our church didn't have their kids in eighteen activities each, then we could get somewhere." "If this older generation wasn't so stuck in its ways, then we could have a ministry to the young families in this neighborhood."

In each case, we identify an obstacle to the mission that is "out there." It is our contention that this way of thinking is the biggest obstacle to real change.

Look back at the sentence you just jotted down in your journal. Read it out loud (more than once) and let it stand in contrast to the preceding statements. What feelings are stirred up as you speak those words out loud?

I Can Only Change Myself

We don't promote this way of thinking as some pious form of self-flagellation. Nor are we seeking to riddle you with guilt—please don't read that sentence as "you are a terrible person." Rather, we adopt this way of thinking in order to focus on the one part of the entire congregational system that we can actually change: ourselves.

I can only change myself. I cannot change the people around me—I can only influence them through my way of being. I influence them by changing myself and my ways of being.

This living systems concept will be explained in greater detail in later chapters, but here's the basic idea we want to introduce now: If the congregational system is not getting the results I want, the first fact I need to acknowledge is that I am part of the system. Thus, I am—at least in part—responsible for creating the results the system is currently getting. If I want the results to change, and if I am the only part of the system I can truly change, then it stands to reason that the best way to change the system is to change myself.

You may say, "Okay, it's true . . . I contribute to the dysfunction, but I am *not* the number-one obstacle to change." Since you can only change you, it is not worth considering whether you contribute more or less dysfunction than others. From your perspective, you are, indeed, the number one obstacle and you must adopt the attitude that you are.

As those of us in the Ridder process adopted this way of thinking and focused more on ourselves, we came to see the following truth about every system of which we are a part: every change changes every thing. That is, the changes in myself, including higher levels of integrity and authenticity, more courageous love and more loving courage, and ever-increasing emotional and spiritual maturity, cannot help but affect every person around me and every living system in which I operate.

In the early stages of the Ridder process, I remember coming home and telling my wife that "the best thing I can do for you, our family, and our church is to focus more on myself." She was aghast. She later shared that the statement sounded awfully selfish to her. It sounded as if I was abandoning the responsibility I owed to her, our family, and our church in favor of a me-focused way of life. But by taking responsibility for my role in those systems, I was actually taking greater responsibility for those systems themselves. It was counter-intuitive.

This new focus on myself started at home and then moved into every other arena in my life. As God healed me of past wounds and grew my emotional maturity, I began maturely responding—instead of rashly reacting—to the inevitable conflicts that arise in a marriage. When my kids misbehaved, I stopped asking, "What's wrong with them?" and started asking, "How can I change my approach?" As I realized more of my culpability and responsibility, I asked for forgiveness and began to experience life-giving healing in crucial relationships.

As my own heart grew in its capacity for hospitality, loving the stranger, I saw parallel changes happening in our church system that allowed us to unleash the most hospitable people instead of hamper them. As I felt the grace of God extended to me in palpable ways and shared those experiences with the congregation, the desire for the grace of God grew in our congregation and they more deeply extended grace to others. The more I lived into God's design, my love, my courage, my authenticity, and my very way of being brought about more and more positive change in the systems in which I live and move, and have my being.

My Personal Story

Sometimes it's easier to understand an idea than it is to put into practice. At one point, over the span of about six months, I had a series of four relational breakdowns. In each case, I was earnestly trying to follow Jesus as I gracefully sought to paint a picture of the difference between each person's current way of life and the life God actually intends for them. And in each case, the person on the other side of the relationship began to either shut down or act out. Despite my best intentions, the results I was getting were the exact opposite of what I desired.

As the first incident occurred, I immediately placed blame on the other person. I had tried to be delicate in my challenge because I figured he could not handle much. When he reacted the way he did, it only confirmed my bias: He was just as immature as I thought he was.

As the second incident developed, I took a similar, but slightly different, approach—I attributed this person's prickly behavior to the difficulty of being challenged by the teachings of Jesus. As the third and fourth incidents unfolded, I could no longer blame "the other." Instead, I became increasingly discouraged. I had a distinct sense that everything I did was a failure. By the time the fourth situation was upon me, I was swimming in a pool of my own melancholy. As I swam in that pool, I became deeply despondent. I just kept asking, "What is the point?"

Thankfully, I have some important relationships in which I am regularly called upon to tell the truth, to be authentic, to "say what is so." In those conversations, I started by speaking about my melancholy, of which I felt guilty and embarrassed. Speaking about it was deeply unpleasant, but absolutely necessary, because as my trusted friends listened, asked deep questions, and sought to help me get clarity, I realized my gloom was nothing other than shame. Rather than seeing myself as someone who had made a few mistakes or had a few setbacks, I was convinced that *I was a mistake and a failure.*

Yet, something interesting happened as I gained the courage to voice those ugly feelings of being such an unsuccessful pastor and a total loser of a person. First, I was not condemned or judged by those that listened. On the whole, they reacted with profound empathy and became deeply concerned about me and my future. Second, I started to gain insight as I saw that all those situations had a common theme—namely, I have "a way of being" in the face of perceived resistance and/or unmet expectations that is not helpful. In fact, one of the key people in my life said, "Drew, you're never going to make any significant progress as a leader in a Christian community if you can't deal with this reality."

Understanding My Way of Being

If people willingly engage and meet my expectations, then ministry goes very well. People seem blessed by me and tell me so. They are grateful for the interaction and even ask for more. However, if I feel resisted or if people fail to meet expectations (both the stated expectations and especially the unshared expectations I silently hold within), I have a way of being that actually creates further resistance and even more problems. I did not immediately understand the exact nature of my way of being, but as I dug deeper and began to ask people about how I relate to others, I realized that my way of being is very shame-inducing.

I don't intentionally heap shame on people; it happens in a very subconscious manner. It's part of my autopilot way of being; I do it without even thinking about it. And left to my own devices, this is the way it plays out: As I grow disappointed with people, I judge them and blame them: "Gosh, what a slacker." "How can this person possibly be so clueless?" "Oh, how immature! Grow up!" "If you weren't going to do the work, why did you agree to it in the first place?" I'm fairly conscious of this judging and blaming that takes place in my internal monologue. In fact, I am conscious enough that I seek to stop judging, and I ask myself, "How can I show this person grace?" However, even in the midst of this prayerful questioning, the effects of the judging and blaming are not completely undone. Eventually—and quite naturally—this way of being leads to mannerisms and behavior that induce shame in others.

Deep down, I want to see others make godly progress, but I am an agent of my own undoing. I project "disappointment" and they often re-treat to feeling like a child whose parent is disappointed with them. They also have a sense of being "unheard" and are left feeling as though they are "wrong." I become more intense and often uncooperative. I fail to make it safe by affirming their value and reassuring them of my love and ac-ceptance even as I present a word of challenge. *I know all of this because I asked them to tell me about myself. Talk about unpleasant!* Instead of help-ing people make progress, my way of being only causes them to shut down and act out. They exhibit the symptoms of feeling deep shame: "the in-tensely painful feeling or experience of believing we are flawed and there-fore unworthy of acceptance and belonging" (Brown, 2007, p. 5).

The Power of Shame

It was a quite an epiphany when I realized that the deep shame I felt was directly related to the experience people were having of me. I had inadvertently shamed others and as the relationships unfolded, I began to shame myself. It was a nasty cycle. I lived in a pool of shame and as I did, I couldn't help but act out of that reality. Shame begot shame begot shame begot shame.

Thank God for trusted friends who listened with empathy as I gave voice to my pain. As long as the narrative remained in the darkness of my own be-ing, it festered and grew exponentially. The awful growth of the shame was aided by judgment, secrecy and silence. The greatest fuel was contributed by my own self-hatred. In fact, there may be no greater fuel for that mad-ness than self-loathing. That's what shame is: hating yourself. I recently read these descriptions of shame that seem to align perfectly with my experience: "Shame is hating yourself and understanding why other people hate you too. . . . Shame is like a prison. But a prison that you deserve to be in because something is wrong with you" (Brown, 2007, p. 4).

Shame is the opposite of the gospel. Shame says, "Yes, you've made a mistake, which is typical for a total loser like yourself." The gGospel says, "Yes, you've made a mistake, and here's some grace to redeem you." Shame says, "You're not perfect, and consequently, you are unworthy of love." The gospel says, "You're not perfect, and despite your imperfection, you are deeply loved." Shame says, "You're uniquely flawed and absolutely do not belong." The gospel says, "Everybody has flaws, including you. But in Christ, we all belong." Shame says, "You are hopeless." The gospel says, "You may be guilty, but Jesus is your hope."

I see that shame has tremendous power in my life. I see that it debilitates me and those around me that "let me down" (i.e., people who fail to live up to the same inappropriate standards of perfection that I foolishly set for myself). I see that it prevents me from seeing reality, especially gospel reality.

Thank God for the body of Christ and the key members who listened as I spoke my shame. Each time I said more, I gained more freedom. Each time I spoke, one more piece of the darkness was dragged into the light. In the light, all these things lose power. Why? Because they are exposed as the lies that they are and it is vividly put on display that I am not defined by those lies.

I am not healed of shame, but for the first time in a long time, I felt like it could be beat. I knew I would not be perfect in my response to resistance or unmet expectations, but I knew I would be better. As a result of God's internal work, I went out from there and experienced tremendous redemption in a few of these situations. Moving forward, I now show more compassion, exercise more empathy, and make more safe space. Most importantly, I show more compassion, exercise more empathy, and make more safe space . . . for *myself.*

As we engaged this Ridder material, I was challenged to understand that I am the number one obstacle to the deep change that God desires. It did not take much convincing. I could see—plain as day—that my own way of being was standing in the way.

By God's grace moving to transform me and thereby transform the systems of which I am a part, First Reformed Church successfully made the difficult move to become Heartland Community Church. We recently celebrated our third anniversary in the new building. By no means are we the perfect example of a healthy church, but there is a wealth of evidence that transformation has taken and is taking place. We worship with about twice as many people as we once did. We have baptized a few adults, including a sixty-one-year-old man. We have six small groups, and each small group either has a missional partner in the community or is designed specifically to incorporate new people. We have partnered with the local elementary school to mentor children and support their backpack program. There is an air of hunger, vitality and growth, and depending on who tells the story, the successful transition and transformation is a flat-out miracle.

In the beginning, I looked outward and assigned blame to the congregation. As it turns out, the problem was not them. I was waiting for others to change and complaining when they failed to do so. I needed to stop worrying about the speck in their eye and focus more on the log in my own. I needed to focus on the only person I could change: me.[2]

---

2. This is not to say that my personal transformation is responsible for *every* facet of the congregational metamorphosis in a mechanistic, cause-effect sort of way. Rather, we would contend that Edwin Friedman was correct in arguing that leadership is an organic phenomenon and that the leader's capacity for self-definition has unseen, yet profound effects (1985, pp. 220–49).

Practice and Reflect

Take some time to reflect on the sentence you wrote down in your journal about being the "number one obstacle to change." Pay particular attention to any resistance that rises up within you.

Going Deeper

We've shared our conviction that we must change ourselves before we can hope for any change in our church or any other institution of which we are a part. We'll delve into this idea more deeply in Part Three when we focus on growing emotional maturity and understanding the church as a living system. To learn more about the personal transformation, we invite you to check out our on-line resources at http://www.westernsem. edu/journey/ridder.

References and Additional Resources

Brown, Brené. *I Thought It Was Just Me (But It Isn't): Making the Journey from "What Will People Think" to "I Am Enough."* New York: Gotham, 2007.

Friedman, Edwin. *Generation to Generation: Family Process in Church and Synagogue.* New York: Guilford Press, 1985.

Herrington, Jim, Robert Creech, and Trisha Taylor. *The Leader's Journey: Accepting the Call to Personal and Congregational Transformation.* San Francisco: Jossey-Bass, 2003.

Part 2

Core Values: Reconnecting to Our Intended Design

What we do is important. How we do it is even more so. We decided early on that we needed to pay close attention to the core values that drive our process of learning. We wanted to focus on values that were evident in the fully human, fully alive life that Jesus lived and that were robust enough to support the missional life we were practicing. Of course, there were many values that were worthy of our focus, and of those, we chose four: integrity, authenticity, courage and love.

Identifying the values that we would pursue was the easy part. Learning to practice them rigorously in our daily lives was definitely harder. We knew that our usual practice—reading about these values, listening to sermons about them, having good intentions about them—wasn't going to give us the results we wanted. Gradually, we began designing challenges for ourselves to grow our capacity to practice these values and then sharing our results with each other, then making adjustments and trying again.

This rhythm of learning led to the kinds of results that others who knew us noticed and commented on, which buoyed our attempts to continue learning. That process continues to this day, as we intentionally build the core values into our lives and then watch to see what God will do.

Chapter 4
Integrity: Restoring the Design

Trisha Taylor and Jim Herrington

What if integrity means more than being a good person or an upstanding citizen? We believe that it does, and that a deep understanding of integrity helps us to move from good intentions to powerful realities.

Imagine your life conforming to God's design for who God created you to be. Imagine a life that is whole and complete, rather than fragmented and compartmentalized. Imagine being a person who does what you say you will do, accomplishing God's purposes in your life. We believe that integrity takes us back to the deepest biblical meaning about being a fully alive human being created in the image of God who creates with God's word.

*I*ntegrity is one of the four core values that we hold up in our journey and strive to master, personally and with our congregations. When you think of integrity, what comes to your mind? Most of us immediately think that having integrity means being a good person, demonstrating strong moral character, and being an upstanding member of the community.

What if integrity means much more than that? And what if mastering integrity as a way of life means that we can live more creatively and more effectively than we ever imagined possible? That's what we believe.

Think for a moment about the Creation story. There, in the very beginning, we see God as Creator. For God, the whole creative process begins with a word: "Let there be light." When God speaks, things happen—things exist that didn't exist before God spoke. It's important to notice that God didn't *think* the world into existence, but rather brought the world into existence through his *spoken* word. And when God looked at all he created, God said that it was very good.

Later in God's story, as God interacts with his people, God continues to create by speaking. For example, God made a verbal promise to Abraham that he would take possession of the Promised Land, and that he would have a son whose progeny would make Abraham the father of a great nation, the people of God (Genesis 12:2–3, 15:4–5, 17:16, 22:15–18). Abraham waited decades to see the promise fulfilled. It took generations, but the people of God emerged just as God had said.

In the same way, when God gave the verbal promise of a savior to the prophets, they could not imagine exactly what he had in mind. But when the time was right, Jesus came into the world to fulfill the word God had spoken centuries before, creating the new reality of the Kingdom of God.

We can clearly see how God functions in relationship to his word. When God speaks, he commits himself to accomplishing what he says. God says, "Light," and light is created. God says, "Water," and the oceans of the world appear. God also looks into the future and says, "I will _____," and God makes good on his promise. We want to ask you to think of integrity in this same way.

Adding Our Word to God's Word

Since we are created in God's image, we are most fully human and fully alive when we join God in creating. And like God, we create with our word. Unlike God, we don't create something out of nothing. However, God has given us the deep privilege of adding our word to his word, to do his will in the world. We have integrity when we give our word in the present to the very things we see God giving his word to, and we join our energies with God's to create a different future.

We see this co-creation at work in the story of Mary, the mother of Jesus, when the angel comes to her and speaks God's intention to bring his son into the world. In faith, Mary replies, "let it be with me according to your word" (Luke 1:38). She adds her word to God's word, and the Savior is created in her womb.

We also understand this when we say "Amen" during prayer or after a prayer is offered or when scripture is read. The word "Amen" means "Let it be." We are asking God to hear the words we have just spoken aloud and make them real in our lives, creating some new reality that doesn't currently exist.

Creating something new with our word is what happens at every wedding. When two people come before God and their friends and family and make promises to each other, they create a marriage by giving their word to each other to love, honor, and cherish each other until death parts them.

We believe that the God-given ability to join God in creating with our word is at the core of integrity. We also believe that in order to bring about real change in our lives and in the world around us, we must grow in our ability to give and keep our word in ways that help to restore our world to God's intended design.

When God said that the world and the human beings he had made were "very good," God meant that they conformed to his intended design for them; they were what God had designed them to be. We believe that every system and structure in our world has a God-given design. Business, for example, is designed to facilitate commerce, to provide goods and services in society, and to provide income for workers and entrepreneurs. Government, family, law enforcement, education, neighborhoods, church, community, social services—all have a God-given design and purpose.

Practice and Reflect

Stop reading for a minute and think about the place where you spend most of your day. If your work is in your home, think about your neighborhood. If you work outside the home, think about your workplace. Take a minute and reflect on God's intended design for your neighborhood, the school where you teach, the office building where your company resides, or the company in which you work. What is God's intended design there? If the Kingdom of God were to come fully into that place, what would be different? What is God's dream for your home, your neighborhood, your church or your workplace? Reflect prayerfully (don't rush!) and write your thoughts in your journal.

Of course, most of the world no longer looks much like what God intended. It seems that each generation finds new ways to rebel against God's design. The systems and structures of the world we live in look less and less like what God had in mind. We sometimes say that the world is broken because it doesn't work the way God meant for it to. Yet, we know that God is constantly at work to reconcile people to himself and to restore relationships and systems to God's intended design so that they will work the way God lovingly intended them to.

When I (Trisha) counsel a couple who is struggling with their relationship, I ask them to think about what they believe about God's design for marriage. They may talk about love and mutuality and self-sacrifice and faithfulness. Our work together then centers on working with God to align their relationship to God's design as they understand it. When my friend Betty looks around the public school where she teaches and asks herself, "What is God's design for this school? How can I cooperate with God to help to bring that about?" she is acting in integrity. When we work to stop human trafficking, we do so because of our conviction that God's design for human beings is that they live in freedom and are not enslaved. That conviction about God's design empowers our work to end modern slavery.

The context for our definition of integrity is neither absurd presumption nor self-interest. Integrity doesn't mean us saying, as Jesus did, "Destroy this temple, and in three days I will raise it up" (John 2:19). Nor does integrity involve us saying, "I will take up two lanes of highway traffic so I can have more room" and then act on fulfilling that declaration. Those are not the kinds of promises we were designed to make. The context for our understanding of integrity is that we are designed by God to join God on mission in representing Christ and his kingdom. The promises we are called to make are those whose fulfillment would advance God's kingdom purposes on the earth.

Giving Our Word to God's Restoration

The key to our promises is being partners in God's reconciling and restoring work. We see that some part of our life—our family, our cul-de-sac, our local school, our workplace—isn't working the way God intended it to work. As God's children made in God's image to also be creators, we say "yes" to God's ongoing restoring work by taking responsibility for the recreation of those places so that they are restored to full functionality. We do that by giving—and then keeping—our word.

Pause and ponder that for a minute. In our experience, most Christians think of their work in this manner: As a follower of Christ, I should do a good job in my workplace and be a person of high moral character. I should also look for and take advantage of opportunities to witness. If someone responds to my witness, I should then invite that person to church.

What we are suggesting is different. We are suggesting that as followers of Christ, we must think about the intended design of our family, cul-de-sac, school, or workplace and then actually "give our word" to being part of their restoration. What does that assertion stir up in you? Do you experience resistance when you read this? Many people do. So, pay attention to that resistance and hold it before the Holy Spirit. You might say, "Lord, this is such a different way of following You than I've ever been taught. It seems really big—almost overwhelming. Lord, help me to stay open to the possibility that You are speaking to me through this experience as I continue to read."

Living Within Our Design

In the context of Christ-followers being called to give our word to the restoration of things to God's design, we want to describe integrity in two ways. First, integrity is synonymous with workability. In other words, things have integrity when they work the way they are designed to work. On August 1, 2007, a bridge spanning the Mississippi River in Minneapolis collapsed during rush hour traffic, killing thirteen people. It doesn't take an engineer to know that the bridge lacked integrity. It didn't do what it was supposed to, and the results were tragic.

In 2005, I (Jim) had a heart attack. I was well informed about the design of the human body. I knew about the importance of exercise and eating habits. I knew about cholesterol and triglycerides standards. Yet, for years I lived outside of the design, and the consequence was a heart attack. I was living out of integrity—out of the design of human health.

The word integrity derives from the Latin word *integritas*, meaning "wholeness" or "perfect condition." Jesus referred to this idea when he taught us to "be perfect (sometimes translated "holy"), therefore, as your heavenly Father is perfect" (Matt. 5:48). Many of us have felt so anxious or intimidated about the idea of perfection or holiness that we have dumbed it down to mean "be a moral person." When we conflate holiness and morality, we seriously dilute what Jesus was calling us to.

While we are certainly called to live moral lives, the word *perfect* in this text is best rendered "whole" or "complete." When God says that he is perfect and holy, God means that he is not compartmentalized or inconsistent, but that he is complete and whole. God's perfection is in the fact that God always acts consistently with who God is. For instance, in God's very being, in God's very essence, God is good. Therefore, because God is good, God does good. Who God is and what God does are always the same.

As we have seen, we were created according to a design. When we are who God designed us to be—and when what we do lines up with who we are—we have integrity. We are holy, whole, and complete—that is, we have integrity—inasmuch as we act consistently with who we are designed to be. In the opening chapter, Brian Stone suggested that we are designed to dream dreams about making the world a better place. We believe deeply that at the heart of the design of what it means to be human is that humans are designed to live missionally. Out of a personal relationship with God, we hear God speak to us about our design and our calling. When God speaks, it is a calling to join God in restoring some part of our world—to establishing God's shalom in our families, our cul-de-sac, our school, or our workplace.

Giving Our Word, Keeping Our Word

Our second definition of the word integrity is profoundly practical: *Integrity means that I do what I say I am going to do when I say I am going to do it, in the way it was meant to be done.* Another way to say this is that when I give my word, I keep my word.

We know that God has integrity because God always does what he says he will do. Much to our chagrin, God doesn't always do it immediately or on our timetable, but God always accomplishes what he promises. Likewise, because we are created in God's image, we do the work of restoring the broken places in our world by giving our word to God's purposes.

Because I (Trisha) believe that God's design is for husbands and wives to live together in loving unity, I have joined with a small group of others who have given our word to restoring marriages through marriage education in the city of Houston. Members of Midland Reformed Church have given their word to serving distressed single parents, believing that it is God's design for these parents to be supported by the church in their neighborhood. Another group at Haven Reformed Church have given their word to the healthy functioning of a mobile-home park near their church building. These are just a few examples of what we are talking about.

We are not suggesting that you give your word to the restoration of everything that is broken. Like Jesus who heard the Father and obeyed, God will call you to some specific people and places where you give your word to work toward restoration. Then, with God's help and over time, you do what you have said you will do. Think about God's call to Moses to deliver his people from Egypt. It took Moses decades to keep his word and get the people from Egypt to the Promised Land. They eventually got there because day after day, year after year, Moses kept his word.

There are two possible pitfalls here. One is that we will not give our word wisely. The other danger is that we will give our word wisely but will not be able to keep it. Fortunately, we can guard against both of these dangers.

Many of us are stressed and overextended because sometimes we give our word unwisely. We say "yes" to things and to people even though we have no room for them in our lives. Then we wear ourselves out trying to hold it all together. If you're one of those people, you may hear the call to "do what you say you will do" and want to erupt in frustration. One church member exploded, "You've got to be kidding me! I'm already killing myself trying to do everything I said I would do!" Later though, she wondered aloud whether everything she had given her word to was actually part of God's plan for her life or was even hers to do.

Hearing from God is central to this conversation. When we agree to do things because we are afraid to say no or because we are not thinking about the alignment of our commitments with our values, we are giving our word unwisely. When we are more motivated by pleasing others or being all things to all people, we may agree to things that are unworthy of us or to things that are inconsistent with our own design.

Sometimes, when we have a history of giving our word unwisely, we may start refusing to give our word at all. We become people who rarely commit to anything, afraid that we won't follow through. We encourage others not to have real expectations of us just in case we might fail. We may make halfhearted promises and then try to get out of our commitments or act passively, hoping that someone else will step up to take them over.

At the risk of confusing the issue, let's also think about all the implicit promises we make. For example, when we became followers of Jesus, we implicitly gave our word to live our lives in the way Jesus lived his. We made implicit promises to love God with our whole hearts and to love our neighbors as ourselves. We promised to learn to love our enemies and to care for the poor. Many of us have spent our adult lives learning to follow Jesus in ways we didn't even know we had signed up for when we originally gave our lives to him.

Keeping Your Word When You Don't Know How

Now let's go ahead and complicate things further. Sometimes God asks us to give our word to things that are currently outside our ability to keep. In fact, in our experience, if you are going to participate in God's mission of restoration and reconciliation, initially you will be called on to make some promises that you can't currently keep. Marriage is a good example of this kind of promise. When two people get married, most of them have no idea what "for better, for worse" or "in sickness or in health" will involve. They give their word to God and to each other and create a new family with that word. They then spend the rest of their lives learning to "love, honor, and cherish" each other in real life.

When Mary said to the angel, "let it be with me according to your word," adding her word to God's word, she could not have known what the future would bring. She gave her word to God, but she could not have been fully prepared for the life that would unfold over the next few decades. When Simeon said to her, "a sword will pierce your own soul also," she could not have known what that meant or how to respond. When the time came, however, Mary lived out her faith in God and continued to keep her word of submission to God.

Mission Houston and Houston's Public Schools

As we were learning this process of giving our word to God's purposes, I (Jim) was founding executive director of Mission Houston, an interdenominational ministry helping congregations impact their communities. The staff and the board of Mission Houston had been engaged in a city-wide initiative called CityFest Houston with Luis Palau. As a part of that experience, teams of congregational leaders across the city had engaged the public schools in their neighborhoods, focusing on schools with a large Title I population, children living at or below the poverty level.

The teams went to neighborhood school principals and asked whether there were any short-term projects they could do that could help improve the educational environment for their students. The relationships between Houston congregations and public schools were at that time apathetic or even adversarial.

Twenty-six teams engaged twenty-six schools and completed school improvement projects. They painted buildings, built playground equipment, upgraded teacher lounges, installed new and better lighting, and built gardens. The experience was transformative for schools and for congregations.

After CityFest, the Mission Houston staff and board committed to a several-month process of seeking and discerning God's call. During a morning of prayer and planning, we had a clear sense that the Lord was saying, "I want you to give your word to the transformation of the public schools in this city."

You can imagine our response. "Are you sure Lord? The whole system— not just some of the schools? How is that possible? We are just a staff of four and a board of ten?" As we pressed into prayer, we had the definite sense that God was speaking clearly to us. So, with some fear that we would be seen as crazy or arrogant, but convinced that this was God's call in our lives, in April 2007, I stood before the four hundred people attending a Mission Houston fundraiser, and on behalf of the staff and board, gave our word to the transformation of the Houston public school system.

Steve Capper, from the Mission Houston staff, reflected what many of us felt:

> It is clear to us that while we have given our word to the transformation of the public schools, we are not yet capable of keeping that word. Sometimes we'll fail because we choose to avoid the inconveniences that selfless serving requires. Most often, though, we'll fail to keep our word because we don't know how to: we don't yet have the skills, the resources, the depth of love necessary to succeed. These things will come to us through faith and through failure, when we are desperate to know what we don't currently know and to have what we don't currently have. In humility, then, we are prepared to honor our word until God gives us the capacity to keep it.

The story of the transformation of the Houston public schools is still unfolding. It hasn't gone the way the Mission Houston team thought it would. There have been some dead-end trails, and several times when the team members have had to reassess how to fulfill their word. But what is true in Houston is that more people are more focused on the transformation of the public schools than ever. The work is not done, but real progress has been made.

Why on earth would we say that it is important to give our word to things when we are presently unable to keep that word? We believe that this is the way God leads us into a larger life in the Kingdom of God. Since we are created in God's image, giving and keeping our word is part of being Christlike. So, too, is living "on mission" for and with God, joining God in his mission to reconcile, redeem, and restore. This is a big calling and it's possible that if you are able to always keep your word as a Kingdom agent, then you are living far too small a life.

When we make integrity simply about being moral rather than about living on mission, we often create a small world of fewer commitments where we only promise what we're fairly certain we can deliver. This is not the world of Abraham, Moses, Ruth, Esther, or Jesus. On the other hand, when we commit to living a life that is intentionally on mission, we find ourselves facing hurdles we've never experienced before. Abraham, in response to hearing God's call, ventured toward a land that "he knew not of." He set out to go somewhere but didn't know exactly where!

If you give your word to live on mission with God, God will take you places where you've never been and where you don't quite know how to navigate. This is what it means to walk by faith. That's ultimately what it means for you to be perfect, holy, and whole—walking by faith in God and joining God on his mission.

When We Can't Keep Our Word

In all of this, we can be sure of one thing: we will not always keep our word. Whether we are living a big life with God or whether our circumstances have prevented us from following through or whether there are personal flaws that get in our way, we will sometimes fail to do what we said we would do when we said we would do it.

Some of us will be tempted to wallow in shame and guilt over this. We learned growing up that if we made a promise and didn't keep it, we were bad people and deserved to be punished. Some of us will be tempted to ignore the gap in our integrity completely, leaving a long trail of broken promises behind us. Since we are promised that our sins are forgiven and there is no condemnation in Christ, we want to invite you to put any shame and guilt aside and simply consider what it will mean to your life if you embrace the call to integrity and learn from your failures. This is not something that will come easily. Learning to embrace failure as a necessary part of the learning process is a habit that must be cultivated over time.

When we are not able to keep our word, we can still honor our word. By honoring our word, we give weight to the belief that our words have power to help create the world that we live in. In other words, rather than pretending like we never made the promise or pretending like our failure to keep our promise doesn't really matter and then moving on to the next thing, we can stop and engage in a process of cleaning up our messes and learning to keep our word in the future.

Cleaning Up Our Messes

Here is the process for cleaning up our messes (honoring our word) that we have found to be a practical guide in growing our integrity:

1. First, we acknowledge that we have not kept our word. We actually stop and take responsibility for the breakdown. When we do this, we will fight the internal voices that encourage us to hide in shame, defensively explain our situation and how it wasn't our fault, or pretend that things are better than they are. We resist these temptations by remembering that this is an opportunity for us to learn.
2. Second, we get present to the impact that our failure to keep our word has created in the lives of others—the mess we have created. We can start by asking the people who were affected by our gap in integrity to tell us what the impact was. As they do, we listen. We don't make excuses or justify ourselves. We don't deflect what they are saying. We actually allow the sting of the impact to touch us. This does two things: It makes it easier for the other person to believe that we really care about them and to forgive us, and it gives us added incentive to keep our word in the future, in order to avoid hurting people in these ways again. At this point, we look for ways to make amends and minimize the negative impact on others and then we follow through.
3. Next, we offer a sincere apology and ask forgiveness. We have all been victims of insincere apologies that either refuse to take responsibility for the problem or even make us to blame for the mess that someone else created. A sincere apology starts with us taking responsibility for our part in the mess we have created and ends with a plea for forgiveness.
4. Last, we re-promise. We make a new commitment and we work to keep it. We get back into action and attempt to keep our word. In some cases, we may need to modify our promise or we may need to clarify what we are actually giving our word to. In almost all cases, we need to give the situation an increased place of priority in our lives. We may need to make changes in ourselves or learn new skills in order to better do what we say we will do in the future.

Out of this experience we will grow in our capacity to keep our word. Then we will have some more breakdowns. And when that happens, we repeat the process of honoring our word. Then over time two things happen. One is that because we persistently work over a long period of time, things begin to change. Sometimes *we don't do what we said we would do when we said we would do it in the way that it was meant to be done*—that's our second definition of integrity. When that happens and we get present to the impact, God uses that to grow us up. God uses that to mature us and to conform us to the image of Jesus. And that increases our capacity to keep our word.

Consequences When We Fail to Keep Our Word

Even when we clean up our messes, there are consequences when we don't keep our word. (This is simply a fact, and is not related to guilt.) There is a correlation between keeping your word and how well things work. The more you keep your word—or honor your word when you can't keep it—the better your relationships will function. *When we do what we say we will do when we say we will do it in the way it was meant to be done,* our relationships and other efforts work better and look more like they were intended to look by God. When we don't keep our word but we do stop and clean up our messes, our relationships function more smoothly and healthily.

Practice and Reflect

Many of us have taken on the assignment to ask five people, "What can you often count on me for? What can you rarely count on me for?" The answers we have heard have changed our lives. Being confronted with the full weight of the consequences of the gaps in our integrity is a gift from God to wake us up, not throw us down. The pain we cause is meant to jolt us not into judgment but into learning.

I invite you to stop and pray about taking on this assignment. Who are five people you can ask these questions? Write down their names. Make a plan about asking these questions. Write down what you learn. Share what you learn with at least one other person or with your small group or learning community.

Integrity gaps in the congregation. Breakdowns (subtle or otherwise) in integrity impact the trust church members have in their leaders. Ridder pastors Brian Stone and John Sparks faced these consequences when they realized their integrity gaps were costing them credibility with the congregation:

> **John:** *Brian and I started as co-pastors almost nine years ago, and we had some definite ideas about where we wanted to go as a church and what it meant to be leaders. We began to share those ideas with the congregation. We became aware that there was a large integrity gap in our midst that was getting in the way of moving forward toward what God was calling us.*
>
> *Part of that gap was called "the flavor of the month" and that's where we just had a long season of time where we would run to this program or that model, and we would adopt it. We would promise that it would bring church growth, and that it was going*

to help us with outreach. We'd stay with it for eighteen months and then abandon it for the next box, program, or church growth conference.

When we would talk about what we were going to do or what we wanted to do, many people would just sigh and say, "Here comes the next flavor of the month." And people realized that if they didn't like the idea, they just had to hang on long enough because we would abandon it for something else.

Brian: They could just outwait us and pretty soon we would pick up the next good idea that the big names put out there for churches to grab hold of. We had a sense of what God's vision for our church was, but this was a huge roadblock to getting there.

John: Well, there was just huge resignation and cynicism . . .

Brian: Right!

John: We would talk about these things that we were excited about and believed in and had this huge conviction around, and there would just be this force field of resignation and cynicism in conversations we would have.

Brian: *We knew we needed to clean that mess up, that there was an integrity gap there. Not all of it was ours, but because we were pastors, it was ours to clean up. On one Sunday morning, we decided to clean the mess up. I remember looking back over the last ten years or so—Haven Church had had seven different vision or mission statements. To put that in context, in a way that was a little lighter, and to not point fingers at previous pastors, I put them all in three long sentences—hang on tight, it's a lot!*

"At Haven Church, we are working together with him because we are a fellowship of Christians who are being built up in the word and trained in various ministries for the purpose of reaching out to others with the love of Jesus Christ. As such, we are reaching out to people with God's love in order to help seekers, unchurched believers and members to become fully devoted followers of Jesus Christ. We do this by connecting people to God in every season of life so they can become love squared, loving God and loving others because we are each disciples of Jesus Christ rooted in God's word and empowered by the Holy Spirit to carry out the ministry of Christ in the world."

(Laughter)

John: So, along the way, we went to every conference offered by the major ministries—we associated with Willow Creek; we did the Saddleback Baseball Diamond; and then we did Seasons of Life. We signed up for many programs. Part of the story is still ongoing—even though we owned the fact that we often hadn't done what we said we would do, and we sought to "say what was so" and close the integrity gap, I think that particular gap was of such size and importance over those ten years that there is still some cynicism remaining: "When are they going to give up on the current vision?"

Brian: One of the pieces that is in play is that none of these vision and mission statements were wrong—they are all rooted in Matthew 28 and the purpose of the church—but as each statement was adopted, systems, structures, and mental models were never really addressed and the substance behind the statements never got traction. I think we're still looking at what it means to address the underlying mental models and structures in order to move forward into what we really want to be about as a church.

John: So the story continues. . . .

Brian: Yep. We're still learning. Hopefully we can out-wait the people who want to go back to Egypt . . . wherever Egypt is! (Laughter).

Integrity gaps in the community. In addition to integrity gaps impacting the trust of church members, there are also consequences when we lack integrity in our missional efforts as disciples and as congregations. One pastor led his congregation to serve a local public elementary school by becoming involved in tutoring, mentoring, supporting teachers, and contributing resources. After a few months, the principal told him that the school would like to give the church a volunteer award. The pastor protested, saying that they hadn't really been serving the school very long. The principal replied, "Well, yes, but churches never follow through and we appreciate that you've done that." This principal's experience with a lack of integrity from congregations had negatively influenced her perspective of church, a sad consequence of well-meaning people not doing what they said they would do.

The world knows that we are designed to function in loving and sacrificial ways. It knows that we have implicitly given our word to forgiveness and to sacrificial love and to the care of the poor. When we fail to live this out—or even pretend that we don't know about this promise—there are consequences to our ability to positively influence the world.

Cultivating Integrity Is a Lifelong Process

As you can imagine, cultivating lives of integrity is not a short-term process or a self-improvement project. It takes a lifetime. Sometimes it's a generational process. Earlier we mentioned that I (Jim) had a heart attack in 2005 that was a result of my living out of the design for the human body. I had surgery to put a stent in one of the large arteries of the heart, and as I left the hospital my doctor gave me good information about healthy eating, exercise, and sleep. There was nothing in the information that I did not already know.

What was new was that I had a sense of urgency to make a change. So, I gave my word to some lifestyle changes. I wish I could say that I immediately came out of the hospital and made dramatic changes in eating, exercise, and sleep patterns. Here is what actually happened.

I gave my word to cutting out processed carbs, sugar, and the kinds of fats that contribute to high cholesterol. I gave my word to running more regularly, and I gave my word to being in bed by 10 pm each night. I did all of that, and initially very little changed. When I went in for my six-month checkup, I had actually gained five pounds. My doctor was alarmed and expressed this to me.

The first breakthrough came after that visit. I shared the doctor's report with my wife, and she became an accountability partner with me in my eating habits. She expressed the impact that my poor lifestyle choices were having on her. She was living in fear that I would have another heart attack. She was living with the fear that she would live the last years of her life alone. As she shared this impact, I allowed her fear to penetrate my heart, and I asked her to forgive me. Then I promised that I was going to change my eating habits. Today I weigh seventeen pounds less than I did when that conversation took place. There were multiple occasions over the eight years between my promise and today that I failed to keep my word. I wish I could say that I immediately cleaned up the mess and honored my word. The truth is that sometimes I would gain four or five or six pounds before I would tell the truth that I was not honoring my word. However, when I honored my word, that honoring provided the impetus for me to get back on track.

The weight loss fed the exercise program. I've been a runner since college, but in these years since my heart attack I've run with more discipline and intentionality. I've trained in a way that has allowed me to run four half-marathons. I just had my annual physical for my sixtieth birthday, and my doctor says that I am healthy—cholesterol, triglycerides, and sugar measures are all within normal ranges. I attribute that in large measure to the practice of learning to keep my word around my health.

Getting to a place of deep integrity in every area of your life won't happen without struggle and, at times, that struggle will be intense. Even Jesus experienced this struggle. In the Garden of Gethsemane, the night before he was beaten and crucified, Jesus agonized over submitting himself to torture and a brutal death. But because doing so was the Father's will, as he had previously repeatedly said to his disciples, and because he had already verbally declared his commitment to doing whatever the Father wanted, Jesus followed through. You can hear the promise he made being kept at the end of his prayer that night: "Yet (despite any objections or fears) I want your will (to which I have committed) to be done" (Matt. 26:39, NLT). Jesus had integrity and kept his word, and in so doing created the future world of forgiveness and salvation and victory over sin. As we build our integrity, we join Jesus in that life-changing work.

Going Deeper

It is our deep conviction that as we become people of integrity— where we actually commit ourselves to the full workability of the systems and structures of our homes, neighborhoods, and workplaces—God will add his creative power to our efforts. Gradually, significant changes will happen as these places move closer to God's intended design for them. And then *when we do what we say we will do when we say we will do it in the manner it was meant to be done*—when we keep or honor our word— we will become people who can be trusted by God and by others with big things and small things. God will use that faithfulness to transform people, to transform families, and to transform communities.

References and Additional Resources

Collins, Jim. *Good to Great: Why Some Companies Make the Leap and Others Don't*. New York: HarperCollins, 2001.

Lencioni, Patrick. *The Five Dysfunctions of a Team: A Leadership Fable*. San Francisco: Jossey-Bass, 2002.

Senge, Peter. *The Fifth Discipline: The Art and Practice of the Learning Organization*. New York: Doubleday, 1990.

Chapter 5

Authenticity: Naked and Not Ashamed

Chip Sauer

We were designed to be authentic. In the garden, we were created "naked and not ashamed" and God's intention that we live honestly with him and with others never changed. We find countless ways to hide, however, especially in our churches. We posture and pose. We manage our image. We conceal who we really are—or what we're really doing—to avoid being judged. We pretend to be someone we're not. We live in fear of being exposed.

The stakes are high because the judgment is real. But when we learn to tell the truth about ourselves—to God and to others—our lives change. We are filled with the power of the authentic life that Jesus lived and calls us to. As we spend less energy on managing what others think of us, we have more energy for the abundant life and our stories have more power in the lives of those we serve. When we learn to live authentically, we can ask for help—and get it. We can form communities of grace and truth with other believers. Our message has the ring of truth to those who don't yet believe.

As we asked God to transform us, we learned that bringing all that we know of who we are to all that we know of God opens the door for the transformation we craved. We practiced taking off the masks (or as Genesis 3 describes, the fig leaves), and God blessed us as relationships were restored and our own hearts were healed.

*I*t was one of those moments when I was fully present. I didn't want to be anywhere else. The moment was real and raw. The person speaking was chronicling her experiences with loss, abuse, faith, and sin. She didn't hide. She didn't minimize. She didn't justify. She was, like Adam and Eve in Genesis 2:25, "naked, and . . . not ashamed." Her courage to share her experience created an environment where one after another, we were compelled to reveal more of ourselves. It was not the typical self-pity dialogue where our stories are manipulative, hopeless, and meant to draw attention to the sorry state of our lives. No, this moment was different. It was hopeful. It was life-giving. It was authentic. I yearn for more moments like that. Don't you?

We Want to Fit In

Words convey meaning and conjure up images. The word naked as used in the Bible carries important meaning in this conversation on authenticity. Typing "naked" into Google (not recommended!) reveals that our definition of naked is focused on the unclothed human body. Naked means we are not covered up. Yet covering up is a prevalent and finely honed skill in today's world. We learn young "to keep a stiff upper lip," "hold it together, " and "not let them see you sweat."

Do you remember the pressure as an adolescent to cover up and conform? Instead of being myself, I was driven to be like everyone else. I wanted to fit in. So I covered up. What I wore, how I spoke, who I liked and didn't like were all about being who I thought I needed to be in order to be accepted.

I remember trying to explain to my mother why I "needed" the $70 Girbaud jeans. "*Everyone* is wearing them, Mom!" I wanted to fit in because I believed this was how I would be accepted.

It's the irony of adolescence. Teenagers looking to identify themselves apart from their families, seek independence and freedom, yet what do they do? They conform and try to be like the people from whom they seek acceptance. The Goths look like the Goths. The skateboarders look like the skateboarders. The cheerleaders . . . well, you get the picture. Instead of seeking our identity from the One who gave us our identity, we look for acceptance and affirmation by putting on what we deem necessary to be accepted and covering up our true self.

This isn't just a struggle in adolescence. Our struggle continues into adulthood, except now it's about homes, cars, net worth, power, prestige, or the right set of golf clubs.

Our son recently started playing golf. What a riot! He began participating in Junior Golf opportunities, and his first day at Junior Golf was a tough one, especially for his mom, my wife. As he walked up to the group of boys outside the pro shop, my wife became keenly aware that our son's bag of clubs did not measure up to the full sets of clubs that his peers had. He had four clubs including a putter in what seemed to her a "Little People's" size golf bag. And sure enough, my son was teased by some of the other boys as they pointed to his set of clubs. The next day it became our life's mission to find him the appropriate set of clubs. We wanted him to fit in, or really, we wanted to fit in. He actually didn't care and was fine with his mini-clubs. But *we* didn't want to be the parents whose son had the wrong clubs. What would people think?

Each of us seeks acceptance in the world in our own way. In *The Different Drum*, Scott Peck describes this tension between authenticity and acceptance. Our desire for acceptance stops us from being authentically ourselves. For Peck, true community is the place where we are both accepted and authentic (1987). Is there really such a place where we can be both?

Genesis reminds us of our intended design. We were not designed to cover up our true selves and conform to the world. We were not designed to hide. When we are able to focus on our Creator, we find the freedom to be authentic with others.

Hiding Our True Selves

Hide and Seek is one of the first games we learn. It's fun to hide and anticipate being found. It's fun to be found. It's fun to look for what's hidden.

My daughter is two. She loves her Dad. She especially enjoys when I come looking for her in her pop-up playhouse. She hides and waits with incredible delight for me to come "find" her. As I walk step bystep toward the playhouse, her giggling increases. She can hardly contain herself as she hears me moving closer. Often, she can't take it, and she pops her head out of the playhouse, "Here I am!" She wants me to find her. She loves being found.

The joy of being found significantly and progressively changes as a child moves into adolescence and adulthood. There is no longer joy in being found, but the pain of guilt and shame. We hide now, not because it's fun, but because we've *become afraid to be found, to be seen for who we really are.* Take a moment to feel this tension. What would happen if you were found, if people saw you for who you really are? What would people see? Yet, don't we all want to be found—to be known? We ask ourselves if being found is worth the risk. Many of us have been wounded when we've let ourselves be found. We've been abused, used, ridiculed, or rejected. There was a cost, maybe a very significant cost, for exposing the truth of who we are. How many of us have shared something deep and private with a "friend" only to find out later how this information was used to ridicule and expose us to others? How many of us have shared something vulnerable and private with our parents only to have it minimized, ridiculed, or ignored? Or how many times have we shared a deep need or feeling we have with our spouse only to be judged and reprimanded for our feelings or needs? I'll never forget the look on my wife's face when, on more than one occasion, I shared something personal about her in public. She experienced hurt, betrayal, and a decrease in her trust of me.

These hurtful experiences have encouraged many of us to embrace a life where we try to avoid getting hurt; where we get what we can for ourselves; and where we maintain the self-image that is most workable, acceptable, and as shame-free as possible. But is this really living? How is that working for you? I've spent so much of my life trying to perform for others, thinking that if I'm good at academics, sports, girls, friendship, *then* I will be loved and accepted. What I've found tells a different story. I do feel better when I perform and get the kudos that come, but I also realize then that I'm loved for what I do, not who I am. The kudos don't last long, and I'm left with a lot more questions about my worth and value. Plus, if loving others is foundational to my life as a follower of Jesus, then using people to get approval is not loving but selfish. It's me-centered, and I really don't find what I'm looking for.

Who Told You That You Were Naked?

The first three chapters of Genesis are critical to understanding the world we live in and our inherent desire to hide. It is a key to understanding ourselves. It is the source of the definition for authenticity I'd invite you to live with for a while: *Authenticity is being naked and not ashamed.*

To understand and embrace this definition, we must allow God to change our story. Tim Keller, pastor of Redeemer Presbyterian Church in New York City, shared a message entitled "Nakedness and the Holiness of God" that has profoundly impacted my understanding of Genesis 3 and the thoughts that follow relating to authenticity (Keller, 1993).

First, what happened after humanity chose to take God's place?

> They heard the sound of the LORD God walking in the garden at the time of the evening breeze, and the man and his wife hid themselves from the presence of the LORD God among the trees of the garden. But the LORD God called to the man, and said to him, "Where are you?" He said, "I heard the sound of you in the garden, and I was afraid, because I was naked; and I hid myself." He said, "Who told you that you were naked? Have you eaten from the tree of which I commanded you not to eat?" The man said, "The woman you gave me to be with me, she gave me fruit from the tree, and I ate." Then the LORD God said to the woman, "What is this that you have done?" The woman said, "The serpent tricked me, and I ate" (Genesis 3:8–13).

After Adam disobeyed God, God asked, "Who told you that you were naked?" Adam had always been naked, but now he was hiding. He never felt the need to hide before. What had changed?

Adam's nakedness went from a reality he was unaware of to a problem he could not tolerate. What led Adam and Eve to hide from God, from each other, and even embrace a commitment to hide from their very own self? What led them into a place where they blamed so naturally and quickly, and where shame was ushered into their feelings about themselves and their physical bodies?

They could not stand to live under the gaze of truth. They could not stand to be seen for who they had become. They could not stand to live under the perception they were now unacceptable or unlovable. And neither can we.

"Don't look at me, Dad." I hear this phrase whenever one of two things happens with my nine-year-old son. Either he is in big trouble or he's embarrassed. When either is true and I look intently at him, my son says, "Don't look at me, Dad." He can't stand the gaze that he feels exposes his shame.

We were created to be fully known and fully loved. This is God's design for us. Adam and Eve, as they walked in the garden with God, naked and not ashamed, experienced what it was to be fully known and fully loved. They had nothing to hide in their relationship with their Creator, with each other, and how they viewed themselves. When they decided to reject God, take God's place, and try to become like God, they rebelled and disobeyed. In their rebellion came shame and a profound change to their perspective. They came to believe they were no longer acceptable, lovable, or worthy of being known. They believed that if they were to be known, they would be rejected. They would not be loved. They would experience more shame. The game of hide and seek began. But it's no longer a game for us—it's the difference between living fully and just existing.

Fig Leaves to Hide Behind

Adam and Eve used fig leaves to hide what they perceived led to their shame, the exposure of their most private parts. Like Adam and Eve, we sew on figurative fig leaves to hide ourselves from God, from each other, and even from ourselves. We all have them. We all use them. We have all become professional pretenders.

I've heard it said that none of us really go to church; we send our best representative. We hide what we don't want seen and try to be the person we want to be seen as. Theologians and psychologists call this our false self. It is the self we create over the course of our lives. It is the way of being we've determined helps us avoid being hurt and helps meet the needs we have. It's our best representative. As we grow older, our fig leaves are not simply tools to hide behind—they become who we see ourselves to be.

One of my favorite fig leaves is looking good. I hide my true self by trying to look good to everyone else. My false self is "I got it all together. I'm an all-star." If I acquire your respect, your admiration, your affirmation, *then* I am lovable. So I strive to please people. I get wrecked when I disappoint someone or let him or her down. My identity is wrapped up in what others think of me, so I am in a state of constant turmoil trying to maintain my image, look good, please others, and receive affirmation. I can never receive enough affirmation to bring me peace, so one negative comment can derail me for days.

What are the figs leaves you use that have helped determine your identity? Are you hoping that people will see you as busy, important, independent, funny, talented, wealthy, influential, powerful, successful, rich, educated, or different, so you try hard to be this person? Sometimes our fig leaves are ways of being that keep people away for fear that they might see us for who we are. Are you presenting as a victim, a loser, a loner, someone who is angry, needy, sad, desperate, or judgmental, or someone who blames others?

Practice and Reflect

Please take a few minutes to do this important exercise we call the Public-Private-Secret Exercise.

Please don't skip this.

Take out a sheet of paper and label three different sections: Public—Private—Secret.

Public: Under the public section, describe how you are in public. How do people experience you in public? How do you see yourself in public?

Private: Under the private section, describe how you are in private— with your immediate family. How would your family describe you at home? How would you describe yourself at home?

Secret: Under the secret section, describe what the voice in your head says about you. When you are alone and quiet, how would you describe yourself? What wounds have you hidden from others? What dreams have you squelched and feared disclosing?

Once you've completed the exercise, answer the following questions:

1. What stands out as you compare the three sections?
2. Who are you really?
3. Does the secret section reflect what you believe God says about you?
4. What do you imagine it would look like if you were authentically you in all three sections? What would be different? What would remain the same?

Conclude this time by asking God to help you see yourself as you are and to grow in your capacity to love yourself as God loves you. Ask God to give you courage to begin sharing more of your private and secret self. When we walk in the light, we find life.

Hiding Keeps Us From Love

After an excellent message I thought I'd preached, I received a poke—a critical word or a perceived, non-verbal slight. A poke hurts and as someone whose survival mechanism is looking good, I processed the poke for days. It impacted everything else I did that week.

Desperate to find affirmation, I did hospital and shut-in visits. I wrote encouraging emails. I worked extra hard on the upcoming message. I looked good. I felt good. Yet, my behavior was selfish. I was thinking about myself throughout the week even though I, from an outsider's perspective, was serving and caring about people. What I was doing was hiding my hurt by trying to overcome it with affirmation. The affirmation made me feel good and it masked my pain. What I wish I had done instead was reach out to the person who poked me to have a clarifying conversation— a conversation that would have helped me understand what the real issues were, which I then could have addressed in an authentic manner.

Practice and Reflect

Have you embraced the lie that if you are fully known, you will not be loved?

Take a few moments to reflect on the possibility you have embraced this lie. What if people really knew the state of your marriage, prayer life, thought life, use of money, places you visited on the Internet, things you've said to your children, lies you've told? What if people really knew your hurts, fears, hopes, regrets? Do you believe you'd receive less love and acceptance? What does that stir up in you? Consider the implications this has on your life (marriage, friendships, family, etc.) if you believe this is true. Write about it briefly in your journal.

Settling for What Won't Satisfy

Instead of accepting God's love, we settle for the world's "love." We settle for experiences that make us feel important and valued. We don't believe being known will lead to being loved, so we hide and look for anything we can get which makes us feel better about ourselves. Settling is a short-term gain with a long-term cost. Settling is fleeting, unfulfilling, self-centered, and like a drug addict, only leads to an increased desire for more and more of the same that never satisfies. We perform. We consume. We hoard. We judge. We get busy. We pursue perfection. We change our appearance. We choose the "right" friends. We do what brings attention and admiration. Like the performer in the circus trying to keep all the plates spinning, we work constantly to put on our Sunday's best for the world. Yet, the emptiness remains and the tension doesn't go away.

Deep down, we know who we are trying to be is not who we are, so even if affirmation and love come our way, we know it is only the image we've created that is receiving this attention. This love and attention is better than nothing, so we settle for what cannot satisfy. We also have the aching suspicion that there are two eyes that cannot be deceived. Regardless of how hard we try, we live under the gaze of a Creator who sees the truth. God knows who we are. God is the just Judge. God is the one who removed Adam and Eve from the garden and put a flaming sword at the door to keep them out.

Our new, shame-based story might sound like this:

> We can't be fully known and loved. We can't even be loved—maybe admired, respected, but not loved. As Adam and Eve were known, they were rejected. They were unacceptable. They were removed from the garden. They are on their own and have to settle for what they can find. This is not only their story, but it is now *my* story.

Even though this is not the end of the story, some of us live as if it is. If this is the story we embrace, we cannot be authentic—naked and not ashamed. This "hide and get what you can" perspective makes perfect sense apart from the radical, unconditional, redeeming love of God expressed in the gift of Jesus Christ. This way of being makes perfect sense if there is no gospel.

Authenticity Is Being Naked and Not Ashamed

Genesis 4 through Revelation 22 expresses the truth that rejection from the garden is not the end of the story. The rest of scripture reveals to us a God who relentlessly and lovingly pursues us. God's story for us is restoration, redemption, reconciliation, and a return to the garden—a return to a restored relationship with God, with each other, and a peace within allowing us to love ourselves as we embrace the call to love others.

God's vision for us is to be fully known and fully loved because no matter how much we seek to cover ourselves, it is only in Jesus Christ that we are covered. "Blessed are those whose iniquities are forgiven, and whose sins are covered; blessed is the one against whom the Lord will not reckon sin" (Rom. 4:7–8).

We believed hiding would enable us to be loved, and it is true a covering had to come. But the covering we have received is not intended to hide us, but to redeem us. Our sins are covered by Jesus on the cross, so that we can have the freedom to be who we have been designed to be. We are no longer the unrepentant sinner worthy of separation from our Creator; we are God's child, free to be known, and free to live in the gift of God's love. The world's approval now has diminishing value because we are finding more and more of what we need in God. We are free to be authentic, to be who we are, because we are no longer ashamed. We can be fully known and fully loved. We can live once again in relationship with God, each other, and ourselves without hiding. The fig leaves and the masks can come off. We can let the gaze of our Creator no longer drive us to hide, but fill us with love. In Christ, we are covered. Our shame is gone. *We can be naked and not ashamed.*

Jesus had no fig leaves. He did not hide or conform. In every circumstance and with every person, Jesus lived out of his identity, even in death. He was naked and not ashamed. Nothing separated Jesus from his relationship with his Father. There was no self-deception, and no need to find value and acceptance outside of himself. He lived authentically, spoke authentically, loved authentically, and his life gives us the freedom to live into our design, out of our identity in him, and to encourage others to do the same.

Apart from the embrace of our identity in Christ, authenticity is not possible. We may look authentic, speak authentically, and be perceived by others as authentic, but without an identity in Christ, our motives will be impure and our fig leaves will abound.

Full Disclosure and Authenticity

Often there is the perception that authenticity means full disclosure— that I have to tell everyone my deep, dark secrets if I am to be authentic. This is not true.

Authenticity is not the same as full disclosure. Full disclosure can even be used as a fig leaf. You've probably experienced the person who shares everything with everyone. This kind of sharing can be manipulative, attention-seeking, and counterproductive. Sometimes this extreme sharing is done to avoid taking responsibility for ourselves and to excuse or even justify sinful behavior.

I want to be careful not to minimize the impact and reality of pain. Our fig leaves are often used to cover our pain, to protect us from experiencing it anymore than we already are. We hide because we hurt. These hurts are real and like a bandage on an open wound, we naturally want to cover the sources of pain to avoid further pain, instead of embracing our roles as stewards of our pain. Frederick Buechner explains:

> Being a good steward of your pain involves . . . being alive to your life. It involves taking the risk of being open, of reaching out, of keeping in touch with the pain as well as the joy of what happens because at no time more than at a painful time do we live out of the depths of who we are instead of out of the shallows. There is no guarantee that we will find a pearl in the depths, that the end of our pain will have a happy end, or even any end at all, but at least we stand a chance of finding in those depths who we most deeply and

humanly are and who each other are. At least we stand a chance of finding that we needn't live alone in our pain (1992, p. 99).

Buechner helps us distinguish between disclosing the details of our pain to others, and simply being with each other in our pain. You can be authentically you and not disclose everything. Disclosure is not the prerequisite for authenticity. Disclosure is important, and full disclosure with some people in some contexts can be necessary, but full disclosure in all contexts is inappropriate and unhelpful.

I remember a conversation with a pastor regarding this tension. He wondered about his struggles with lustful thoughts and pornography and wondered if he was required to share this publicly with the congregation. I encouraged him to discuss this with his wife and elders before making any decisions about going public. He does not have to share these struggles in a public setting in order to be authentic. The Spirit may lead him one day to share in this context, but it is not required. The goal is not to emphasize our "horribleness" as if the more horrible things about us we share the more authentic we are. Remember, our identity is found in the One who has rescued us from ourselves, our sin, and our separation from him, so this identity is the one we ought to emphasize, not the old self of sin.

Embracing a Commitment to Authenticity

God desires that we grow more fully into our identity in Christ. As this takes place, we grow in authenticity. How can we open ourselves up to this new way of being?

Follow Jesus

First and most important, we follow Jesus. Following Jesus means abiding in Christ, not going it alone, embracing a commitment to radical obedience which includes confronting places of habitual disobedience, all the while living into God's purpose to restore and redeem all of creation. Not simply setting aside a quiet time, abiding in Jesus becomes a way of life and the source of your power. It is the way the Holy Spirit can work in and through you. As described more fully in Chapter 8, following Christ is about reclaiming our identity as a disciple of Christ.

Refuse to Hide Any Longer

Second, we make the choice moment by moment, circumstance by circumstance, relationship by relationship, to refuse to hide or pretend any longer. We ask God to help us be authentic. Instead of circumstances and people determining our identity, God does. This idea of "self-differentiation" is discussed more fully in our next chapter in the context of courage. Choosing to be authentic does take courage and is a lifelong work. Every situation and relationship carries with it the pressure to conform.

We have to learn to be ourselves and see ourselves clearly. As I grow in my capacity to see myself through God's eyes, to recognize that my value and identity are found in God, I am more able to selflessly love those I'm with instead of using them to affirm my value.

Be Less Secretive

Finally, we need to be less secretive. What we keep in the darkness destroys, poisons, and significantly hinders what God desires to do through us. What we bring into the light, God redeems, heals, and restores.

> For once you were darkness, but now in the Lord you are light. Live as children of light—for the fruit of the light is found in all that is good and right and true. Try to find out what is pleasing to the Lord. Take no part in the unfruitful works of darkness, but instead expose them. For it is shameful even to mention what such people do secretly; but everything exposed by the light becomes visible, for everything that becomes visible is light. Therefore it says, "Sleeper, awake! Rise from the dead, and Christ will shine on you" (Eph. 5:8–14).

Each of us has places of habitual disobedience. We may have wrestled with some of these areas for years and have resigned ourselves to thinking that nothing will change. We may have minimized their significance because of all the other good work we are doing. Yet, they remain, and they are sin. God sees these places in the darkness of our lives as significant areas of growth—growth that can only take place through God's work. We have already changed what we are capable of changing ourselves without God's help. Perhaps we have cried out to God and, because nothing has changed, we've grown resigned and cynical. What is missing may be your willingness to share what you are hiding with another trustworthy human being.

We keep sin in the darkness by hiding it from God, each other, and our own selves. Sin is part of our secret self, the self that only we know about. It's revealing how often the voice of the secret self is condemning and negative. The way we talk to ourselves is often indicative of the fact we know the truth. We are trying to hide, yet as much as we try, we cannot hide the truth from ourselves. We need to let out the "skeletons in our closet" and bring them into the light.

It is important that a few people in your life know everything there is to know about you. These people need to know *everything*—not a watered-down version of the truth, but the whole truth, with no excuses, rationalizations, or minimizations.

"I can't do that," you say.

Yes, you can.

"You don't understand. What will people think? I'll be rejected, looked down on. This will lead to more shame."

That's a real possibility. It's a risk. But remember, your identity is not based on the opinion of others. You are free because you are God's. There is the real possibility these people whom you've chosen to share with really love you. There is the distinct probability that their love for you will only grow because of your willingness to stop hiding. There is the hopeful possibility that by expressing the whole truth you will more fully experience grace, and the shame you've been carrying will diminish instead of deepen because you are bringing what is in the darkness into the light. Not only will you likely experience a deeper sense of God's love and grace through these relationships, but you are also enlisting a small community of support to help you avoid the areas of darkness in which you've struggled. This community of grace and truth provides the accountability we need to address the places of habitual disobedience where we've been stuck, not in judgment and guilt, but in love and truth. This accountability enables the secret self to no longer be a haven for darkness where self-talk is driven by voices other than God's, but instead allows God's light and God's voice to overcome the places of darkness and speak God's words of truth into your life. It is in the context of these relationships that we can grow in our capacity to be authentic and experience acceptance, where we can practice being naked and not ashamed.

Alcoholics don't begin their recovery until they admit they have a problem and ask for help. People trapped in the allure of pornography don't begin to heal until they admit their sin and ask for help. Abused men, women, and children don't begin to find hope until they bring to the surface the abuse and ask for help. None of us came into relationship with Christ without taking responsibility for and telling the truth about our brokenness and asking for help.

We have to confront the places of darkness in our lives and bring them into the light. We need to tell the truth. We need to ask for help. We need to stop hiding.

Remember the alternative. Hiding what's true in the darkness with no possibility that the shame will be addressed, with no community of people to help us address the places we are stuck, and with no possibility that God intends for us to experience his grace and love in very tangible ways through human relationships, will only lead to guilt, loneliness, stagnation, and darkness. Why do we stay here? What keeps us here is fear. What keeps us here is shame. What keeps us here is because we believe the lies of the enemy who is working overtime to keep us right here—alone, resigned, shameful, and hiding. We were not designed for this. This is not the story Jesus has for you. Jesus has invited you into a different, transforming, life-giving story, where you are his, naked and not ashamed.

Taking Off My Fig Leaves

One place where I've grown in authenticity is in my preaching. Not long ago I did a five-week series on love, sex, and dating. One of the greatest regrets of my life is that I was sexually active in college. For a long time I carried a ton of guilt and shame about that season of my life. Now I can see how far outside of God's design I was, but then it was not so clear to me. Two things happened as a result of me being authentic about my college experience in such a public way.

First, I've had a number of authentic conversations and comments from people who hear my preaching. One man stopped me after one of the sermons and said, "It's actually very encouraging to see that you are not Superman. Hearing about your struggles and knowing that you've made some big mistakes makes you more real and more believable. Thank you." I think it helps the congregation to see what it is like to be a work in progress—to see that I have wounding that needs healing. As they hear how I worked that out, they find encouragement for their own journey.

Second, it opened up a wide variety of conversations that I may never have had. One couple said to me, "We waited until we were married, and we didn't get much credit for it, but we are so glad we did." A young man stopped me in that hallway of the church and said, "Thank you so much for telling us the truth about sex and dating from the Bible and for telling the truth about your own experience. My experience was very similar to yours. I wished I had known then what I know now." I encouraged both this couple and this young man to tell their stories. Taking off my fig leaf of needing to look good all the time enabled me to connect authentically with my congregation in a way I hadn't before.

Practice and Reflect

Spend some time in quiet and ask: When have I been willing to take off my fig leaf and be authentically myself? What happened? Who in my life could I authentically share something in my private or secret self? Schedule a time and share. Be bold! Then look for another person with whom you can share. See this as a process of growing your capacity to be authentic in a wide variety of settings. Here's something else you can do: Take a few days in your quiet time and journal the story of your life including the events that resulted in or contributed to the formation of your private or secret self. When you've finished, share this story with someone.

Going Deeper

Practicing authenticity means being willing to take off our fig leaves and disclose who we really are to the world. When we are authentic, we are able to confront the dark places in our lives and we are able to open ourselves to the possibility of real change and real transformation.

To learn more about the core value of authenticity, check out our online resources at http://www.westernsem.edu/journey/ridder.

References and Additional Resources

Benner, David G. *The Gift of Being Yourself: The Sacred Call to Self-Discovery.* Downers Grove, IL: IVP Books, 2004.

Brown, Brené. *I Thought It Was Just Me: Making the Journey from "What Will People Think?" to "I Am Enough."* New York: Penguin, 2008.

Buechner, Frederick. *Clown in the Belfry: Writings on Faith and Fiction.* New York: HarperCollins, 1992.

Keller, Tim. "Nakedness & The Holiness of God" (sermon, 1993). http://sermons2.redeemer.com/sermons/nakedness-holiness-god.

Miller, Donald, *Scary Close: Dropping the Act and Finding True Intimacy.* Nashville: Thomas Nelson, 2015.

Peck, M. Scott. *The Different Drum: Community Making and Peace.* New York: Touchstone, 1987.

Chapter 6
Courage: Stepping off the Sidelines

Jessica Shults

Be strong and courageous. . . .
—Joshua 1

One isn't necessarily born with courage, but one is born with po-
tential. Without courage, we cannot practice any other virtue with
consistency. We can't be kind, true, merciful, generous, or honest.
—Maya Angelou

How do you grow courage? We started to ask that question when it became clear that living this fully human, fully alive life was going to require
us to be a lot braver than we were used to being. We needed courage for
seeking God, courage for defining ourselves, courage for facing opposi-
tion, courage for missional living.

We learned that we grew courage when we practiced doing hard
things. We got braver when we did the things that scared us and when we
shared our fears and victories with each other. When we practiced giving up looking good and staying safe, we found reserves of courage we
didn't even know we had. Then God gave us more opportunities to practice being brave and we tried hard to take them on. We grew our capacity
for obedience to God by "doing it scared" and watching to see what God
would do in and through us.

*W*e have asked you to risk dreaming dreams, to risk identifying and closing integrity gaps, and to risk being authentic. I want to begin this chapter by asking a question about courage: Was Joshua able to be a courageous leader because he was blessed with the "adventure gene"?

The Adventure Gene

The science on the genetics of personality is still in its infancy. It landed on the world in 1996, with two papers attempting to link Novelty Seeking and Extraversion with the DRD4 gene coding for a particular dopamine receptor in the brain (Ebstein, 2006). "Novelty Seeking" is a specific personality used by researchers and professionals to make comparisons from one person to the next. A non-technical explanation of novelty seeking includes:

- Tendency to respond strongly to novelty
- Exploratory activity in pursuit of rewards
- Active avoidance of monotony
- Active avoidance of punishment
- Less influenced by emotion (especially fear) in risk assessment (Roussos, et al., 2009).

This research has made me wonder whether in order to be faithful to the instructions found in scripture to be strong and courageous followers of Christ, must we possess the adventure gene? More specifically, I've wondered about congregational leaders. Do those who have the adventure gene have an advantage over those of us who do not?

My question is a deep and personal one because I am pretty convinced I was born with quite the opposite gene. High school mock elections are rarely a boost to one's ego unless you are one of the select few voted "most likely to take your breath away," "most likely to save the earth," or "most likely to run a Fortune 500 company." During my supposedly celebratory senior banquet night in 1997, I received the honor of finding out I was voted, "most likely to be boring." Who approved the list of what we voted on anyway? Years after the embarrassment faded, I realized that what my classmates saw in me was that even as a high school student, I was not likely to go outside the rules. Extremely consistent in my personality and standing for what I believed in, I would usually make the safe choice in every circumstance. *So does this mean that because of the way God created me I am starting with a handicap as a leader?*

For years I held this question in tension, believing God created me for the epic life. Over time, I have become fully convicted that for me, learning to be courageous means that I must choose to step into the adventure of life, even while being scared. This is how I grow my own personal courage. This is the place where I take on radical obedience. Jesus beckons me to enter a place where I risk everything that I am comfortable with, even though on most days I would rather play it safe in case God does not show up. I can see clearly that if I continue life in that posture, I will miss the opportunity to live the epic life God calls me to live.

Safe and Stuck

"Stuck at the Visitor's Center" is a powerful story about courage. Gary Haugen (2008) tells of a camping and hiking trip he took with his dad and two older brothers on Mount Rainer. Seeing a scary warning sign on the trail, young Gary opted to spend the day at the visitor's center while his father and brothers climbed the mountain.

> One of the biggest regrets of life, I think is a sense of having gone on the trip but missed the adventure....
>
> The visitor's center was warm and comfortable, with lots of interesting things to watch and read. I devoured the information and explored every corner, and judging by the crowd, it was clearly the place to be. As the afternoon stretched on, however, the massive visitor's center started to feel awfully small. The warm air felt stuffy, and the stuffed wild animals started to seem just—dead. The inspiring loop videos about extraordinary people who climbed the mountain weren't as interesting the sixth and seventh time, and they made me wish I could be one of those actually climbing the mountain instead of reading about it. I felt bored, sleepy, and small—and I missed my dad. I was totally stuck. Totally safe—but totally stuck.
>
> After the longest afternoon of my ten-year-old life, Dad and my brothers returned flushed with their triumph. Their faces were red from the cold and their eyes clear with delight. They were wet from the snow, famished, dehydrated and nursing scrapes from the rocks and ice, but on the long drive home they had something else. They had stories and an unforgettable day with their dad on a great mountain.

Do you ever feel like that? Totally safe but totally stuck in life, especially with respect to your personal relationship with Christ. If so, then I want to ask you these questions: How do you develop your capacity to be courageous? How do you move beyond your fears or whatever is stopping you in order to take up the adventure? These are important questions because I am convinced that deep down none of us want to miss the adventure God created us to experience. Do you?

Courage to Live as Wholehearted People of God

How do you develop the courage to live as the wholehearted people of God, believing that you deserve to and should be on this adventure? The door is swung wide open by research done by Brené Brown (2010) dealing with the pull that shame and fear have on each of our lives. When shame and fear are allowed to control the inner parts of our being, they unravel our ability to accept who God has created us to be. In the face of the shame and fear, we are busy protecting and covering up things about ourselves of which people might not approve. We keep our distance from others and aren't willing to risk connection.

Brown has discovered that what separates those who risk connectedness and those who do not is that they believe they are worthy of love and belonging. Wholehearted people live with deep courage ("the ability to tell the story of who you are with your whole heart"), compassion ("being kind to yourself first"), and connection (because they are willing to be authentic and have the courage to be imperfect). People who live wholehearted are people "who are willing to say I love you first, to do something where there are no guarantees, to breathe through the doctor calling after your mammogram" (Brown, 2011). This is the type of people we are called to be as followers of Christ.

What stands in the way of you living as the wholehearted person God is calling you to be? I've learned from personal experience that whatever it is that stops you, to get unstopped, you must take on the hard work of growing your courage muscles.

When we recognize that we are all imperfect, we can begin to believe that we are all worthy of love and belonging. When we work from a place where we believe we are enough, we are kinder and gentler to those around us, and kinder and gentler to ourselves. In addition to this, we have laid the groundwork for stepping into the adventure, to having the courage to begin our epic life, the life to which God is calling us.

Systems and Courageous Leadership

In the last chapter, Chip talked about the value of authenticity and the fact that it takes courage to seek our true identity in God rather than seeking our identity through the eyes of others. In his seminal work entitled *A Failure of Nerve*, Edwin Friedman (1999) suggests that leaders often fail to live courageously because the systems in which they live and serve have so much invisible influence on the choices those leaders make. While we will discuss systems thinking in more detail in later chapters, I want to introduce the idea here as it relates to courageous leadership.

Systems thinking is a way of *thinking*. A comparison to linear thinking may be helpful. Linear thinking is the thinking that I do when I look at my lack of courage and think that I lack courage because "A" causes "B." In systems thinking, I am empowered to see that my lack of courage has multiple causes that grow out of the interactions I have with others to whom I am connected.

So as a leader, one contributing factor to my lack of courage may be that I don't have the adventure gene. With that as a given, I believe I have heard from God about a course of action that scares me, but I decide that I will grow my courage and take this action despite my fear. Then when I share what I am about to do with my friend, she has a fearful response and expresses that to me, and my courage diminishes. My friend tells someone else what I am considering doing and that person comes to me calmly and says, "I really don't believe that is a wise course of action." I can feel my resolve diminishing. This simple example illustrates the point that the lack of the adventure gene is only one of the factors contributing to the choice I make.

Self-Differentiation

Friedman suggests that effective leadership—here, growing one's courage—is about an emotional process of regulating one's own anxiety while staying connected to the system. He refers to this process as self-differentiation. At its most basic level, self-differentiation is about knowing where "one person ends and another begins" (2007, pp. 183, 199). Said another way, it is about knowing what I am responsible for and recognizing that when I act responsibly, those actions will have impact on those to whom I am connected. My actions may make others anxious (for a whole variety of reasons) and their anxiety can have an impact on me and on the choices I make.

In human systems, often when an individual acts as a differentiated self, others get anxious. And in the face of the anxiety of others, I am tempted to become less differentiated, less able to regulate my own anxiety. To go back to my earlier illustration, I heard God say to me, "Jess, this is the course of action I want you to take." Though I was afraid, I was determined to obey the Lord. Then, as I interacted with others, their anxiety diminished my resolve until I learned to see the impact of other people's anxiety on me. When I learned to see the impact of their anxiety, I was more able to take a stand and stay with my choices.

Friedman (2007) suggests that an individual person can stay connected to others without losing her identity and without taking on the emotional anxiety of others or of the group. A self-differentiated individual can take a well-defined stand even when others disagree while remaining connected with others in a meaningful way.

Now, let's dig a little deeper. While I can stay with my course of action while staying connected to those who are anxious about my choices, here is something that makes it really challenging. A family or a congregation is made up of people who possess varying levels of differentiation. For those who have extremely low levels of differentiation, Friedman (2007) argues they can be like viruses in the human body.

Viruses do not have a nucleus or a core organizing principle, so they cannot exist on their own. They look for other poorly differentiated cells to latch on to. They infect the organization with their anxiety. They cannot handle one-on-one conflict with another person. So they try to rope in a third person in an effort to lessen the anxiety. This is called triangulation. If you are the one being triangled, it is so tempting to enmesh yourself in the drama and to feel good about being needed or included in the conversation (Friedman, 2007).

Friedman (2007) suggests that a well-differentiated leader, one acting with great courage, acts as the emotional immune system of an organization. By managing her own anxiety, she resists being triangulated and this situation forces others to take responsibility for themselves. This may be counter-intuitive to those of us who are used to being part of anxious systems. Many pastors and congregational leaders act as though it is their job to be responsible for reducing the anxiety of others. Differentiated leaders have the courage to take responsibility for their own anxiety and allow others to take responsibility for theirs. (See also Herrington et al., 2003.)

Courage to Move Ahead with Our Mission

We can learn about the courage to move ahead from Joshua's life. God speaks to Joshua about courage and about carrying out his mission. God begins by saying, "Be strong and courageous; for you shall put this people in possession of the land that I swore to their ancestors to give them" (Josh. 1: 6).

God's call on Joshua's life was to lead the Israelites out of the desert into the Promised Land. God's call to join the adventure always involves moving in some aspect—from Point A to Point B. Moving from our current reality to God's emerging future—the future that God desires for our congregation rather than the default future we arrive at based on decisions made out of fear, anxiety from congregation members who have other expectations, or from making no plans at all—demands deep courage.

My Courage Story

I have already told you of my natural inclinations in life, my temptation to stay at the visitor center or maybe take the paved trails. It is not my natural inclination to head right towards the mountain of adventure.

I grew up the daughter of a pastor, and very early on in life sensed a call to full-time ministry. As I headed to college, I internalized this call as a call to youth ministry. I spent my college years immersed in any ministry experience available—interning at a local church, participating in Northwestern College's campus ministries, and spending my summers working at church camp.

It was during this time that my college advisor, professors, campus pastors as well as others in the church began to encourage me to consider attending seminary. My first reaction to their well-meaning encouragement was, "No thank you, not in a million years. After all, women can't be pastors anyway." And yet our conversations, along with the uneasiness in my spirit, led me to wonder if this was an adventure I was called to take. So in January of my senior year of college, I courageously enrolled in seminary, taking the firm stance that I would attend but would certainly never be a "real" pastor. God used my passion for students to place me in a local church to lead their college ministry, but my time there became about so much more. For the first time, I experienced a congregation thinking deeply about missional living and asking the hard questions about how they might serve their neighborhood. During my summers I ran a ministry for the neighborhood kids that became a source of deep joy and provided me with immense hope about the ways the local church could join God in the work he was doing in the world around them. God was helping me fall back in love with the local church that I insisted I would never serve.

During the final months of seminary as I was seeking employment, God was up to something in the congregation my husband had been serving during the past two years. We discovered that they had begun the work of developing a new position and the job description just happened to be in the areas where I was comfortable saying I had gifts. At the end of a process, led by the Spirit, I joyfully accepted the position of becoming the Pastor of Discipleship Ministries, close to being a "real" pastor in a local congregation, but still hiding under the safety net of not being *the* pastor. There was still plenty of room to defer to the other person if things got too tough.

After a few years of serving in this discipleship ministry role, my senior pastor moved on to a different ministry experience. I found myself filling new roles and found great joy and fulfillment in doing so, though I hesitated to admit it. After almost a year of searching for the next perfect senior pastor, intended to be male, thirty to forty years old, and a stellar leader who would take the congregation to the next level, the search committee came to a point of frustration and began to ask themselves why they weren't finding that individual.

It was at this very same time that I left to go to Texas for my first Faithwalking experience with Ridder Church Renewal. (Faithwalking is a spiritual formation process that includes a three-day weekend retreat, a twenty-four-week small group process, and a leadership course.) In the stack of church work I took along with me to do in my free time, there was a document created by the search team clarifying what they believed they were looking for in the next pastoral leader of the congregation. The team had asked me to review the document, and I looked at it periodically throughout my three-day Faithwalking experience. Repeatedly I heard God say, "This is you they have just described. This is who I have called you to be."

As the sense of these promptings became clearer and stronger, there was plenty of push back and resistance from me—this was not who I wanted to be! This was not the cross I wanted to bear because I knew full well the pain and loneliness that came with this role. I returned from that Faithwalking experience with more passion for my faith and more hope for the church.[1] I also returned with a clear commitment that I would *not* reveal the ways God was calling me to step out in courage and take on the challenge of being a different kind of pastor in my current context.

Two days after landing back in Grand Rapids, a small group met to review this document summarizing the type of leader Standale Reformed Church was looking for. One of the members opened the meeting by asking me to share about my experience in Texas, and then we would get to the real business we had gathered to do. I'm not sure what I said in those moments that followed. But when I finished, one of the deeply in-tune and courageous members of this group said, "I think we are here to talk about something different. I think we need to talk about you being our next pastor and what might be standing in the way of that happening."

On that day my journey, my adventure, the one that I had tried with all of my might to avoid, reached a whole new level. And you know what is still so incredible? In the days, months, and years that have followed that moment, there has been an overwhelming sense of peace received from God that this is just where God would have me be!

This journey has also been deeply painful at times. But what sustains me and gives me the courage to continue on is thinking about what I would have missed if I hadn't been willing to be on this adventure. My default future would have been to remain in the backseat of leadership and service for my entire life. I would have been much more comfortable there, and I probably would have accomplished some great things for the Kingdom. But I would have missed something, and we as a congregation would have missed something as well.

Courage Is a Choice

Take a look at Joshua 1:6–9:

Be strong and courageous; for you shall put this people in possession of the land that I swore to their ancestors to give them. Only be strong and very courageous, being careful to act in accordance with all the law that my servant Moses commanded you; do not turn from it to the right hand or to the left, so that you may be successful wherever you go. This book of the law shall not depart out of your mouth; you shall meditate on it day and night, so that you may be careful to act in accordance with all that is written in it. For then you shall make your way prosperous, and then you shall be successful. I hereby command you: Be strong and courageous; do not be frightened or dismayed, for the LORD your God is with you wherever you go.

---

1. For more information about Faithwalking, go to www.faithwalking.us.

Three different times God says to Joshua, "Be strong and courageous." For those who think that courage is the same kind of emotional reaction as fear—that it's just something you feel—then God's words may seem impossible. But the fact is that we don't experience courage the same way we experience fear. Fear is a feeling; courage is a stance we take. Courage is a value we intentionally embrace, a choice we can make. God told Joshua to be strong and courageous because courage was a choice that Joshua was capable of making. It's not as if God told Joshua, "Be tall!" or "Be left-handed!" or "Be Dutch!" These are things a person can't control. You're either tall or left-handed or Dutch or you're not. But God told Joshua to be courageous because courage is a choice that is based on faith and trust in God. The more you choose courage, the more you grow in your capacity to live courageously. Experience transforms, and courage transforms our ability to get into action that makes real change possible.

My personal example of courage is an enjoyable one to share because my risk-taking ended well. That doesn't mean that while I was in the midst of it I was not afraid. Most people watching the transformation I have experienced in my life during the last five years would describe me as one of the most courageous people they know. While they have witnessed my courage, I would have rarely described myself that way. There have been plenty of times when I was shaking internally, feeling the burden of fear creeping in more days than not. Yet, I continued to choose courage.

Courage Needs to Be Nurtured

Because fear is a very natural feeling we experience each day, we need to recognize that courage must be continually nurtured. We're rarely given the luxury of only being courageous when we are no longer scared. Rather, radical obedience in our life will mean "doing it scared." Like me, most Christians are not blessed with the adventure gene, but we can grow in our capacity to have courage.

Just like the Spirit cultivates love, joy, peace, patience, kindness, generosity, faithfulness, gentleness and self-control (Gal. 5:22–23), we must pray for ways to increase our ability to choose courage so that courage grows to a place of maturity and wholeness in our lives.

Follow Courageous Examples

One way to nurture courage is by following courageous examples.

Moses was a leadership example for Joshua. God said to Joshua, "act in accordance with all the law that my servant Moses commanded you; do not turn from it to the right hand or to the left" (Josh. 1:7). Though Joshua was his own man, his own leader, God reminded him from the beginning that he needed to hang on to the lessons he learned under the leadership of Moses.

Practice and Reflect

Take some time and reflect upon the following questions: Do you know a few courageous people whose examples you can follow? Have you seen how they react to challenges and setbacks? Have you noticed how they stand up to difficult situations? Learn from them. Learn to do what they do. This is why Paul said to the church in Corinth, "I appeal to you, then, be imitators of me" (1 Cor. 4:16), and "Be imitators of me, as I am of Christ" (1 Cor. 11:1). Look for examples to follow in your own life.

Courageous Colleagues in Ministry

A story I would hope to have the courage to imitate is the story of my friend Chris, a fellow pastor in Ridder Church Renewal, and his congregation at Pillar Church. Dedicated in 1856 and located near Hope College and Western Theological Seminary in Holland, Michigan, Pillar Church has a deep, rich history.

When Pastor Chris arrived, Pillar's membership was declining. Six years later, things weren't much better, with the pews filled mostly with individuals who were past age sixty. There was one baby in the nursery and one or two children in Children and Worship. Early on, Chris and the church leadership tried a few initiatives hoping to change this picture, but despite a lot of really hard work, things didn't seem to change.

A year into the Ridder process, Pastor Chris and his team were given the specific assignment of creating a "Current Reality" document—a document that described the "what is so" in their congregation. Pastor Chris and his team took on this assignment with great courage. They wrote down on paper what many had danced around for decades. At the end of this process, it was pretty clear that some significant changes would need to be in their future.

A vision team was formed with representatives from Pillar Church, First Reformed Church, and the community around Pillar. This team began to ask what God might have in mind for the future of Pillar Church —what we call "God's emerging future." Why had God placed them in this specific location at this specific time? What might need to change for fruitful and faithful ministry to take place? At the end of that process, they discerned this particular vision:

> *Pillar Church is the embodiment of a unique history and vision of reconciliation. Reconciliation is key to the vision and experience of Pillar Church. Pillar Church is a dual-affiliation church of the Christian Reformed Church in North America and the Reformed Church in America. This dual affiliation reflects a deep hope for reconciliation between these two historic churches and is an expression of God's heart for the reconciliation of all things to himself through Jesus Christ.*

Pillar Church, strategically located on the campus of Hope College, desires to participate in the faith formation of young women and men for life, work, and ministry of all kinds in all places. Pillar Church desires to partner with Western Theological Seminary in the pastoral development of women and men for ministry in and with the church.

Pillar Church is an historic church founded as the city of Holland was being established and longs to experience the continual movement of God's revitalizing spirit in the church.

Pillar Church is a church committed to mission both globally and locally and is especially eager to extend itself in missional efforts for the continued renewal of the city of Holland.

When they asked themselves what it would take to bridge the gap between their current reality and God's emerging future, they knew they lacked the people and financial resources necessary. Believing that this alone should not stop them and that this alone was not more than what God could accomplish, they decided to raise the money and recruit people to join in fulfilling the vision they sensed God gave them. This was a way of "doing church" that none of them had ever experienced before. Three members of the vision team approached a local foundation with a grant proposal for half of the needed funds. They received a phone call the next day with the news that the entire amount was granted! That phone call was a profound "and God will go with you wherever you go" moment.

These days, their landscape is quickly changing. Their current reality today consists of new pastoral and staff leadership, a worship attendance five times larger, and a significant shift in the demographics of the people filling the pews. Four themes have sharpened the purpose at Pillar: reconciliation, raising up leaders, renewing the city, and revitalizing the church. The church is active in refugee resettlement, mentoring college and seminary students, partnering with local social agencies, and offering hospitality to the city by way of its beautiful green space downtown. The leadership recognizes that courage is still needed to stay focused on this vision and implement ministry to fit the goals.

The story is fun to tell because it is a story of success. The reality is there would not have been much of a story to tell if courageous action had not been taken by both Pastor Chris and the church leaders around him. There were moments in the process that they were risking everything. They risked the current congregation dismissing them and choosing to remain just as they were for as long as they could. Pastor Chris risked his job. The vision team risked rejection by the local foundation. They risked rejection from their denomination when seeking to become a dual-affiliation church. They also faced the ever-present risk that the initial excitement of a new vision might fade as they stayed committed to the difficult and challenging work of gospel reconciliation.

Courageous Friends

Not only must we surround ourselves with courageous colleagues in ministry, but we must also surround ourselves with courageous friends who take the words found in Joshua "be strong and courageous" to the next level in their own lives. My friend Beth is one of these individuals. Here is her story in her own words:

> My journey into single motherhood in the city started when I was in college. I was happily and comfortably studying youth ministry at a Bible college. God slowly but surely started turning my heart towards changing my career path to helping others in need, not just suburban youth like I had planned. My major ended up becoming social work although I wasn't quite sure what I would be doing with it. I did know it would not be something comfortable and familiar. God started speaking to me through classes, sermons, chapels and conversations with friends and advisors. I felt God calling me to urban ministry. I resisted. Growing up a country girl, I had no interest in working in or living in the city. In fact, I was a bit afraid of the idea. I felt there wasn't much I could offer any "city people."
>
> When I was told I couldn't work a third summer at my favorite summer camp but was offered a position I hadn't even applied for at an urban ministry, I still resisted. One evening while driving on the highway that overlooks the city, God finally spoke loud enough and made my heart ache hard enough that I had to give in. I was listening to a song by Bebo Norman for the first time called "Walk Down This Mountain." The chorus says, "So walk down this mountain with your heart held high. Follow in the footsteps of your Maker. With this love that's gone before you and these people at your side, if you offer up your broken cup, you will taste the meaning of this life." Tears. Fine. I'd go. With my heart held high, I willed myself to trust as I followed my Maker's steps, my support system at my side. Little did I know it was in the act of following, being radically obedient, that I really would begin to taste the true meaning of this life.
>
> That summer, working with children and families in the city, and living in their neighborhood, I fell in love. Life as it had been before was over! This was where I had to be. I wasn't comfortable. I was unsure about future details. It sure wasn't my dreams or my family's for my life, but it was God's plan, and I was finally willing to follow it!
>
> That summer I met a young single mom, not much older than me. She had six kids and obviously needed help that I was able

to give. Over time we built a mutual friendship full of love and trust amidst our numerous differences. I became the godmother to one of her sons and am helping raise him to this day. And then when she became pregnant with her eighth child, she admitted she couldn't raise the baby alone. She needed help. I had no doubt that I was to become this child's godmother and help raise her. When her little girl was born, the baby came home with me. Now six years later, I'm her legal guardian and her "mom" and I intend to be that forever!

During this time God's call to the people in this city remained clear. I graduated from college and took a full time social work job at a non-profit agency downtown. I also took a part-time job at the same urban ministry. God opened up an opportunity to purchase a home right in the neighborhood. I had been living comfortably (and for free) with my parents in the country, not even thinking of moving out. But God had other plans. Now eight years later, I'm a homeowner in this part of the city, and there is nowhere else I'd rather live.

Living out God's call to me to be a single mother in the city has meant experiencing things I never expected or even wanted to be part of my story. I've had my home broken into. I'm helping raise a teenage boy who has learning disabilities and a history of stealing. I've had a gang threaten my godson while he was under my sole care. I've dealt with multiple health issues with my little girl. I've had the heartache of turning in my godson to the authorities, leading to incarceration. I've had meetings with Child Protective Services in an effort to advocate for my children's biological mother. I've endured rude looks, questions and opinions offered about our "family" situation, and I've dealt with the everyday stress of owning a home and raising children alone.

I was never and am never really alone though. I have my support system and most importantly, I have the One who called me to this life. I have my Maker's footsteps to follow. My Rock. My Strength. My Courage to taste the meaning of this life.

Do life with people who are at least one step ahead of you on the courage scale.

Your Courage Collage

As a native of West Michigan, I have grown up hearing heroic stories about President Gerald R. Ford. When visiting the Ford museum, I watched a video showing President Ford receiving the 2001 John F. Kennedy Profile in Courage Award from Caroline Kennedy: "As President, he made a controversial decision of conscience to pardon former president

Nixon and end the national trauma of Watergate. In doing so, he placed his love of country ahead of his own political future" (Kennedy, 2001).

That humble, grateful, and somewhat relieved expression on President Ford's face as he received the Profile of Courage award will be a moment burned in my memory forever. Courage was defined for me—it was put on full display and the foggy glasses were taken off. As I exited the museum that day, I stopped by the gift shop and purchased a magnet with President Ford's picture on it, so that each day when I go to open my refrigerator, I am reminded of my conscious decision to choose courage so that I don't miss the adventure.

I need another magnet for my office or maybe a large poster with the words of Joshua 1:9 plastered in a prominent place: "do not be frightened or dismayed, for the LORD your God is with you wherever you go." Most days I still need that reminder. Next to those words should be testimonies of transformed lives, pictures of people with whom I have had the privilege of journeying, and places I have gone that have been way less than boring. Around those words, these images would make up a collage of this epic life that God designed me for.

If I looked at this collage, I guarantee you that on most days my heart would beat faster and a smile would come to my face and maybe even tears to my eyes seeing the reminders of God's big dream for me. Really! I was someone who thought I preferred a much more boring life. Even though I may not have been born with the adventure gene, now that I've experienced a taste of the epic life God has invited me into, I would never go back to that safe, boring life on the sidelines.

Practice and Reflect

In solitude: Please get out your journal and set some time aside for quiet reflection.

1. Where do you consider yourself to fall from 1–10 on the "courage scale"? Prayerfully consider moments when you have lived courageously. Write them down. What allowed you to act courageously in those moments? What happened when you made that choice? What stands in the way of you living more courageously, or as Brené Brown puts it, more wholeheartedly?
2. Prayerfully consider the stories of courage God has placed in your life. Make a plan to interview two courageous individuals. When you ask them their stories, think about whether they label themselves courageous. What happened in their lives to enable them able to step into the adventure God had planned for them?

In your small group: Please bring your journals and the following supplies: poster board, markers, scissors, magazines, and glue sticks.

1. Share what you learned in your reflection time about your own moments of courage and those of the people you interviewed.
2. Consider making a collage of courage, including images and testimonies of courage from your own life and the lives around you.

Going Deeper

Courage is a choice. It is essential to nurture our ability to be courageous if we want to move off the sidelines and into the epic life that God intends for us. To learn more about nurturing the value of courage, we invite you to check out our online resources at http://www.westernsem. edu/journey/ridder.

References and Additional Resources

Brown, Brené. *The Gifts of Imperfection: Let Go of Who You Think You Are Supposed to Be and Embrace Who You Are.* Center City, MN: Hazelden Press, 2010.

_____. "The Power of Vulnerability" (TED talk), 2011. http://www.ted. com/talks/brene_brown_on_vulnerability.

_____. *Daring Greatly: How the Courage to Be Vulnerable Transforms the Way We Live, Love, Parent and Lead.* New York: Gotham, 2016.

Ebstein, R.P. "The Molecular Genetic Architecture of Human Personality: Beyond Self-report Questionnaires." *Molecular Psychiatry*, 11, no. 5 (2006): 427–45.

Friedman, Edwin. *A Failure of Nerve.* New York: Seabury Books, 2007.

Haugen, Gary A. *Just Courage: God's Great Expedition for the Restless Christian.* Downers Grove, IL: InterVarsity Press, 2008

John F. Kennedy Presidential Library and Museum, "Gerald Ford, Award Announcement," 2001. http://www.jrflibrary.org/Events-and-Awards/Profilesin-Courage-Award-Recipients/Gerald-Ford.

Roussos, P., S. G. Giakoumaki, and P. Bitsios. Cognitive and Emotional Processing in High Novelty Seeking Associated with the L-DRD4 Genotype. *Neuropsychologia*, 47, no. 7 (2009): 1654–9.

A Wholehearted Courage Story

Brené Brown defines courage as being able to tell the story of who you are with your whole heart. It has taken me a long time to have courage. Finding courage was hard because my story seemed radically different than the story told by other women in my community. In the Christian circles I grew up in, no one told my story and those who tried paid a great cost.

My story, the one I tell with my whole heart, is about being a wife to an incredible man, a mother of two precious boys, and a pastor of a daring congregation. My story is different than the story my mom tells, my sisters tell, the story other wives and mothers in my congregation tell, and in many cases the story the church universal tells of the right way to be a Christian woman. Stories that differ are often made wrong and so for a long time I only told part of my story because of the shame I experienced when I told it with my whole heart.

Before I found courage, it was easy to allow others to tell my story. That way I didn't have to. And along the way, others took joy in trying to do so. They would tell the story they wished for me or a story they believed was more faithful to God's role for women. For a long time, without even knowing I was, I let them. Why? Because just like everybody else I wanted people to like me, to accept me, and I thought the way to do that was to hide who I really was or only tell part of the truth.

My fears were reinforced by events along the way and the meaning I made from those experiences. One of those included a phone call a week after we began sharing the news that we were expecting a second child. The phone rang at about 9:00 p.m. and on the other end was one of the current church leaders offering his congratulations. After a little small talk, the real reason of the call was revealed. He said something like this, "As I work on the church budget for next year, I assume that I can write you in with a part-time position, rather than full-time, since you will have two kids." In shock, I fumbled over my words lacking the ability to have a crucial conversation in that moment.

Even in the midst of my lack of courage, God was powerfully writing my story even when I resisted letting him. Experience taught me that the place of greatest peace for me and my family was when I choose to be faithful to my story. God's story for my life included weaving together the roles of wife, mother, and pastor in very full yet faithful ways.

In the midst of my struggle, I was invited to reflect on scripture passages where God had called his people by name: "Samuel, Samuel!" "Mary!" "Saul, Saul." I heard, "Jess! This is what I made you for. You don't have to hide, you don't have to be filled with shame, and you don't have to pretend you have not clearly heard your name."

When God called "Jess, Jess!" God was saying, "Jess, I have created you to be a wife, a mother, and a pastor, and until you are willing to courageously tell that story and accept that this is your unique story, you won't experience wholehearted life with me."

This is my story, and mine alone. And I'm learning to tell it with my whole heart.

Chapter 7
Love: Nobody Wins unless Everybody Wins

Brian Stone

I have found the paradox that if you love until it hurts, there can be no more hurt, only more love.

—Mother Teresa

Love is not affectionate feeling, but a steady wish for the loved person's ultimate good as far as it can be obtained.

—C.S. Lewis

It takes courage to live this life to which God has called us. In particular, it takes courage to love the way God requires us to—to love the people who aren't like us, the people who don't like us, the people God loves. We realized that we had settled for being "nice," when God had called us to a fierce missional love.

We wanted to learn the kind of love that could transform us, the kind of love that could empower lives of sacrifice and big dreams. We took the challenge of practicing that kind of love in the relationships we already had, especially with our families, the people we go to church with, the people in our neighborhoods and in the broken parts of our communities. Of the values we intentionally embraced, the greatest of these is love.

*L*ove. It's a small, dangerous word, isn't it? It's been used over and over in songs to convey a feeling that might be as fleeting as a one-night stand. It's used to express how much we enjoy the flavor of ice cream or the color of someone's shirt. It's a word that's been used by hormonal boys to manipulate their dates and by abusive spouses to sugarcoat their brutality.

Love. Love is also the value that is necessary to everything you are as a follower of Jesus. When love is absent, nothing you read about in this book—no other core value, no mental model, no leadership skill—really matters.

While love can mean anything from sex without consequences to our feelings about the appetizer menu at our favorite restaurant, I want to look at love as a value that is to be cultivated and grown in our lives as we pursue transformation toward missional living.

As you read, I encourage you to listen from the posture that asks, "What if this is true?" Let the Holy Spirit speak to you.

Confessions of One Who Doesn't Love As Well As He Should

I'm going to be honest with you. I didn't take on writing this chapter because I am the most loving person in the world. In fact, my co-pastor, John, told me he finds my writing this chapter to be very ironic and humorous! It isn't that I'm not loving, but there are many people who don't *experience* me as loving.

It isn't that I don't care about others. In fact, I am very sensitive and have a high capacity to empathize with others. Don, one of my elders and a good friend, often jokes about which one of us will cry first while listening to someone's story. However, by utilizing the DiSC® behavior assessment tool, I have learned that in addition to being a highly extroverted "people person," I am also highly task-driven. And in my autopilot way of being in the world, this means that I can go from having a great time in the midst of all the people around me to becoming so focused on the task that there is a trail of carnage behind me. I can be the most judgmental and selfish jerk you have ever met.

And so, I took on this chapter not because I am the expert on love, but because it is a value I need to intentionally grow in my life! Will you join me on this journey?

Practice and Reflect

Stop! Will you do something very courageous? Before reading on in this chapter, have a conversation with three people who know you well and ask them two questions: How do you experience me as loving? When don't you experience me as loving? As soon as you can afterward, spend time in solitude with God and journal what that experience was like for you.

We Are Commanded to Love

In the last chapter, Jess explained that courage isn't a feeling; it's a value that we choose in spite of our feelings. Love, as we understand it biblically, is a value, a way of being that we can choose.

In Leviticus 19:18 we are told, "love your neighbor as yourself." In John 13:34 Jesus expands this idea by commanding us, "Just as I have loved you, you also should love one another." Paul, in his letter to the church in Colossae says, "Above all, clothe yourselves with love, which binds everything together in perfect harmony" (Col. 3:14).

It seems, then, that love is something we can choose. It wouldn't make sense for the Scriptures to call us to love if it was something we couldn't choose, would it? And yet, that is how many of us live so much of the time. We choose not to love because we don't "feel like it."

God created us with the ability to choose love. We are made in God's image and God is love. We see that most perfectly in the person of Jesus Christ.

Jesus Is Loving Always

The first chapter of the Gospel of John makes it very clear: Jesus is God made flesh. When we look at Jesus, we see the Father: "In the beginning was the Word, and the Word was with God, and the Word was God" (John 1:1). And later, in verse 18: "No one has ever seen God. It is God the only Son, who is close to the Father's heart, who has made him known." And in 1 John 4:8: "Whoever does not love does not know God, for God is love."

Jesus, the Son, comes to earth and in doing so reveals who God is. God is love. If we want to see what love looks like, we look to Jesus. Jesus, who is God, is love—always.

- When Jesus turns water into wine late into the wedding, that is love.
- When Jesus touches the leper and heals him, that is love.
- When Jesus spits to make mud for the blind man, that is love.
- When Jesus doesn't condemn the woman caught in adultery, that is love.
- When Jesus tells her to stop, that is love.
- When Jesus invites Peter onto the water, that is love.
- When Jesus tells Peter to get behind him, that is love.
- When Jesus washes the disciples' feet, that is love.
- When Jesus turns the tables on the sellers in the temple, that is love.
- When Jesus calls the Pharisees whitewashed tombs, that is love.

In every situation, with every individual that he interacted with, Jesus always perfectly loved. When he was angry, he loved. When he was tired, he loved. When he was frustrated, he loved. Always.

You can read about it in the Gospels. I did. As a part of my own transformation and recognition that I didn't love the way Jesus calls me to love, I reread the Gospels. I did my best to read them from two perspectives. I tried to read them again as if it was the first time, and I read them specifically to see how Jesus expressed love—in every situation. Very quickly I discovered that love, as it is expressed in the person of Jesus, is so much more than I thought it was. At times I was annoyed, at times I was frustrated, and at times I was just downright confounded—that love could look like that.

Practice and Reflect

When was the last time you read the Gospels, or one of them, with fresh eyes? If you are going through this book with a learning community, consider taking the time to do that together.

Defining Love Differently

In our learning community, we have used two definitions or images for love that have helped us take love on more deeply as a value.

One way we define love is, *I will and act for your good.* In *Renovation of the Heart*, Dallas Willard defines love in this way: "It is to will good—or 'bene-volence.' We love something or someone when we promote its good for its own sake" (2002, p. 130). We add to his definition the word "act" to bring into sharper clarity both intention and action.

You see, unlike Jesus, we struggle along with Paul in Romans 7 in the battle between what we desire to do and what we actually do. When God wills something, what he wills comes to be.

So when I see you, I truly desire what is best for you and I align my actions around that. This desire causes me to align myself with the message of Philippians 2:3–4 to set myself aside and look to your interests instead, considering them more important than mine. I begin to take on the very attitude of Christ, "Who, being in very nature God, did not consider equality with God something to be used to his own advantage; rather, he made himself nothing by taking the very nature of a servant" (Phil. 2:6–7, NIV).

A second definition of love we use in our learning community is *nobody wins unless everybody wins.* OK, right now, let me ask you: How well you are listening? If you are like me, you immediately said something like this to yourself, "What? That doesn't make sense. Everybody? That's impossible; everybody can't win. That would mean we all have to give up what we believe." Or, you at least maybe you *thought* something like that.

When we use the word "win" in this sense, we are using it differently than we typically do—especially in the context of relationships. Most of us, most of the time, have an approach to relationships where winning (getting our way, being right, having our needs met) is our motivation for how we are with one another. We want to redefine the word win in this context to mean something different. What if winning had more to do with emotional maturity than being right? What if winning had more to do with being able to define what you think, feel, value and believe than it did with getting your way? What if winning had more to do with helping the other person "say what is so" for them than for you trying to get your needs met?

The Bible doesn't tell us that we have to agree on everything, but it does tell us to get along. It doesn't tell us we have to think the same way about the same things, but it does tell us to keep the unity of the Spirit. It doesn't tell us to compromise our values, but it does tell us that the world will know we follow Jesus because of how we love others.

Four Movements of Love

In *Renovation of the Heart*, Willard describes the four movements of love. The first move is "he first loved us" (1 John 4:19). We know this because Jesus laid down his life for us (1 John 3:16). God's love shown to us empowers us then to love God with all our heart, soul, mind and strength—the second move of love. We love God because God loved us first.

The third move of love is deeply connected to the second move. When Jesus answers the question about which is the greatest commandment, his response in Matthew 22:37 is followed by "and the second [greatest commandment] is like it: 'You shall love your neighbor as yourself'" (Matt. 22:39). The fourth move comes as we fully love God and then love others, we become the "others" in the lives of those around us, and then we can receive their love (Willard, 2002).

The fourth move is where we need to focus our attention—it is here where we get stuck. What does it mean to love others as we have defined it: *I will and act for your good* and *nobody wins unless everybody wins*?

Being "For You"

In *Love Walked among Us*, Paul Miller (2001) tells us that Jesus saw other people and had a mind full for them. Love sees people and develops a *for-ness* toward them. In other words, when I see you, I make a decision to be *for you*. As I mature and become more like Jesus, this for-ness becomes more natural, but when I start intentionally developing this value, for-ness might seem foreign. This for-ness is my will, the place in my being where decisions are made, for your good.

Practice and Reflect

Do you remember a time in your life when you felt deeply loved and understood by someone? That you knew they were for you? Who was it? What did they say? How did they listen? What did they do? What could you learn from them? Write your reflections in your journal. Consider sharing what you wrote with someone you can trust.

Love Sees People. Notices Them. Is for Them.

This means that when I see you, I am to be cultivating the value of love in my life in such a way that I see you as created in the image of God and full of possibility. I develop a for-ness for you in such a way that I understand that I have a responsibility to you, to will and act for your good. I have a responsibility *to* you, but as Mike discusses more fully in Chapter 9, I am not responsible *for* you.

I will and act for your good, but I do not own your decisions and behavior. I do not need to take on your anxiety and make it my own. When your life breaks down, I don't need to allow that to shatter mine—even though it might break my heart.

We see this kind of love in the life of Jesus very clearly. His engagement with the rich young man who had obeyed all the law but was unable to give all he had to the poor in order to follow Jesus is just one such example. Even on his way into Jerusalem, Jesus's for-ness is expressed in his tears; but he does not take responsibility for their hardheartedness (Luke 19:41ff). Then, upon entering the city, acting in love, Jesus drives out the merchants. It is a love that is shown not only to the people gathering to worship and sacrifice to God, but it is also a love that is shown to the merchants who have made the temple a den of thieves—because Jesus is always love, all the time.

Willing and acting for your good, as we see with Jesus, means at times I act in a way you do not appreciate. To act and will for your good does not mean making your life easier. It does not mean doing all the hard things for you.

There were times, I'm sure, when my kids would have loved their parents to do their homework for them. There were times my wife and I thought it would be easier and more peaceful in the house if we had. But we didn't. In love, we understood that acting in love meant allowing them to struggle through the hard work of algebra.

I co-pastored for many years with my good friend John Sparks. There were times when he would ask me to take on a difficult ministry situation for him and I would say no. I didn't say no to be mean. I said no because he knew I loved him and that he was really asking out of his anxiety about that situation. And in those times I offered to talk through the situation with him. Then there were times when John, out of love for me, would ask me to take on a difficult ministry situation, and I would say yes. I said yes because I knew John willed and acted for my good and was encouraging me to stay in action in a situation that required loving courage.

Sometimes John and I had to dialogue about it—passionately. We could do this because we loved and trusted one another and because we both held to the value of love in that *nobody wins unless everybody wins*. I said what there was to say about what I thought, felt, valued and believed in such a way as to be understood. I deeply listened, asking questions and reframing what I heard, in order to understand. In those situations, even when I was doing something I didn't want to do, I won. I won because we both were able to clearly define ourselves around a particular issue.

As we led our church through change, John and I both continued to develop the ability to dialogue around difficult issues. However, when we understand love in the sense that *nobody wins unless everybody wins,* we change the game for how change takes place. A top-down process that says, in effect, "If you don't like it, don't let the door hit you on the way out," is a lose-lose approach.

When we want everyone to win, it doesn't mean everyone gets his or her way. It means that we courageously love them and create an environment where people have the opportunity to say what there is to say without blaming or shaming. We model this first by authentically "saying what is so" for us in love, and then listening deeply to those around us. As is discussed more fully in Chapter 12, we learn to remain less anxious in the system and remain emotionally connected in the midst of disagreement.

Then, when a decision is reached or made in the congregation, we have helped people move toward the transformation process with deep commitment. Often when congregations make decisions, they are simply giving permission for the pastor or key leaders to do what they want to do. Their decision is one of compliance—not commitment. When people feel that they have helped shaped the future and are willing to fully invest their lives for it, you get a different outcome. And if some in the congregation feel that they cannot stay in the community because of the direction it is going, we have helped them define themselves so that they are able to *leave well.* There may be sadness in the leaving to be sure, but also present is joy, hope, health, and relationship.

Mature Discipleship and Love

To lovingly take a stand in the face of no agreement requires a tremendous amount of emotional and spiritual maturity that can only be found through intentionally partnering with the Holy Spirit in the process of personal transformation. Unless we engage in personal transformation, our own anxiety will get in our way of being loving in the midst of an anxious relationship. As my friend Chip likes to say, "anxiety makes me stupid."

When we're stupid, we are unloving. When we are highly anxious, our autopilot ways of being take over and we take the 1 Corinthians 13 message about love and live it in reverse. When we are immature and unable to live out our beliefs and values, we become rude, self-seeking, angry recorders of wrong who celebrate the failings of others because we can use them to our advantage. It is true about me and it is true about you.

Unless we grow in our capacity to love, *everything* in this book can become manipulative and dangerous. Unless we grow the value of love in our lives, every skill or accomplishment is nothing more than the noise of cymbals at best and can become harmful to others at worst. We cannot grow in our capacity to love until we courageously face the things in our lives that cause us to get stuck in our immaturity.

However, with the help of the Holy Spirit and in the context of a loving learning community, this kind of deep change is possible. As we practice bringing every area of our lives into radical obedience to Jesus, choosing to live reflectively through the spiritual disciplines, and letting God use others in our lives in a truth-filled authentic community of love and grace, transformation at a very deep level will begin to take shape. We will begin to live into a way of being that fulfills God's design for us—love.

Mission and Love

It is love that caused God to create. It is with love that God created you. It is love that moved the Father to send the Son. It is with love that the Son took on our brokenness all the way to the cross.

As we intentionally disciple ourselves to the person of Jesus Christ, if we do so fully, we cannot help but grow in the value of love. It is one of the fruits of the Spirit, after all! As we grow in this value, we will become more and more like the person of Jesus and we will fall more and more in love with the pinnacle of his creation—others. We will begin to deeply listen to them and allow them to change our perceptions. We will hear them as they share what is really *so* in their lives. We will begin to understand their brokenness.

We will begin to see the systemic brokenness that impacts and perpetuates patterns of abuse, divorce, drug use, promiscuity, poverty, and homelessness, and our hearts will break. Because of love, we won't be content with high divorce rates or abandoned families. Because of love, we will make commitments to take on those broken systems—commitments we can't yet keep. Love helps us grow the capacity to keep those commitments.

On December 17, 1988, I married the girl of my dreams. We had been great friends for over eight years when I made a promise I couldn't keep. I promised Cathy that I would honor her, cherish her, protect her, and be faithful to her—regardless. I didn't have the capacity to keep that promise. We were young and had no idea what life would bring. For many years, we developed our capacity to keep those promises. Today, twenty-eight years later, and following the devastation of an affair, we are relearning how to keep our promises and love each other well. We have given ourselves (sometimes successfully, sometimes less so) to listening deeply and courageously to one another and willing and acting for the good of the other. This has meant challenging conversations of listening to "what is so" for each other, encouraging one another as we learn depths of faithfulness we could not have imagined when we made our vows to each other.

What if followers of Jesus lived that way with the world? I once heard Michael Frost, pastor, author, and missiologist eloquently say that we are called to a deeper intimacy with our communities so we might truly love them. Anybody can serve the community and do something "nice," but it takes courage as followers of Jesus to become intimate with our communities, to deeply understand our communities, to love our communities.

That is what mature Christian love looks like—deep, intimate engagement to restore our communities to their intended designs.

Practice and Reflect
Take a break from your reading and do some journaling around the following questions:

1. Think of an important relationship in which love is difficult. Take a few moments to imagine that person and to connect emotionally to the current relationship with that person. Ask God to guide you during this time of solitude as you reflect on what it would be like to love that person better, more completely or more maturely.
2. Experiencing someone as difficult to love says at least as much about you as it does about the other person. In this case, what does your difficulty loving this person say about you? What is it that you need to give God access to so that you can be changed more fully into a person who can love with the mature love that we see in the life of Jesus?
3. Where do your habitual ways of being come into play affecting your ability to love this person?
4. If one definition of love is that "nobody wins unless everybody wins," what might it look like for both of you to "win" in this relationship? Do you see ways that you are trying to win at the other person's expense? Do you see ways that you are allowing that person to win at your expense?
5. Another definition of love is the commitment that "I will and act for your good." What might it look like to take that on in this relationship? What gets stirred up in you when you "act for another's good" and that person doesn't receive it in love? If your relationship with this person exists in a larger system or community (a congregation, a workplace, a family), what is the role of that larger system in your relationship with this person? What would it take for you to become less "fused" with that person?

Jesus instructs us to love our enemies by "blessing" them and by praying for them. Take some time now to pray for your difficult relationship, for the other person and for yourself. Write down any impressions or promptings that come your way as you pray.

Change Is Possible
I began this chapter by confessing that people don't always experience me as loving. As I told you earlier, my task orientation can lead me to be selfish and judgmental with the people around me. I'd like to share a story with you that illustrates that change is possible when we engage in the transformational learning necessary to cultivate the value of love.

One day I got back from lunch and headed to my office to finish the sermon that I was preaching on Sunday. I had a lot of work yet to do on the sermon and was feeling pretty pressed. I sat down at my desk and opened my laptop and was just settling in when a key staff member showed up at my office door. He was visibly upset.

"Do you have a minute?" he asked.

Internal gut check. I was really feeling pressed to finish this sermon but the work I had been doing over the past year on becoming a more loving person kicked in.

"Sure, come on in." I shut down my computer and looked at him. "What's up?"

For the next fifteen minutes he told me the story of a vitriolic attack that he had just experienced at the hands of one of the members. The member was furious about something that had happened a couple of days earlier, and he showed up in the staff member's office full of anger that he vomited that anger all over the place.

He told the story quickly. He was shaking as he talked.

When he paused, I said, "I am so sorry this has happened. What are you feeling?"

When I asked that question, he came uncorked. He raised his voice. He cursed, and eventually he cried. He was simultaneously furious and terrified. It was clearly a traumatic experience for him. I simply let him vent . . . and this went on for a while.

When it finally seemed that he had no more words, I responded:

"I want to say again that I am so sorry this happened. I don't think you'll get over this quickly. Is there anything else you need to say?"

More hurt poured out from my colleague.

The next day when I got to the office, I stopped by to see him.

"You okay?"

"I'm not sure. . . ."

We talked for a bit and I helped him strategize about how he could step fully into this and not let it push him into a tailspin. It would take a lot of courage and authenticity on his part. I expressed my confidence that he had what it takes to find his way through this.

After the weekend I checked in again.

"I'm still hurting, but I think I'm better."

We made some small talk and then he said,

"Thank you. You sure have changed in the last few years."

"Really? Tell me what you see," I said.

"There was a time in our relationship where I would have come to you with what happened. You would have listened for a few minutes, and then you would have told me what I needed to do to fix the problem. And, the only other conversation we would have had would be you checking to see if I had fixed the problem. Last week you listened. You prayed for me. You checked in on me (tears appeared in his eyes as he spoke) and you offered to support me as I figured out what to do."

Going Deeper

Love is a value that is central to all of Christian life. Without love, nothing else matters. Love is a choice that can be nurtured by living a reflective life. When we learn to love in this way, our love will cause us to will and act for the good of others.

Available on our website http://www.westernsem.edu/journey/ridder in the resources section is the *Emotional Maturity Worksheet* that will help you see how your own anxiety stops you from loving others fully as well as the *Love Solitude Exercise* that is designed to help you get into action in a relationship where you want to be more loving.

REFERENCES AND OTHER RESOURCES

DiSC Profile, http://www.discprofile.com.

Goff, Bob. *Love Does: Discover a Secretly Incredible Life in an Ordinary World.* Nashville: Thomas Nelson, 2012.

Miller, Paul E. *Love Walked among Us: Learning to Love Like Jesus.* Colorado Springs: NavPress, 2001.

Willard, Dallas. *Renovation of the Heart: Putting On The Character Of Christ.* Colorado Springs: NavPress, 2002.

A Love Story

I met Marilyn when she moved in with my friends, Steve and Nanette. She was escaping from an abusive marriage. In the midst of separating, divorcing and healing from such an abusive marriage, Marilyn experienced the powerful and transformational love of Jesus through Steve and Nanette. Today, Marilyn is a close friend, and she leads a missional community in a mobile home park. What follows is an interview I conducted with her:

Steve and Nanette opened their home to you as a refuge in the storm, but they clearly didn't want your marriage to end. What was it like to have them clearly define their beliefs about marriage and at the same time give you freedom to say what you believed and wanted?

> I remember them having lots of talks with me alone. They tried to see both sides and were open-minded, but they clearly didn't want me to just give up on the marriage. They made that clear. They thought it would be a good idea for me to seek Christian marital counseling while being separated from my ex and living with them. I, on the other hand, just had it made up in my mind that they wouldn't

understand how bad it was because they weren't living at my house to see it. I didn't really want to seek counseling—I had made up my mind and there was no going back. I remember thinking that no one but my daughter and me would understand what we went through, but I learned that wasn't true.

They wanted to hear from me about what was so unrepairable about the marriage. Over time, through many conversations, where it seemed like I was always repeating myself, Steve and Nanette began to understand. I knew they understood my pain when the conversation shifted from "fixing" my marriage to my daughter and me being able to stay with them until we can get on our feet again.

When you really knew they were deeply listening to you and not trying to "fix" things, what was that like?

Having late talks with them and spilling my guts to them and then having them finally deeply understand me was a relief!!! I felt loved and supported. I felt safe and protected by them. I didn't feel so alone. We didn't feel so alone. We knew there was hope and that we would be all right.

Was there a time when they acted for your good, and that of your daughter, even though it was really hard because it might not have felt good at the time?

Yeah.… I believe they were acting for my good when they would talk to me about not reacting to my ex. Whenever he did hurtful things to me, all I wanted was to hurt him back, make him pay. I thought it would make me feel better. Steve and Nanette, however, did not want me to retaliate. They reminded me that I have friends and family who love me; that I now have a church family who loves me and that I would be okay—material things could be replaced.

In those moments when you wanted to react, how did you know they were responding out of deep love for you, even though it didn't feel like it from your perspective?

It wasn't easy. But I knew they loved me and that they were protecting me. I had a lot of people tell me I should make him pay for what he was doing to me and they didn't understand why I was just turning the other cheek. But I also began to understand, thanks to Nanette, that my ex was hurting me because he was hurt.

Anything else you want to say?

I remember Nanette telling me I had a thorn in my flesh. Removing that thorn was really painful but Satan does *not* win! She said I had an open wound but it would heal leaving only a faint scar. That scar would be just visible enough for others to ask me about it. And then I could tell them how I grew to depend on God and love God even more during my weakness. God has my heart and I have the ultimate prize, Christ!

Part 3
Mental Models: Shifting the Way We Think

They say that the definition of insanity is doing the same thing but expecting a different result. If we want different results—and we do—we have to learn to do different things.

This means that we have to learn new skills for leadership and we have to learn them on the mental model level. A mental model is a set of assumptions we have about the world and how it works. Our mental models usually operate outside of our awareness, on the level of beliefs and expectations that seem instinctive to us. For deep change to happen, we must consciously replace one set of mental models for another.

In Part Three, you will read about the new skills we developed and the way they began to replace our old assumptions about ministry, about the church, and about leading change. Using the transformational learning model, we got good information from a variety of sources about the skills that great leaders master. We practiced with each other and in our congregational settings. We reflected with our leadership teams and our ministry partners, and then we went back for more comprehensive information. The learning continues.

Chapter 8
Reclaiming Discipleship: From Membership to the Mission Field

John Sparks

Jesus was clear: "Go and make disciples." But what is a disciple? How do you make one? For that matter, how do you *be* one? As we began to ask those questions with renewed intensity, we realized that our confusion was not unique. Christians in every era and every locale have to discover what discipleship means in their own context.

A basic tenet of systems theory is that a system is perfectly designed to get the results that it gets. When we realized that our congregational systems were better at producing good church members than they were at making mature disciples of Jesus, we wondered what it would look like to change the design at the mental model level.

Interacting with the Gospels produced a simple guide: Disciples of Jesus are radically obedient to Jesus and join him on his mission to reconcile and restore the world to himself. They live in intimate connection with God and discern God's calling and work in their lives through an authentic practice of the disciplines found in a reflective life. They join together in communities of grace and truth, on mission together, while pursuing a shared vision.

As we sought to align our lives with this vision of discipleship, following Jesus took on new meaning for us and our lives were filled with renewed hope.

*I*n the name of authenticity, there are some things that you should know about this chapter and me. First, the subject of discipleship to Jesus is a passion of mine. I have ridden this hobbyhorse personally, educationally, and ecclesiastically since I was eighteen years old. For more than thirty years, I have been working out my own discipleship to Jesus while helping others to do the same. With much imperfection, I have sought to increase my capacity to be a disciple of Jesus and to help the church fulfill its mission.

My second confession is that I love all things Dallas Willard. From all the books I have read on discipleship outside of the Bible, Willard's words and ideas have informed my thinking and practice more than any other. Many of his thoughts appear directly and indirectly in the pages that follow. In my opinion and experience, Willard clearly and accurately diagnoses the reasons why many churches fail to make the kinds of disciples described in the New Testament. In addition, he also provides thoughtful and practical insights for anyone desiring to reclaim the rightful place of disciple-making in the local church—that is to impact the world.

My third confession is that while this chapter directly addresses discipleship, this entire book is in fact about reclaiming, recovering, and re-engaging discipleship (personal, congregational, and societal) as Jesus's plan to carry out the mission of God. I have come to the conclusion that the entirety of the Christian life is about discipleship. When my church began developing a process for discipleship, we quickly came to see that discipleship is at the heart of everything that we should do and be as a church.

The State of the American Church

The Church Is Losing Impact
My fourth confession regards my assumptions about the state of the church in the United States. Assumption number one: The church is quickly losing its impact on the marketplace and its societal institutions. This assumption is validated in the research of authors like David T. Olson, the director of the American Church Research Project. He makes the case that the American church is in crisis simply by noting the growing separation between church attendance, which is generally stagnant or declining, and the growing American population. Looking to the year 2020, Olson concludes, "The future looks grim for the American church. The conditions that produce growth are simply not present. If present trends continue, the church will fall farther behind population growth" (2008, p. 179). Beyond counting the number of people attending worship services, Olson's research also indicates, "Seventy-percent of Americans do not have a consistent, life-giving connection with a local church" (30). Seven out of ten people have no contact with a church community. If Olson is correct, this

trend is likely to get worse. Research like this is not news to pastors who have long suspected through firsthand experience that their churches are losing influence on the growing and changing populations around their congregations[1] (Olson, 2008).

The current state of Christianity is also not lost on church members. I recently asked forty-five adults in a Sunday school class to give me the first word that came to their minds to describe the state of Christianity in America. After some conversation in small groups, dozens of people shared their word. To my surprise, none of the words were hopeful or positive. The tone and choice of words was negative and did not speak well of our current situation. They used words like "weak," "ineffective," "diluted," and "distracted." The decline or stagnation in church attendance and the troubling sense of a growing and changing population that finds itself more and more outside the influence of the church, demands that we rethink our current understanding and practices of discipleship. To do otherwise is to keep working harder at what we are already doing while expecting different results.

We Don't Need More Information on Discipleship

Assumption number two about the American church: Pastors and church members do not need more information on the subject of discipleship as the way to reclaim it. I remember my first semester of Bible college and the pre-semester visit to the campus bookstore. I was there to buy my first set of college books. Table after table was stacked high with piles of books. I was both overwhelmed by this sight and excited, excited because I love books. What I remember most about this occasion was the computer printed banner that hung over the room. With dot-matrix print quality, the banner read, "The writing of many books is tiresome" (based on Eccl. 12:12). As I write this chapter on the subject of discipleship, I am very mindful of the legion of published books and articles on this subject in the last thirty-five years.

What can one chapter possibly add to the conversation, and does more information on the subject make any real difference? I do not want to add more information. Instead I want to offer a corrective in light of what may be missing, forgotten, or corrupted by culture and self. I want to present a clear way of thinking that will enable the church and individuals to reclaim a kind of discipleship that can take effective action in our world in order to fulfill the mission of Christ.

While information plays an important part in our understanding of what it means to be a disciple of Jesus, information alone will not transform a person into the image of Christ (1 Cor. 3:18). I have spent the ma-

---

1. Olson's research indicates that between the years 2000–2005, "In no single state did church attendance keep up with population growth" (2008, p. 39).

jority of my life studying discipleship. I can say with humility that I have mastered the information, but at the end of the day, I often fail to obey the words of Jesus that I know so well. As a Christian for more than forty years, I have areas in my life of habitual disobedience, not from lack of information, but from failure to practice mastering the teachings of Jesus in my daily life. My belief is that the task of reclaiming discipleship is not so much a matter of information as it is about clear thinking and consistent practice concerning what a disciple is and how disciples are made. With that in mind, I believe it's essential to look at what is keeping you and me from actually living more fully as disciples of Jesus.

In this chapter, I invite you to reflect on how you think about discipleship. We are getting the results that we are seeing in and outside of the church because of how we currently think or do not think about discipleship. In an effort to reclaim the rightful place of discipleship in our lives, churches, and world, I will first present a different, but ancient, Mental Model of Discipleship. I will then identify and critique some rival discipleship models, and finally I will share what my church has been doing to reclaim discipleship in our congregation.

The Mental Model of Discipleship

A mental model is a way of thinking that enables one to take effective action in the world. For example, I have a mental model of how to take care of a headache. I do not have to give the issue any conscious thought. When I have a headache, I simply act—and so do you. That is the power of a mental model. However before the invention of aspirin, people had a different mental model for curing a headache. In this way, mental models represent the best practices and information for their time, but they are never complete. New models are always needed because, as C.S. Lewis and others have observed, there is no such thing as an ultimate model.[2]

Even when a model closely resembles reality, changes in society, environment, or new information can render the model less than accurate. This explains the variety of discipling models that have emerged through the ages by reformers such as Ignatius of Loyola (1491–1556), John Calvin (1509–1564), Philip Jacob Spencer (1635–1705), and John Wesley (1703–1791).

Practice and Reflect

Take some time right now and sketch out on paper what you think of when you think about discipleship to Jesus. In other words, what assumptions do you hold about what a disciple is? What actions would you take in order to make a disciple who lived his life the way that Jesus would live it? What is your current mental model of discipleship?

---

2. See Brian D. McLaren's (2001, 28–38) creative description of C.S. Lewis's view on the limits of human perspective and models.

The discipleship model[3] illustrated in Figure 8.1 is a way to identify, describe, and picture a model of discipleship that leads to personal
transformation and to a missional life. In my experience, the model provides an effective way for church leaders and congregations to develop a
clear picture and shared language about the nature of discipleship. This
clarity has the power to create a new and powerful culture of practice
within a church.[4]

Figure 8.1—A Mental Model of Discipleship

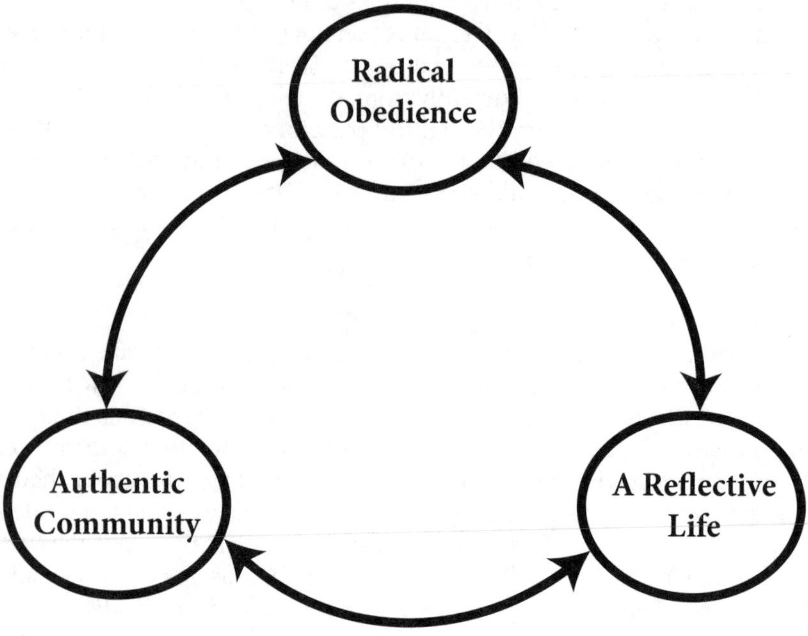

Each of the three circles depicts a significant mark of a disciple of
Jesus. The two-way arrows illustrate that there is no sequential order and
that all three circles overlap and interact with one another. In fact, the
power of the model is in the arrows. One cannot make much progress
as a disciple by overemphasizing one aspect over the others. To overstate

---

3.　This Mental Model of Discipleship is presented in *The Leader's Journey* (Herrington et al., 2003, p. 7)
and refined in *The Faithwalking Complete Notebook* (Herrington et al., 2013). Faithwalking is a spiritual formation process for individuals and churches that fosters personal transformation and leads
to missional living.

4.　This describes my experience. We have made great progress in becoming disciples of Jesus by
simply becoming clear about what a disciple of Jesus is. We further enhance this clarity by use of
a common language, which the mental model provides. While it may seem a rather simple effort,
we have made great strides forward in our discipleship to Jesus simply because we know what we
are all talking about and we have a common language to talk about it.

obedience is to court legalism (Matt. 23:23–26; 1 Cor. 13:1–3). To focus only on reflection is to give no time to mission (Luke 6:64; Isa. 29:13). To give oneself entirely to community is to end up as another self-help group (Matt. 5:46–47). This Mental Model of Discipleship illustrates a dynamic interplay of obedience, community, and reflection that must interact and support one another for transformation to happen.

What Is Transformation?

Before we consider each of the three components of discipleship, let me describe briefly what we mean by transformation. Transformation is not a destination, but a lifelong journey towards wholeness. Human beings need to be transformed because our disobedience—our sinfulness—has moved us away from God's intended design. In Genesis, Adam and Eve were created to be fully human and fully alive, but following their rejection and rebellion against God, they became de-formed from their original design. The good news of God and the gospel of Jesus Christ is that human de-formation is not the last word. Human re-formation has been God's project since the fall of Adam and Eve, a work that God initiates and sustains. This work, however, involves human effort. This work of re-formation or trans-formation takes humanity back to the creation mandate (Gen. 1:20–2:3) to have stewardship and responsibility for the land, and to the blessing of Abraham, where the people of God are to be a blessing and to serve others (Gen. 12:1–3). This kind of transformational life is what lies behind the process of discipleship. New Testament scholar Michael Wilkins puts it this way: "Discipleship means living a fully human life in this world in union with Jesus Christ and His people, growing in conformity to His image, and helping others to know and become like Jesus" (1997, p. 111–112, 119). Transformation is an ongoing effort that moves de-formed humans towards becoming healthy, whole, and complete persons according to God's design, as a means to steward and bless the land. By engaging the three components of this model simultaneously, you find a pathway to being transformed back to God's design.

Radical Obedience

Radical obedience to the commands of Jesus addresses the require-ment that all disciples obey their master-teacher (John 8:31; 14:20–22; 15:9–11; 1 John 2:2–6). This obedience produces disciples who are capable of love of God, self, neighbor, stranger, and enemy. Radical obedience is choosing "yes" to *everything* Jesus commands. Furthermore, being obedi-ent disciples and teaching obedience is what the Great Commission re-quires (Matt. 28:20).

To speak of radical obedience is to admit there are areas of habitual disobedience. There are many areas in our lives where we obey Jesus, but there are also other areas in our lives where we habitually disobey Jesus.

This disobedience may be the result of a less than accurate understanding of discipleship, a syncretistic relationship between culture and faith, an expression of our brokenness, and/or sinful rebellion on our part. Whatever the cause, habitual disobedience negatively impacts our lives, relationships, and the world in which we live. In the case of our impact on the world, the world wonders why we so often ignore the commands of Jesus. Dallas Willard observes, "More than any other single thing, in any case, *the practical irrelevance of actual obedience to Christ* accounts for the weakening effect of Christianity in the world today" (1998, p. xv, emphasis his). Radical obedience is not only an essential mark of a disciple of Jesus, it is also an essential means to missional living.

There are many stories that describe the negative impact of disobedience on the mission of Christ in our world. People cannot hear the good news concerning God's kingdom because of firsthand, hurtful experiences with mean Christians and churches that condemn. Why would anyone want to become a disciple of Jesus when Jesus appears to make so little difference in the lives of those who take on his name? Could this be part of the answer to why the American church is in crisis? Our lack of intention to be obedient in everything that Jesus commanded not only impedes personal transformation, but it also hinders the ministry of Christ in our churches, families, and communities.

There appears today to be a lack of seriousness around the subject of obedience. After all, we think, "Christians are not perfect, just forgiven." However, we short-circuit the work of transformation if we Christians do not intend to obey everything that Jesus commanded. We must come to clearly see that disobedience is a barrier to the transformational work of Jesus in our lives, and the lives of others, and that is why he would have us confront it head on. When we confront our disobedience by the grace of God and the help of others, we find healing. This is what a good friend of mine, Tom, experienced when he confronted some longstanding disobedience toward his father:

> *Today at sixty years old, I am able to think of my dad and smile. That was not the case for many years. My dad was an angry, abusive man, and my memories of him would well up inside of me much anger. I did not care to see him and when I spoke of him, I usually said nothing good. I decided to attend a Faithwalking 101 retreat in October of 2011 with no real idea of what would happen. I was not expecting anything big. As it turned out, I was wrong.*
>
> *I learned through the various sessions about the Mental Model of Discipleship and the importance of how the three parts need to work together, with no one part more important than any other. The retreat concluded with a time of ministry where we could admit our habitual disobedience, describe the impact that our lack of obedi-*

ence had on others, and ask forgiveness through the confession and naming of the lies that have kept our habitual disobedience in place. I was undone by this process.

I sat at a table with three friends. It was quiet and I started reflecting on my dad, on the things that were so imbedded in my soul, the things that injected such pain into my being. I became overwhelmed and suddenly tears began to well up in my eyes and drop onto the papers in front of me. I sobbed uncontrollably. The Holy Spirit was showing me the impact on my soul; the pain, anger, and hatred I carried for over fifty years. Even though it poisoned me and my relationship with God and others, it was my ammunition to justify my habitual disobedience, "You son of a bitch! You will never do that to me again! I will never be like you!"

With my habitual disobedience clearly in mind, I looked up through my tears and Kleenex so that I could share and pray with one of the presenters. I got up, walked to him sobbing every step of the way. I was able to put words to my pain. Following a time of prayer, I felt such a cleansing. Before I returned to my seat, I was encouraged to press more deeply into my habitual disobedience to come to a point where I could forgive and love my dad.

I worked hard and continued the process of healing that had started at the retreat. I moved through my pain and my anger, and was able to confess my habitual disobedience. I came to realize the negative vows I made at an early age were to protect myself. I realized that I didn't need them anymore. I realized I had been harboring a sin of an unforgiving spirit, but in my mind my dad deserved nothing from me, especially not forgiveness. Through some spiritual coaching and the Holy Spirit's power, I was able to forgive my eighty-two year-old dad. The story didn't end there.

In April of 2012, my dad fell and broke his hip, developed pneumonia, and died in June. I was able to sit at his bedside and hold his hand as he accepted Christ into his heart and life. I have never had greater joy than in that moment. Today at sixty years old, I am able to think of my dad and smile.

We have some idea about the goodness and rightness of obedience, but we underestimate the power of disobedience in our lives. Until we confront habitual disobedience, and the brokenness in our lives that keeps us in that place, we will never be able to experience the freedom and healing that come with living in radical obedience to Jesus.

Practice and Reflect

If you were consistently living a life of radical obedience in the life you currently have, what would your life look like? As you have read this section, has any area of habitual disobedience surfaced in your thinking? If you are able to identify an area of disobedience, pause for a few minutes and reflect on the impact of this disobedience on you; on your relationships to those closest to you; and on your relationship to God. Describe the reasons or justification you have given to remain disobedient. Are you experiencing any sense of resistance as you reflect on these questions? What does that resistance reflect?

Authentic Community

A community of grace and truth is a place where disciples can lovingly and honestly help one another with areas of habitual disobedience and provide encouragement and accountability for the reflective lifestyle that brings power to this journey. Discipleship to Jesus happens best when sisters and brothers fellowship together, in the presence of God, "in an atmosphere of honesty, openness, indiscriminate acceptance of all, [and with] caring" (Willard, 2002, pp. 245–246; see also John 1:14, 13:35; Eph. 4:15; Heb. 10:24–25). Grace-giving communities are safe places free from any sense of condemnation or shame because "Judgment, criticism, guilt, or shame can produce short-term change, but meaningful, long-term inside-out change is nurtured by grace" (Herrington et al., 2003, p. 9; see also John 20:27; Rom. 8:1).

Truth-telling communities create an environment of accountability and authenticity that seeks and welcomes correction (Prov. 10:17; 12:1). Members of an authentic community serve as mirrors for one another, graciously helping each person to see what they cannot see on their own. The combination of grace and truth provides an environment where individuals can safely hear or share difficult things that we often keep hidden.

I have discovered that the things that we hide from others and God act as barriers to transformation. Unfortunately, authentic community is something that American Christians have rarely encountered. Church, as it is often experienced, has become a few short hours of life each week where we often sit passively watching others do some religious activities while remaining isolated from God and each other. A community of grace and truth is a group of people where no one needs to hide, and, in the choosing not to hide, there is much healing (John 3:21; 1 John 1:5–7; James 5:13–16).

An authentic community has been an important part of my transformation. I had an off-again/on-again slavery to lust. For decades, I could find no freedom from this habitual sin even though I read a number of books, prayed mightily, and listened to a variety of speakers on the topic. In a remarkable community to which I belong, I found a safe place where there was no condemnation or shame. No one communicated that I was a bad pastor or rejected me because of my disobedience. With this knowledge and experience, I was invited to "say what was so" about my habitual disobedience by confessing to God and others in the community. I was terrified to bring to light what I had hidden for so long, but I was so tired of losing the battle of lust. One of the great lessons that I have learned about my sin and brokenness is that God cannot heal what I choose to keep in the dark. Following my confession of habitual disobedience and confronting the possible sources of this sin and its impact on my relationship to God and others, I renounced lust and made a new promise to live a life of purity for God.

As I submitted to this process and brought my habitual sin before God and a few others, I found healing and freedom that I had never experienced up to that point. Authentic community helped me get unstuck from my habitual disobedience and encouraged me to be honest with God in the midst of my reflective life. Transformation happens best when we belong to a grace-giving and truth-telling community.

Recently I was struck by the number of people who come to my church each week hiding from others and God. I had just finished a Faithwalking retreat where we teach authenticity and invite people to practice authenticity as a natural part of our God-given design. In this particular retreat, all four of the people that I listened to and prayed with shared with me what I can only call heavy-duty sins accompanied by years of guilt, shame, hurt, and unforgiveness. These people told me that either they had only told a very few people what I was hearing or that I was the first person they had told. In their sharing, I could see transformation as they gave up clinging to the secret parts of their lives and offered them up to God and another human being. There were expressions of relief, tears of joy, and expressions of freedom and healing, much of what I had experienced when I got authentic with my issue of lust.

However, my spirit was disturbed. I had known these people for more than ten years through the ministries of my church, but I had no idea of the burdens they were carrying. Furthermore, I did not want to imagine how many other people like them were hiding in plain sight in our worship services where we regularly sing and talk about transformation. I am beginning to understand how important authenticity is to our churches. We will not make much progress in our churches toward living the life that God intended until we learn to be authentic with one another. In a way, authentic community can be like "Drano," helping us get unstuck so that we can flush out the stuff in our lives that keeps us from transformation.

Practice and Reflect

What if authentic community became a regular part of your discipleship? How might your life be different? What have you been hiding or pretending about? What would the impact of releasing the pretense or that which is hidden? What draws you to this kind of community and what repels you? Have you ever experienced community as described in this chapter? What would it take to create or join such a group? How would your involvement in an authentic community increase your capacity to obey Jesus and to live a reflective life? Take a few minutes to journal the answer to some of these questions.

Reflective Living

A reflective lifestyle is one where the disciple of Jesus regularly practices a variety of spiritual disciplines, alone and in community, as a way to abide deeply with Jesus. The classic Christian disciplines,[5] solitude, silence, fasting, worship, fellowship, confession, and study, "are essential to the formation of Jesus's character in our lives" (Herrington et al., 2003, p. 11). Reflective living is an intentional and thoughtful way to order the hours, days, and weeks of life around spiritual practices in order to stay connected to Jesus (John 15:4–5). The disciplines are a means to embody a way of living in relationship with Christ that is dynamic and continuous. Willard describes these practices and their effect in the following way:

> These are root-level practices that slowly bring us to an understanding of who and what we really are—often producing occasions of profound repentance—and that allow God to reoccupy the places in our lives where only he belongs. They require lengthy times and extreme intensity to do their work, though at the beginning we must ease into them in a gentle and nonheroic manner (2002, p. 157).

A reflective lifestyle is an intentional and rigorous way of being that puts us in contact with the resources of the kingdom of God. However, this is more than adding a quiet time or Bible reading to our day. A reflective life is about arranging and rearranging our lives around practices that empower us to be continuously empowered by the life of Jesus (Herrington et al., 2003; see also cf. Luke 14:25–33). You cannot live into this aspect of discipleship by adding a morning devotional to your already busy life because, "Marginalizing these practices robs them of power in our lives" (Herrington et al., 2003 p. 11; see also cf. Luke 9:23; 57–62). A lifestyle around the classic Christian spiritual disciplines provides wise tools for the Spirit of God to confront habitual disobedience and to equip the disciple to be a person of grace and truth for others.

When we consider engagement in spiritual disciplines, I find it helpful to remember that Jesus and others like the apostle Paul modeled, taught, and practiced such disciplines. As disciples of Jesus, we are to observe and imitate our master teacher. Willard writes:

---

5. *Spiritual Disciplines Handbook* is a very helpful book listing a variety of spiritual disciplines and how to practice them (Calhoun, 2005).

We do not just hear what Jesus *said* to do and try to do that. Rather, we also notice what he *did*, and we do that too. We notice, for example, that he spent extended times in solitude and silence, and we enter solitude and silence with him. We note what a thorough student of the scriptures he was, and we follow him, the Living Word, into the depths of the written word. We notice how he used worship and prayer, how he served those around him, and so forth (1998, p. 352, emphasis his).

If Jesus and Paul found it necessary to engage in what we are calling a reflective life, how much more do we need to?

I was thirty-eight years old before I understood the important part that spiritual disciplines play in the life of a disciple. I had grown up in an atmosphere where the disciplines were suspect. They were either closely connected with the idea of punishment, legalism, a way to earn salvation, or extreme and weird asceticism. However, I learned that the spiritual disciplines are none of these things. With time, I came to understand and experience spiritual disciplines in my life as a power pack for daily living, strengthening my ability to love God and to love others. Along the way, I came to understand that the disciplines of the Christian faith are not laws, a checklist, as means to produce self-righteousness, harsh, abusive, strange, or something I had to add to my already busy life. Instead, they became a way of life for me.

There was a time when I thought of my spiritual practices in terms of whether I did them or not. Now I evaluate my spiritual habits on the impact that they are having on my life. More recently, I have learned the powerful connection between authenticity and my practices. In my spiritual exercises, I do not use pretty words, cover up my true thoughts or feelings, or follow a mindless script. Instead, I bring the raw, ragged truth of who I am to God right in the midst of my solitude, prayer, study, fasting, silence, and so on. For me, this means that I sometimes study with doubt, pray with anger, and sit in solitude with hopelessness, but whatever is true about me I bring to God, and God has met me right where I am.

Practice and Reflect

If you were consistently living a reflective life, how would your life be different? How do your spiritual practices differ from the reflective life described in this chapter? What would need to change in your life to keep spiritual disciplines from merely being an add-on to your life or a checklist? How would growing in your capacity to live a reflective life impact your obedience to Jesus and your community?

I suspect that most readers will find some degree of agreement with the Mental Model of Discipleship. After all, disciples should obey, be with and love others, and do things like pray and study the Bible. If this is so, what keeps the church in America from fully living into such a model?

Why do we continue to see a growing lack of influence by the church in our world today? I believe that rival discipleship models and cultural influences are part of what keep us from completely engaging in the practices the Mental Model of Discipleship depicts.

Rival Models and Cultural Filters

Over the last fifty years, there have been many different views expressed about what makes someone a disciple and about how the church is to accomplish the work of discipleship. The views range from describing a certain kind of person engaged in particular activities to churches offering specific kinds of programs. With the church's current and growing loss of impact and influence in our neighborhoods, workplaces, and cities, we believe it is time to rethink our mental models of discipleship.

Our assumption is simple: Incomplete or inaccurate mental models of discipleship lead to the inability to live according to our created design, as Jesus taught and modeled. Wrong thinking results in wrong living, which results in the lack of missional impact upon our world. So, let us consider some of the discipleship models in light of our cultural context and the teachings of the New Testament in an effort to forge a more complete and effective model.

Christian-Only and Super-Christian Models

Through the influence of some parachurch organizations, authors, and pastors in the 1970s, a model of discipleship emerged where a disciple was defined as an advanced or Super-Christian (Wilkins, 1992; Willard, 2006). This model separated a Christian from a disciple by creating a two-tiered relationship with Jesus. The first level was one of being saved and taking on the name "Christian." The second, and more advanced level, involved a greater level of commitment and generally took on the name "Disciple." The result of such a view allowed one to remain on the first tier forever without ever needing to become a disciple, while still enjoy the forgiveness of sins and eternal life (Willard, 1998). The Christian-Only model takes seriously the important matter of salvation. The Super-Christian model takes discipleship to Jesus seriously. It stresses Jesus's radical call, cost of discipleship, and the small number of committed disciples who left everything to follow him, but both models mistakenly make discipleship a voluntary and optional next step for a special and select few.

I believe the Christian-Only model has contributed more to the stark lack of difference between the lives of Christian and non-Christian than any other thing. Willard sums up the impact of this kind of thinking on the contemporary church:

> For at least several decades the churches of the Western world have not made discipleship a condition of being a Christian. One

is not required to be, or to intend to be, a disciple in order to become a Christian, and one may remain a Christian without any
signs of progress toward or in discipleship. Contemporary American churches in particular do not require following Christ in his
example, spirit, and teaching as a condition of membership—
either of entering into or continuing in fellowship of a denomination or local church. . . . So far as the visible Christian institution
of our day are concerned, *discipleship clearly is optional* (2006, p.
4, emphasis his).

While there are exceptions, the church has been deeply influenced by this
mental model that makes a clear distinction between being a Christian
and being a disciple, and unfortunately, our world has been deeply impacted by this way of thinking and acting. If Christianity is only about
missing hell and arriving in heaven, and discipleship is a special classifi-
cation reserved for a special few Super-Christians, no wonder there is so
little interest in hearing and obeying Jesus. Without discipleship, Christianity centers on getting people into heaven when they die rather than getting heaven into people while they live.[6] The Christian-Only model creates
people who are then ready to die, but not ready to live. Unless we confront
the nondiscipleship in our churches, we will continue to see "Christians"
who are not Christlike. We will continue to see "Christians" who see the
example and teachings of Jesus as an enigma without any relevance for
their actual lives. With discipleship removed from what it means to be a
Christian, the mental model of Christianity is often limited to a profession
of faith, church membership, worship attendance, and maybe the avoidance of certain "big sins." For many today, these key areas define what it
means to be a "good Christian."

Imagine Tim, an eleven-year-old boy, going forward at the end of a
worship service to accept Jesus Christ as his personal Lord and Savior.
In that moment, someone tells him that he is forgiven and now has the
gift of eternal life, but he is left to figure out what to do with the rest of
his life because the gospel he heard was a gospel about what happens to
you after you die. Without a clear understanding of what it means to be
a disciple of Jesus, this eleven-year-old will grow up in the church hearing the teachings of Jesus in terms of personal salvation and morality,
while leaving his current life and the world around him untransformed
(Willard, 1998). With Jesus having little to do with his everyday life, one
can see how such a boy could easily fall into the cultural norms of the
day. Safely secured in his personal salvation, he is then free to pursue
the American Dream—consumerism, and a life of comfort and ease—
while boldly responding to a pollster's question that he is a Christian

---

6.   I am here reliant on Willard's (2002) thinking on the failure of inaccurate models of discipleship.

who believes in Jesus as the Son of God. However, according to the polls, he is just as likely to cheat on his taxes, watch pornography, and get a divorce as his non-Christian peers. Is this what Jesus had in mind for his followers who would take on his name?

The Super-Christian model is not only inaccurate because of its disturbing lack of impact on the "Christian" and the world—it is also inaccurate for distinguishing between Christian and disciple because there is no biblical evidence to support the view. The word "disciple" appears 269 times in the New Testament. "Christian" appears only three times and was unmistakably used to refer to the disciples of Jesus: "The *disciples* were called Christians first at Antioch" (Willard, 2006; Acts 11:26, emphasis mine).[7] Nowhere in the New Testament do we see a class of Christians and a class of disciples. The entire New Testament "is a book about disciples, by disciples, and for disciples of Jesus Christ," who were also called Christians (Willard, 2006, p. 3). Therefore, we should understand and use the terms "Christian" and "disciple" interchangeably. There is no class of Christian-Only and Super-Christian in the teaching of Scripture.

Practice and Reflect

How do you see the difference, if any, between "Christian" and "disciple?" You may not believe that there is a difference, but does this kind of thinking show up in practice? If you were to gather fifty people from your church and ask them by show of hands if they were Christians, and then you were to ask by show of hands how many considered themselves disciples, would you see the same hands go up each time?

Learner Model

There is a model of discipleship that stresses the idea of learner, student, or pupil. A correct view of disciple is to connect the noun with the verb "to learn." However, this is confusing in western culture because we have a particular view of *learning* that is different from the New Testament understanding of *learning*. For many of us today, learning is only about information, as Peter Senge rightly observes:

> Most people's eyes glaze over if you talk to them about "learning" or "learning organizations." The words tend to immediately invoke images of sitting passively in schoolrooms, listening, following directions, and pleasing the teacher by avoiding mistakes. In effect, in everyday use, learning has become synonymous with "taking in information" (1990, p. 13).

---

7.   Outside the Gospels, disciples of Jesus are referred to as "saints," "followers," "believers," and "brothers," to name only a few. Surely these names are not separate classes of Christians, but are descriptive names used for disciples of Jesus (Longenecker, 1996).

Senge makes the point that such an understanding of learning falls short of reality: "It would be nonsensical to say, 'I have just read a great book about bicycle riding—I've now learned that'"(1990, p. 13). Real learning is about transformation, not about passively receiving information. From his decades of experience as a college professor, Willard also notes:

> In our day learners usually think of themselves as containers of some sort, with a purely passive space to be filled by information the teacher possesses and wishes to transfer—the "from jug to mug model." The teacher is to fill in empty parts of the receptacle with "truth" that may or may not later make some difference to the life of the one who has it. The teacher must get the information into them. We then "test" the patients to see if they "got it" by checking whether they can reproduce it in language rather than watching how they live (1998, pp. 112–13; see also pp. 316–318).

The idea and actual practices of a disciple or learner in first-century Judaism had a very different look than those of a learner in the twenty-first century. The clear expectation of first-century master-teachers was for their disciples to master the practices that were contained in their teaching. This mastery transformed people. Willard summaries the difference between learning in the two centuries:

> We must recognize, first of all, that the aim of the popular teacher in Jesus' time was not to impart information, but to make a significant change in the lives of the hearers. Of course that may require an information transfer, but it is a particular modern notion that the aim of teaching is to bring people to know things that may have no effect at all on their lives (1998, pp. 112–114).

The nature of discipleship-learning is to bring about a formative change or transformation in the life of the learner. A disciple then is not only a learner, but also an apprentice or practitioner who has come to Jesus to learn how to do the things he did (John 14:12). This is the meaning of the words of Jesus in Luke 6:40: "A disciple is not above the teacher, but everyone who is fully qualified will be *like the teacher*" (emphasis mine). In this way, Jesus's view of discipleship has a lot more in common with the idea of apprenticeship than a classroom student or pupil. An apprentice is learning from a master-teacher so that they too can become a master. For example, a plumber's apprentice learns how to become a master plumber through transformative learning. The apprentice is not with the master-plumber to learn information she will never need or use. The same is true for those who are with Jesus today through his promised presence, the Word of God, and the Holy Spirit; we are with him to become like him (1 John 2:6).

In my experience, the learner model of discipleship has negatively impacted the church's ability to make apprentices of Jesus. There is a stark difference between knowing something and being transformed through mastering the practices of what you know. The problem with our understanding of information is that information alone will not make me more like Jesus. If that were so, I would have been Jesus-like a long time ago. Sadly, this cultural understanding of learning has infiltrated the church. For example, many small groups and Sunday school classes in my experience exist to consume information. I know this because at the end of a small group's study, the question I am most likely to hear is, "What should we study next?" and not "How can we put into practice and learn to master what was presented to us in this class?" George Barna discovered through research that most small groups fail to achieve transformative learning:

> Our research shows that most small groups do well with fellowship but falter when it comes to facilitating transformation. Even the teaching delivered in most small groups has little enduring influence in the lives of group participants (2001, pp. 54–55).

A small group has great potential to be a discipling context, but because of traditional mental models about learning they miss the opportunity to facilitate transformation. We suggest that the Mental Model of Discipleship can provide a wonderful corrective for small groups who have gone off course from their original intent, because our neighborhoods, workplaces, and cities do not need learned Christians, but transformed followers of Jesus who are taking responsibility to bring peace and blessing to the land.

Practice and Reflect

Identify some clear teaching of Jesus that you struggle to incorporate into your daily life. Read Galatians 5:22–23 and identify a fruit of the spirit that you struggle to master. Or review the seven deadly sins—pride, envy, gluttony, lust, anger, greed, or sloth, and identify one of these sins that continues to plague you in some key relationship.

Now, go to three people in your life who have a stake in your spiritual growth and be authentic with them. Acknowledge that, though you know the clear teachings of Jesus regarding the issue you have chosen, you struggle to master this as a practice in your own life. Ask them to pray for you as you take on practicing mastery in this particular area.

Now, find an accountability person—your pastor, a trusted friend who has some mastery in the arena that you have identified, or a coach. The key is this should be a person who is farther down the road of mastery with this particular challenge than you are. Dialogue with that person about what actions you will take to increase your mastery. Take that action and regardless of how it goes, report back to your accountability person. Reflect on what you have learned from getting into action. Then decide on the next actions you will take. Keep repeating this until mastery comes.

Divider-Plate Model

My older brother hates when food on his plate runs into and touches other food on his plate. In his perfect world, he would have every meal on a cafeteria-style divider plate where all the food is separate. Like this divider plate, there is a mental model that comes from church language and structures that pictures discipleship as a distinct or separate ministry among other ministries of the church. Distinct staff titles and ministry department headings all contribute to what we think of discipleship in the church. The clearest practical example of defining discipleship as a separate ministry or department in the church is through the discipleship/ evangelism dichotomy, where the two rarely run into or touch each other. Many churches make a distinction between the ministries of evangelism and discipleship by creating separate committees or programs, or in larger churches, of hiring pastoral staff members with distinct responsibilities for evangelism and discipleship. This and other arrangements create the impression that discipleship is a part of what the church does, but not the whole. The problem with this dichotomy is twofold: First, with evangelism separate from discipleship, we invite people to trust in Jesus for the forgiveness of sins and eternal life, but say little about the need to be his disciple or apprentice in kingdom living, because that is a separate division of the church. Second, with discipleship disconnected from evangelism, it is easy for people to turn spiritually inward and to ignore bringing God's good rule to bear in the places where we spend most of our waking hours, because that is a separate division of the church. This unfortunate dichotomy is due to a misunderstanding of the aim of discipleship, as Willard makes clear:

> The focus of discipleship to Christ is not the church, but the world. If it is focused on the church it will stagnate and leave most people at a dead-end, for their life is not the church. Discipleship is *for the sake of the world*, not for the sake of the church. It is carried out in those situations where people spend their lives (2001, p. 209, emphasis his).

In this way, discipleship is missional in nature and there is no need to segregate discipleship from other departments of the church. The Great Commission of the Church is to equip disciples to live out their discipleship wherever they go.

Instead of separating these ministries from one another, we believe that these are all the same work. Separating them has resulted in a special class of people who are on mission. We believe that every follower of Christ should be on mission. A person comes to faith in Christ and is discipled in the midst of missional engagement.

By making or suggesting that people in our congregations can choose between discipleship, mission, and evangelism (or none of the above!), we set up a situation where church members abdicate their God-given responsibilities and justify not being salt and light or a city on a hill (Matt. 5:13–16). What if Christians and churches understood that the primary ministry of the church is to make disciples? What if the primary impact of this singularly focused ministry was a discipleship directed toward our homes, workplaces, neighborhoods, and cities?

Practice and Reflect

How do you and your church view the ministry of discipleship? Is there any sense in your church where people pick and choose between evangelism, discipleship, and mission? Do you feel any resistance to this idea that discipleship *is* the work or to the idea that discipleship is for the world?

Reclaiming Discipleship: One Example

As I noted at the beginning of this chapter, years ago my church sought to develop a clear process of discipleship. After coming to terms with our current reality, we quickly realized that discipleship should not function as a separate ministry within the church, but should be the overall description of who we are and what we do. Simply put, we decided to be make discipleship the main thing, as Willard encourages:

> *Announce that you teach people to do the things that Jesus said to do. Put it out in front of your meeting place on a sign; declare it in local print media and on your Web page. Publicize and run training programs designed to develop specific points of the character of Christ as given in the New Testament. Put the whole weight of the staff and congregation back of this.*
>
> *Who you and your congregation will have to be, and what you will have to do to back this up, will concretize and make utterly real God's plan for the spiritual transformation of human existence on earth (2002, pp. 220–221, emphasis his; see also pp. 235–236).*

What Willard is suggesting is no easy thing. Try suggesting his idea at your next staff or church leadership meeting and watch what happens. In my context, the initial response by the majority was resistance. There were underlying fears and misconceptions that such a thing was not possible or even good to try. What would this decision mean for existing programs? What would have to be turned loose and what would we have to take on in order to implement this decision? In the beginning the anxiety was pretty high.

As pastors and leaders we managed to remain relatively calm as the conversation unfolded. We proposed the idea. We gave time for reflection. We listened to objections. We watched anxiety ripple through the system. We supported one another in standing firm while also genuinely seeking to help our team see the high value in taking this approach. We made adjustments based on feedback.

I wish I could report that we quickly embraced this change. However, there was a good deal of discomfort as we kept this conversation alive. Over time, we made progress. There were people in the congregation who were willing to take this on.

In a brief and nonprescriptive way, I want to share what emerged for us.[8]

First, our leaders have and continue to own and work out our apprenticeship to Jesus. The Great Commission fully assumes that those who are making disciples are themselves disciples (Willard, 1998). Although this may appear to be an obvious statement, I believe that one of the great tragedies of the American church is our ability to sell Christianity, with all our mass production techniques and marketing skills, without buying it ourselves. Before we try and transform the world, we must first be on the road of transformation because personal transformation precedes congregational transformation.

We seek to increase our capacity in obeying everything that Jesus commanded; we work on abiding in Jesus through a lifestyle of spiritual practices; and, we participate in and benefit from a community of grace and truth. In other words, we seek to embody the Mental Model of Discipleship. We take responsibility for our learning. We put the work of radical obedience, authentic community, and reflective life in our calendars. We regularly practice with the goal of mastery, and we hold up the Mental Model of Discipleship as a means for evaluation.

Second, we encourage people to attend our corporate worship service. We value the corporate worship of God as an end in itself, and since public worship services require low commitment and provide little to no accountability, we gently encourage and regularly invite people to a journey of apprenticeship.

Third, we invite people to an apprenticeship journey. The apprenticeship journey begins with a weekend Faithwalking retreat. Here they learn about the work of spiritual formation and are given both language and tools that help them get started on the journey of personal transformation.

The second phase of the apprenticeship is a thirteen-week discussion group where the skills and values introduced in the retreat are reviewed and then more deeply applied and practiced. During these thirteen weeks,

---

8. In our effort to make discipleship the heart of who we are and what we do, we were greatly helped by the book *Simple Church: Returning to God's Process for Making Disciples* (Rainer and Geiger, 2006).

groups experience what it is like to be in a community of grace and truth. After the thirteen-week discussion group, participants are invited to engage in a more formal process that we call the Apprenticeship Training Team.

The Apprenticeship Training Team is a two-to-three-year commitment, in which team members encourage and support one another as each practices mastering the skills and values learned in the retreat and discussion groups. Through regular practice and with the help of a coach, real and deep change comes to their lives.

Our end goal is that our people will be able to live missionally. The experience comes to an end when participants either join an existing missional community or they launch one. A missional community forms around places in our world that are not working according to God's design. Missional communities are where we take responsibility for the land by blessing and serving others as a way to bring the shalom and kingdom of God to bear.

We have and are forming missional communities around schools, mobile home parks, and neighborhoods. These missional communities are where the body of Christ functions outside of the physical church campus, including working with other Christians from area churches who also live and work where we do. This is the end game for the entire discipleship process. Our ultimate goal is to make disciples who direct their discipleship toward the healing and restoring of the broken places within our community back to God's intended design. This is what it means to live a fully human and fully alive life. This is what we believe it means to reclaim discipleship.

I confess that we are still very young in this effort. In some ways, the jury is still out as to whether our efforts will have the impact that we believe God has called us to make. However, the initial signs are very encouraging. Although there has been some resistance, the multiplying stories of transformation both inside and outside of the church are undeniable. For people in our intentional process, it is not uncommon to hear stories like this one. A teacher who is coming to see her school as her mission field came to me just recently. She started the conversation by saying, "I'm not sure I could have made it this year without what I'm learning in the Apprenticeship Program."

"Would you tell me more about that?"

"The school is undergoing seismic changes and it is amazing how I am increasingly able to be calm in the face of that, listening for God's activity in the chaos."

Or there is the mother in our congregation who told me that in a recent carpool, the conversation unfolded in such a way that she was able to share with the girls in her car how God has transformed some deep challenges in her marriage and a strained relationship with her mother. As she told me this story, I asked, "To what do you attribute the deep changes?"

"Learning to be authentic—with God and with some key people in my life has opened up really hard but life-giving conversations that have resulted in deep change. I could never have engaged those conversations without the learning I got in the Apprenticeship Program."

This woman is learning how to be authentic with God and others.

There are still many who say "no thank you" to our invitations to move into our process, but month after month, we keep seeing people coming out from the "crowd" to begin an apprenticeship relationship with Jesus that leads to missional living.

Practice and Reflect

What place does discipleship have in your life and church? Is discipleship a part of your life among other parts or does it address the heart of who you are and what you do? Is discipleship at the heart of your church, and if not, what is? What would the church look like in America if we were to reclaim discipleship and put it in its rightful place? What would Christianity look like if every Christian took on a life of radical obedience, authentic community, and a reflective life?

Going Deeper

Discipleship is the whole work of the church and requires radical obedience, authentic community and reflective living. In order to make disciples, church leaders must be disciples themselves, actively apprenticing themselves to Jesus. In reclaiming discipleship, we make the shift from thinking about members sitting in the pews to disciples out in their communities bringing God's kingdom and healing to broken places.

To learn more about the reclaiming discipleship, we invite you to check out our online resources at http://www.westernsem.edu/journey/ridder.

References and Additional Resources

Ahlberg, Adele Calhoun. *Spiritual Disciplines Handbook*. Downers Grove, IL: InterVarsity Press, 2005.

Barna, George. *Growing True Disciples: New Strategies for Producing Genuine Disciples of Christ*. Colorado Springs: Waterbrook Press, 2001.

Herrington, Jim, R. Robert Creech, and Trisha Taylor. *The Leader's Journey: Accepting the Call to Personal and Congregational Transformation*. San Francisco: Jossey-Bass, 2003.

Herrington, Jim, Steve Capper, and Trisha Taylor. *The Faithwalking Complete Notebook*, 2013.

Longenecker, Richard N. *Patterns of Discipleship in the New Testament*. Grand Rapids: William B. Eerdmans, 1996.

McLaren, Brian D. *A New Kind of Christian: A Tale of Two Friends on a Spiritual Journey*. San Francisco: Jossey-Bass, 2001.

Olson, David T. *The American Church in Crisis*. Grand Rapids: Zondervan, 2008.

Rainer, Thom S. and Eric Geiger. *Simple Church. Simple Church: Returning to God's Process for Making Disciples*. Nashville: B & H Publishing Group, 2006.

Senge, Peter. *The Fifth Discipline: The Art and Practice of the Learning Organization*. New York: Doubleday, 1990.

Willard, Dallas. *The Divine Conspiracy: Rediscovering Our Hidden Life in God*. San Francisco: HarperCollins, 1998.

_____. *Knowing Christ Today: Why We Can Trust Spiritual Knowledge*. San Francisco: HarperCollins, 2000.

_____. *Renovation of the Heart: Putting on the Character of Christ*. Colorado Springs: NavPress, 2002.

_____. *The Great Omission: Reclaiming Jesus's Essential Teachings on Discipleship*. San Francisco: HarperCollins, 2006.

Wilkins, Michael J. *Following the Master*. Grand Rapids: Zondervan, 1992.

_____. *In His Image: Reflecting Christ in Everyday Life*. Colorado Springs: NavPress, 1997.

Chapter 9

Responsible for Myself, Responsible to Others: From Fusion to Emotional Maturity

Michael DeRuyter

We know that we can't change others, that we can only change ourselves. And yet, we spend countless hours trying to get others to change. We manipulate. We fret. We make demands. We throw tantrums. We pull back from relationships when others won't be who we want them to be.

As we moved toward God's emerging future, we learned the power of emotional maturity, focusing on our own choices, managing our own feelings and decisions, and changing ourselves. In the process, we learned to see our own anxiety and the anxiety of others.

We learned that we have predictable reactions to anxiety that keep us limited and stuck. We practiced confronting those automatic reactions and responding differently. We learned to take responsibility for our own lives with God's help.

*A*s congregational leaders, we are first of all responsible for ourselves. We are each responsible for answering Jesus's query, "Who do you say that I am?" (Matt. 16:15), and for not settling for secondhand faith or warmed-over doubt. Rather than merely adopting the handed-down beliefs of our parents or parroting the skepticism of our favorite professor, we are each responsible for attending to our own spiritual growth, grappling with questions and doubts, sorting through perspectives, and incorporating behaviors into our lives so that we reach maturity (Eph. 4:13). Disciples of Jesus are responsible for their own self-denying, cross-bearing, following-Jesus-at-all-costs obedience. Disciples are responsible for persisting in worship and prayer, while acknowledging God with thanks and praise. As a follower of Jesus, these practices are exclusively *my own* responsibility in my own life, and no one can do them for me, and no one else can reject them for me.

You and I are responsible for our own thoughts and emotions. We are each responsible for our own thinking, drawing our own conclusions, and deciding whether or not to follow an emotional impulse. We are each responsible for determining what beliefs and values will govern our lives.

Responsible for Self and Responsible to Others

We are responsible *for* these things because people are made as response-able creatures before God. We are endowed with a stunningly rich array of faculties and abilities to guide and enhance our lives, and responding to God's gifts and presence in our lives with creativity, strength, passion, and increasing Christlikeness is God's high calling and rich opportunity for all of us (Mark 25:14–29).

In addition to being responsible *for* ourselves in all of these important ways, we are also responsible *to* others (Mark 25:34–40). As leaders, we are responsible *to* the congregation we serve and the commitments we have made. We can see the balance between responsibility *for self* and responsibility *to others* in John's gospel where Jesus's threefold "Do *you* love me?" (John 21:17) first invites Peter to affirm responsibility *for* his own love-relationship with Jesus, and then immediately commands him to "Feed my sheep," a responsibility *to* those entrusted into Peter's care.

Later on in the Pastoral Epistles, Paul catalogs a series of responsibilities to others where he instructs Timothy to focus on teaching, encouraging, praying for, standing firm, and being prepared. Paul's summary statement in 2 Timothy underscores the reason for all of this as he urges Timothy, "Work at telling others the Good News, and fully carry out the ministry God has given you" (2 Tim. 4:5, NLT). Timothy is responsible to others in the carrying out of his ministerial role, which is distinct from but connected to his responsibility for his own faith (2 Tim. 1:6). Interestingly, in ministry Timothy is not responsible *for* the belief or rejection that may be evoked in others through his work. He is responsible for *telling* the message. The members of his congregation are responsible *for* their response to the message, for their own faith.

Where else do our responsibilities lie? For one, we are responsible *to* the land, to promote its healing (2 Chron. 7:14). Our prayerful, humble repentance (itself a form of taking responsibility) is linked to this healing, and it fulfills the original cultural mandate given to humans regarding their stewardship of the earth (Gen. 1:26–28; 2:15). Further, we are responsible *to* the poor and marginalized (James 1:27). Jesus's teaching about dividing the sheep and the goats at the final judgment identifies faithful ministry *to* the poor, the imprisoned, the hungry and the vulnerable as the primary factor in distinguishing sheep from goats (Mark 25:33–40).

Adjusting the focus of our lens from the broadest perspective of our culture down to the most intimate level of family, we find that here too we have responsibilities *to* our spouses and children, but I would suggest, not *for* them. When applied to children this may be more difficult to see. We naturally feel responsible *for* our children. Parents who act on this feeling are seen as good parents. However, historian Peter Stearns (2003) has demonstrated that this feeling is a relatively contemporary arrival on the parenting scene. From Stearns' historical perspective, casting children as weak, fragile, and vulnerable is more a product of our own fears as parents, contemporary cultural pressures and demands, and family expectations than any inherent weakness within a child. While it may seem as if it is a positive cultural move to become more responsible for our fragile, vulnerable children, Psychiatrist Roberta Gilbert (1999) argues that parents who become overly responsible for their children actually impair them.

My son Benjamin struggled with math in fourth grade. I felt responsible *for* his learning. The more intense I became about trying to get Benjamin to learn, the worse he did. Seeing myself as responsible for his learning meant that his failure was my failure. And failure meant frustration, anger, and blame expressed towards Benjamin, my wife, the classroom teacher, and school administration. None of this represented responsible parenting or academic improvement. I was not capable of more productive assistance until I recognized the limit of my responsibility. I was responsible *to* set a reasonable bedtime, provide nourishment, bring him to school, and think with him (not for him) about math. That meant my wife and I expected him to ask specific questions about his math homework rather than declare that he just didn't "get it." I also retained responsibility for managing my own fears about how I would look as a parent if my son failed in math rather than making my son responsible for managing my public image. On the other hand, I was not responsible *for* his learning. I was not responsible for his disliking school, his struggling with a teacher, or bringing his best thinking to a math problem. Getting clear about what Benjamin could and should do for himself and being willing to let him fail finally produced the parenting result that I was actually interested in—a son who was increasingly taking responsibility for his education. And it also changed the way I began to think about my work as a pastoral leader.

Responsible Pastoral Leadership

Healthy, sustainable, biblically sound leadership requires us to be as clear and as specific as possible about what actions we are responsible *for*, and who we are responsible *to*. Now, in the real world where ministry actually takes place, confusion about what sorts of things belong where abounds. For example, in our congregation we frequently work with single parents. Several years ago, one young mother received financial assistance from us for more than a year. In hindsight, we clearly took responsibility for ourselves that properly belonged to her. For a time we even had her utility bills sent directly to the church office and paid them *for* her without her involvement. While she was always appreciative of the help, but she also experienced the unfortunate consequences of our overly responsible behavior. This young mom refused to socialize with anyone from our congregation because she was convinced we saw her as weak, needy, and incapable. Of course that's what she thought. That is precisely what our "helpful" actions communicated. And likely too it is exactly what she came to believe true about herself. Responsible leadership requires that we puzzle out the qualities and content of a productive ministry *to* the poor that doesn't morph into our becoming responsible *for* them (and thus actually doing harm to the responsible self of another), just as responsible parenting demands that a parent fulfill his responsibility *to* a son struggling with math (or asthma or heroin) without becoming responsible *for* that child (again, harming the child by failing to nurture the child's own self-responsibility). Well-intentioned leaders, and yes, parents, all too easily slip into the seductive habit of becoming responsible *for* people instead of *to* them. Why? Could it be that we want to become responsible *for* people's thoughts and feelings and attitudes and decisions because by doing so we gain a (false) sense of control over them and experience feelings of success and security?

Or is it that we believe we can make our own world more manageable and predictable? Have you ever noticed that when you act as if you are indispensably responsible *for* the transformation of those around you, that you gain the energy and satisfaction of being needed and valued?

My Story

The drive to be needed, valued, and to appear successful motivated much of my effort to change the people around me. When I first participated in a learning community and was exposed to the material that would eventually become the content of this book, I was forced to confront my persistent tendency to manage the things in others that were properly their responsibility. As I was beginning to grasp the powerful potential of this material, a little voice in the back of my mind was telling me, "This might actually be the leverage you need to get those people in the church to finally change. You will look wildly successful!" I took what I was learning and applied it to the congregation in the hopes that they would soon change. Everyone, I thought, would soon be in deeply meaningful small groups, living missional lives, and becoming masters in all matters of relationships. I just had to make people learn what I was learning. That turned out about as well as trying to make my son learn math. After being frustrated by my inability to change anyone and facing some devastatingly personal "defeats" and setbacks in our congregation, I hit the limits of how far that strategy could take me. My wife came home one night to find me sitting in a recliner in our darkened basement, with the TV flickering in front of me, sound turned off.

I am not a crier. My wife wishes I would cry more often. That night her wish came true as I sat in my chair and sobbed. "Why can't anyone see that my plan for them to change is in their best interest?" I wondered. Through the haze of my self-pity, God brought two sentences to my awareness that night. First, "I want you to *love* your congregation; and trying to change *them* is an act of hostility, not love." (Note, I have come to see *trying to change you* and *longing for your ongoing transformation towards mature Christlikeness while still respecting your own responsibility* as two very different things.) And a few moments later, the second one followed: "The greatest obstacle to change in your congregation isn't them—it's you." How could that be?

Over-Functioning and Under-Functioning

It is a hostile act to *take* responsibility *for* the thoughts, feelings, actions, or values of another person and supplant the other from deciding and directing the life-content for those things that *only* they can properly and realistically be responsible. In fact, the person who oversteps these bounds of responsibility is *over-functioning*. And the one who allows these bounds to be crossed is *under-functioning*. The two always go together, an intricate dance of helplessness and needing to be needed, propping up and pulling down.

One place that the over-functioning/under-functioning dance steps can most clearly be seen is in families gripped by substance addiction. While the alcoholic may very well in fact be acting irresponsibly, and he is certainly not soliciting the family for more responsibility, there is almost always also a family member who is acting over-responsibly (McKnight, 1998), providing the stabilizing counterbalance in the relationship dance. Watching how frequently the so-called "sober" marriage partner begins to struggle and is suddenly off-balance once the "alcoholic" partner becomes sober demonstrates this dynamic.

When Henry sat down in my office, I could tell immediately that something wasn't right. He looked exhausted and distressed. Over the course of our conversation, Henry revealed his wife's problem with alcohol, and his concern that the alcoholism was out of control. Henry was at a loss. He had tried everything to get his wife to dial back her drinking, but now she was becoming intoxicated in the afternoon and then driving their kids around town. And he wondered if I had any ideas about how to control this irresponsible behavior of his wife.

Can you hear the language of over-functioning? How can *I* get *her* to change? How can *I get her* to want sobriety? What do *I do* to make *her* more responsible? All of the focus is on changing his wife's behavior and managing her life choices.

While the issues facing Henry were complicated and extremely serious, with potentially grave consequences attached to any decisions made, what Henry didn't see was that his constant need to become responsible *for* his wife's behavior and manage *her* symptoms instead of focusing on his own behavior actually *contributed* to her inability to be responsible and likely pre-dated the alcohol (McKnight, 1998). The alcohol obscured the ongoing dance that included Henry as much as his wife. Simply asking the question, "What purpose does the alcohol serve in your marriage?" began to shift Henry's definition of the problem.

We do a version of this dance all the time in the churches that we lead, complaining about the lack of spiritual maturity evident in our members' lives while simultaneously and anxiously *taking over* responsibility for their spiritual growth. I wonder how many youth directors or worship leaders have lost their jobs, stumbling in their dance when someone's "needs" weren't being adequately met. The youth studies were too fluffy. Worship was boring. No one communicated clearly about the issue before the vote. Over-functioning leaders are shocked to find themselves surrounded by such helpless people. Yet when church members demand to be spoon fed, church leaders show up with the spoon collection.

The Danger of Fusion

At other times, the reverse is true. When we are lost, overwhelmed, or confused, it can be easy to give up our responsibility and allow the thoughts, feelings, values, and attitudes of others become our own. The pressure to fuse into the thinking and feeling of others around me can be tremendous. I experienced a very simple form of this pressure early in my tenure in Midland when our congregation was rethinking its traditional approaches to Christian education and spiritual formation. I was clear about what I valued and believed. In the course of our board level conversation, one board member said, "Well, what ever changes we make, the last thing we want to do is make anyone mad." Everyone around the table nodded their head and agreed. And my own thinking shifted subtly as the value of "not making anyone mad" attached itself to every other goal. But was that really my thinking? Did that represent my goal for discipleship programming? Was it actually my highest priority and the "last thing I wanted to do"? More accurately, the value of not making anyone mad became my value as I gave up the responsibility for my own thinking in order to fit in with the group. To this day, almost six years later, if someone in the congregation is upset about some aspect of our discipleship program, I feel like a failure, a feeling based on someone else's value. Unfortunately, this pressure to take the less responsible course in favor of fitting in or gaining acceptance and approval can be most intense during times of conflict, transition, and change, precisely when the leader's clear, thoughtful, value-driven input is most needed. When leaders are over-functioning or under-functioning and unclear about their responsibilities, they are not only contributing to the status quo of the organization, but are actually obstacles to positive change.

Practice and Reflect

Sometimes the difference between being responsible *for* and being responsible *to* can seem quite subtle. Take a few minutes right now and reflect on those things you are responsible *for*, and the people or entities you are responsible *to*. As you reflect on your lists, ask yourself what part have you played in the over/under-functioning dance. Making such a list during times of high stress when you are reacting to a crisis is virtually impossible. However, beginning to think about the content of these lists in a time of relative calm can provide a valuable roadmap for decisions and actions when crises do arise, a value that is proven by a more accurate ability to focus time, energy, and thought towards the things that you can change instead of squandering those precious resources in an effort to fix those aspects of a crisis that you can not change.

Letting Go of Trying to Change Others

As I craft my own lists, there is one item that I am neither responsible *for*, nor *to*: Changing Others. The exercise of getting clearer about where my responsibilities lie brings me to reaffirm that the only person I can realistically change is *me*. I can only directly change what I am responsible *for*. And when I do that, I am in the best position to fulfill my responsibility *to* my children, my spouse, my congregation, and my city.

I met with a group of women who were mentors for young teen mothers. Some of them were getting stuck in their relationships with the new moms, and they wanted to talk about how to get things moving again. These mentors couldn't get "their girls" to value the right things and act in the right ways. They were feeling increasingly defeated by the lack of change they were seeing in the girls.

During our meeting I said, "We don't have the ability to control or determine anyone else's thoughts or feelings, motives, or beliefs. We don't cause or originate these things for others, and we cannot change these things in others. Furthermore, your girls can't *make* you feel upset or frustrated without you playing a part. So what are the expectations that you bring to the mentoring relationship that are contributing to your frustrations?" Some of the mentors responded, "Well, if I can't change anyone then what's the point of mentoring?"

This expectation that our role as leaders is to *get others to change* pervades our culture. But others at our mentor training meeting that evening breathed a sigh of relief as I shared that a mentor could have great impact by modeling different choices and allowing mentees to choose for themselves whether or not to change. The realization that we can't change others—alcoholic spouses, teen moms, or members of our congregation— both frustrates and liberates.

People who hold onto the belief that their responsibility is to change others will be deeply frustrated. Those who depend on managing the feelings of others and monitoring how others are thinking about us in order to feel secure will also be frustrated, and may feel as if someone has suddenly changed the music in the middle of the dance, leaving them out of step and off balance, not sure what to do next.

Unfortunately, these feelings of frustration will eventually give way to the deeper frustration of repeated failure. It's one thing to fail; it is another to fail while working hard at the wrong thing. Recall the double-bind despair of the mentor who couldn't understand the point of her work if it wasn't getting her mentee to change, while at the same time admitting that her best efforts to date could not produce the change she thought was needed.

Different Ways to Dance

Addressing this deeper frustration will require getting off the dance floor and reexamining the rhythm that we are dancing to in the first place. We believe that there is a new rhythm, in fact, an entirely new dance that we can master as leaders. And it is this new dance that ultimately offers the freedom to work towards growth and maturity in the one person that I can change. This is the liberating hope that some of the mentors saw opening up before them in our meeting.

We human beings, dancing to an almost instinctive beat within ourselves, want to make sense of our world. When we see a problem or a phenomenon, we desire to identify the source, which we say is the cause. If I observe A, it is because of B. B causes C. C causes D. And D causes E. Notice the powerful rhythm of this cadence in your own life and speech. Unless we stop and listen, we may miss just how automatic and prevalent this style of thinking really is.

One might assume if someone is sick, it is be*cause* of a germ. If a church is struggling, it is because of a troublemaking person or group. If the nation is on the wrong track, it is because of the other political party. The economy is a mess because of unions or wealthy capitalists. If we pay close attention, we will notice the impact of this linear, cause-and-effect thinking resonating throughout our everyday discourse. We say things like, "She makes me so angry," or "If only he would give me more atten-tion, I would be more affectionate." After a board meeting, a chairperson might reflect to his friend that it would have been a great meeting with a positive result if it hadn't been for the backward thinking of one of the other board members. When discussing a colleague who has burned out of ministry, a group of pastors might point to the unrealistic demands placed on their friend by her congregation.

Can you identify in these examples the causes that are ascribed to the observed effects? My spouse is the *cause of* my angry emotions. My hus-band is the *cause of* my lack of affection. The obstinate board member is the *cause of* a rough meeting. The demanding congregation is the *cause of* the pastor's burnout. On the dance floor the equivalent might be, "I tripped because you didn't know your steps." Now, in all of these instances, this logic will lead us to believe that fixing any given problem *requires* fixing the other person who is the cause of the problem in the first place. Here we go again, the old dance steps trying to change others.

Initially, because we want to be perceived as polite and kind, "fixing" attempts begin with gently persuasive overtures. In the event that our subtle efforts to convince or persuade others fail, an all-out attack may be launched—yelling, threatening, demanding, suing, even insisting that the offender take dance lessons! In both cases, the goal of *eradicating* the *cause* of the problem in the other person is pursued with vigor. In other situations, instead of persuading or attacking, a larger group may *isolate* the perceived troublemaker, emotionally and socially cutting that individual off, refusing to dance together any more, perhaps with the ultimate goal of sending the scapegoat off into the wilderness along with the "sins" of the congregation.

One congregation managed to do both of these dance steps with a youth director who failed to meet expectations. Jeff related well to some students. He did not engender trust and respect with parents and church leaders. First there were efforts to "fix" Jeff by giving him more detailed job descriptions and requiring more rigorous reporting on his behalf. As the tide of discontent rose, the positive contributions that Jeff made to the youth group were washed away and forgotten. Jeff was blamed for the low attendance at youth group events. Some congregation members declared that the only way to ensure the high school students would not abandon their faith after they went off to college was to get rid of the youth director.

Cause-and-Effect Thinking Is Too Limiting

While cause-and-effect thinking may seem like the only reasonable way to make sense of our world, perhaps the only rhythm we have ever considered dancing to, it suffers from two significant limitations. First, it fails to appreciate the fact that we are simultaneously embedded in mul-tiple relationships and contexts with each contributing to our experience in the world in endless patterns and reciprocities, making it impossible to pinpoint *the* cause of any one effect. A one simple example: someone sniffles next to you on an airplane as you travel to a job interview and you smash yourself as far as you can into the opposite side of the cramped seat, keeping your distance because germs will make you sick.

And yet we carry bacteria and viruses around with us all of the time—on our skin, in our nostrils, lining our intestinal tracks. These germs don't generally make us sick—unless something else is out of balance with our immune system. What might cause the sort of disequilibrium that would promote sickness? We know there is a fascinating interplay between our emotions and our immune system.

Dr. Esther Sternberg from the National Institute of Health has convincingly demonstrated that our feelings really can make us sick, and they do so by impinging the operation of our immune system—either suppressing it or kicking it into overdrive (2001). The symptoms that we experience after "catching" a cold may be far more about our body's immune system response getting stuck in high speed as our mind and body attempt to deal with the stress of a job interview than with the "germ" we picked up on the plane on the way to the interview.

What is the *cause* of the illness, then? Is it the germ? My stress response? My immune system? The interviewer? Or my history of doing poorly at job interviews? Perhaps the cause is really a complex interfacing of all of these? What if instead of a germ and a body, we were talking about a youth director and a congregation? How accurate could it be to say that a problem is caused by a particular person, without noticing that the congregation's response to that person also plays a part, as does the congregation's history with that issue? If even the most routine human experiences—such as catching the common cold—resist simple cause-and-effect explanations, then how much more important might it be when we are faced with incredibly complex leadership challenges in a congregation or family to avoid overly simplistic, cause-effect based "solutions," acting as if a facet of a problem is the *cause* of the problem?

There is a second important, frustrating limitation to the old cause-and-effect drumbeat. Cause-and-effect thinking tends to blur the very boundaries of responsibility *for* and *to* we have been working to establish. Keeping clear about what I am responsible for, while at the same time remaining committed to a cause-and-effect view of the world, is an impossible dance step to pull off. This is because cause-effect thinking lends itself to the language of blame rather than the very different grammar of responsibility. Blame collapses a highly complex, reciprocal, dynamic web of relationships into a single person and makes the problem either my fault or your fault. Responsibility sees the part one plays within the larger context, without recourse to the causal language of "your fault" or "my fault." When we confuse responsibility with blame, we give up our responsible self.

In the examples of cause-effect thinking noted above, this blurred confusion included someone giving up responsibility for his own feelings (his anger) by blaming his wife as the cause. Loss of responsible self could be seen in the wife who tried to off-load responsibility for her lack of romance by blaming her husband's inattentiveness, and we saw it again in the leader giving up responsibility for the difficult board meeting by making another member *the* problem.

And finally the lines of responsibility were obscured when a pastor gave up the responsibility of boundary setting in her own life while allowing others in the congregation to establish them instead. Cause-effect thinking really is a deep, beating rhythm driving the dance of over- and under-functioning.

When one person takes too much responsibility, and another too little, both parties contribute to the problem. "An over functioning person shapes the attitudes, feelings and behaviors of the under functioning spouse *as much as* the under functioning one shapes the attitudes, feelings, and behaviors of the over functioning one" (Kerr and Bowen, 1998, p. 55). Both parties are equally responsible for the status quo.

Yet, if I locate the cause of the problem in the other person, then I won't see that I have any personal role or responsibility for the problem, so the energy to solve the problem is directed towards the other person. In fact, any desire in me to fix, convince, isolate, avoid, or retaliate against the perceived problem-person in a church or a family is strong evidence that I have slipped into cause-and-effect thinking and failed to see my own part in the problem.

The reason this way of thinking and problem-solving inevitably leads to a stalemate no matter how hard we work towards change is that while I am busy expending energy on those things in others that I blame but can not change, the things that I *can* change in myself fail to receive attention.

My Conflict Dance

Here's how it works for me: A few months ago I had a misunderstanding with our worship leader. It was a minor conflict that I uncharitably blamed her for. When she didn't see things quite my way, I went a little quiet, pulled back, and avoided the problem. For me, this is the most natural first step in my conflict dance—avoid it!

From my comfortable distance, I began to find all sorts of evidence confirming and justifying my feeling that this worship leader was someone to be avoided. My plan was to wait out the storm of her anger and then come out of my hole when conditions seemed safer.

However, my disappearing act was actually fueling the storm. I was growing more and more angry and frustrated because my feeble attempts to control and fix the problem (in her, of course) by avoiding it, were not only failing to produce positive results, but were counterproductively making her more upset and confused at the same time.

Of course, it is no surprise I don't have the ability to manage other people's feelings, impressions, or behaviors. In fact, doing what was perfectly natural for me, namely, blaming someone else as the *cause* of the problem, and then trying to avoid that person as a way of avoiding the problem, was actually driving what started out as a mild disagreement up into the red zone.

Fortunately for me, the worship leader did what was *un*natural for her and drove to my house, knocked on my door, and said, "Please talk to me. Nothing hurts worse than being ignored. Help me understand what is going on between us."

This ending to the story was possible because my coworker took responsibility for herself in the dance and saw the problem as between us. The problem wasn't in me or in her, but in the dance of actions and reactions and interactions going on between us.

Living Systems

This shift of perspective illustrated in my colleague shows us a way out of the double bind that cause-and-effect thinking creates for us. Exchanging a linear, cause-and-effect perspective for a more nuanced living systems perspective allows us, in fact requires us, to remain clear about what we are responsible for in our own lives. And it allows us to leave behind the frustrations and blind alleys of trying to get people around me to change, while paradoxically opening up the possibility and freedom of genuine movement towards increased congregational health.

Nature of a Living System

So what then is a living system? We can begin by saying what it is not. A system is not a linear chain of causes and effects. Linear, non-system perspectives might see that A causes B, and then that B causes C, and C causes D and so on. Stringing together a whole series of causes and effects does not make a system. Further, seeing a system is more than simply recognizing multicausality, no matter how complex.

For instance, the other night on the Weather Channel I was listening to an explanation of how hurricanes form. No one factor causes a hurricane. In fact, unless all of the conditions are met—sea and air temperature, wind speed and direction, amounts of precipitation, and so forth—the hurricane will not form at all. A system is more than a complex array of causes for any one effect. Rather, a system is characterized by *reciprocity*. In a system, each of the component members influences each of the other members and in turn is influenced by them. Our solar system is a good example of this reciprocity. The mass of each planet and the sun contributes to the force of gravity present in the system and each planet is subsequently governed by the force of that gravity.

A living system is organic rather than mechanical. A natural, living system occurs without the intervention of human beings. You have observed a living system if you have ever stood in front of the Open Sea exhibit at the Monterey Bay Aquarium and watched the school of Pacific Sardines race around and around, countless fish swimming as if they are controlled by a single mind. Each fish seems to be connected to each of the other fish, perceiving in each other the minutest signal prior to a perfectly coordinated mass direction change. No one fish can be identified as the *cause* of a shift to the right or a sudden reversal, yet no fish is left behind. Many insect colonies, primates in the wild, and even flocks of birds reveal evidence of complex interdependencies and reciprocities that allow for the survival of the group.

Churches and families are also examples of living systems. In fact, any time human beings spend prolonged time with other human beings who are deemed to be important, a living system is formed. Granted, humans seldom seem to be able to read one another and respond with as much graceful precision as a school of sardines.

Nevertheless, members of a family, a work group, or a congregation do monitor one another for clues about how to act, feel, or decide. And in turn the behavior or attitude that has been adjusted in one as a result of this constant monitoring is picked up on by other members of the family and becomes a part of the basis for their own behavior. And so it goes in the living system, a constant interplay of actions and reactions moves through the entire group, as if everyone were wired together.

Learning to see my family or my congregation as a system has two important advantages beyond the fact that it gives me a more accurate and nuanced, and therefore more empowering, picture of how reality actually seems to function. First of all, when I keep the interconnections and interactions of a system in mind, I will be reminded to see myself as a part of the system. Rather than locating the problem in another person, I am forced by virtue of the system's interconnectivity to notice my own role in maintaining the characteristics and behaviors of the system.

For example, in the conflict that I described with my staff member, it was a systems perspective that allowed her to get beyond blaming either me or herself as the cause of the conflict, and to recognize instead that the problem was in the reactive interaction between us, almost taking on a life of its own. And that realization leads to the second advantage of systems thinking. While the conflict was not caused by either one of us, both of us *played a role* in keeping it alive.

Therefore each individual retains genuine responsibility for his or her part of the system without being blamed as the "cause" of the problem. When one of us simply took responsibility to change the part we were playing, the conflict resolved itself. It is as if my role was the negative pole and hers was the positive pole of a relationship circuit, and as long as both poles were present the power was able to flow through the system. To turn the power off only requires disconnecting one of the poles. While my co-worker had neither the ability nor the responsibility to manage my side of the polarity, by managing to thoughtfully alter her side she was able to change the whole system.

Back on that miserable evening in my darkened basement when God penetrated my tears and self-pity long enough to remind me that *I* was the greatest obstacle to meaningful transformation in my congregation, God wasn't piling on guilt and condemnation—God was giving me hope! If I can thoughtfully and meaningfully change the one and only thing that I actually have functional control over, namely, my part in the system, then the entire system, by definition, will change to adapt to my move.

Anxiety in Living Systems

In living systems, it isn't electricity that moves between people, but rather anxiety, which can be just as electrifying and just as deadly. Anxiety is more than just a feeling of being worried, but is the total functioning of the threat-response system that is hardwired into all living things by the Creator (Steinke, 2006). Automatic physiological, psychological, and behavioral responses to threats in our environment are gifts to us that keep us alive. Unfortunately, this automatic response is triggered regardless of whether the threat is real or imagined. The *perception* of a threat produces the same result as a factual threat: reduced capacity for thinking, increased automatic emotional reactivity. And the form that this increased emotional reactivity takes may include features such as loss of imagination or flexibility, demand for certainty, and a reduced tolerance for complexity in favor of simplistic all-or-nothing, yes-no, good-bad thinking.

As thinking decreases, "people will have difficulty recognizing and utilizing new information." Anxious people may become more guarded and vigilant or critical. Anxiety-soaked behaviors are guided less by thoughtful principles and careful assessment of the situation, and more by the instinctive survival urges of the individual or group, and include behaviors such as attacking, defending, withdrawing, pursuing. or peace-making (Papero, 2000).

Anxiety, then, is generated in response to threats, real or imagined. And anxiety is incredibly contagious. When one member of a living system is experiencing heightened anxiety, the whole system can be infected. Picture a single bird getting spooked by a noise and the entire flock taking to flight. In a congregation, one person becomes anxious and before long three others are reacting *as if* they have been threatened as well.

How would it make a difference for you as a leader if you were able to see the nasty, unsigned note that you find on your desk on Monday morning as a sign of anxiety in the system rather than as evidence that there is something "wrong" with someone out there in the congregation who needs to be fixed? Or as an indication that there is something "wrong" with you? What kind of thought process would it take to become curious about that anxiety and its influence rather than defensive or angry or despondent?

We can imagine some of the obvious sources of anxiety in a congregation. The death of an influential leader, a significant budget shortfall, or the
abrupt departure of several young families, can produce vast amounts of
congregational anxiety because of the perceived threats to congregational
survival. Families in congregations can bring along the anxiety they have
accrued outside of the congregational system—from home life or workplace
or school, for instance—and share it with the members of the congregation.
Under any of these circumstances, systems thinkers will be especially aware
of the heightened level of anxiety in the relationships of their system and be
able to notice the evidence of it. This gives leaders a perspective other than
feeling personally attacked or rejected.

There is another source of anxiety that we may not find so obvious,
but it is nonetheless a powerful contributor to the amount of anxiety in
a system and, further, it influences individual levels of sensitivity to that
systemic anxiety. To see this second, less obvious anxiety amplifier in operation, you need to know that anxiety in relationships is often governed
by the balance between individuality and togetherness forces.

Togetherness and Individuality Forces in Living Systems

Human beings in relationships work out a balance of time, energy,
thought, and emotion that will be directed toward others and that will be
reserved for self. Human beings need one another for survival, so we often
feel motivated by the desire to fit in, get along, and be part of the larger
group. We find that we are often willing to make concessions and give up
important parts of who we are in order to fit with the group. This human
need is sometimes called the "togetherness" force, and it is not good or bad
(Kerr and Bowen, 1988). God's design for human beings includes the fact
that we legitimately depend on one another in cooperative community. Indeed, being fruitful and multiplying and filling the earth *requires* that we
form relationships. In the New Testament, one of Paul's favorite metaphors
for the church is that of a body, an image that becomes grotesque unless one
assumes togetherness. And at the very heart of all reality we believe that
God himself exists in the togetherness of Three Persons.

On the other hand, we are designed as individuals who have God-
given dreams and gifts and abilities and purposes. The legitimate need
to pursue these is sometimes called the "individuality" force (Kerr and
Bowen, 1988). Separate and unique individuals are just as much a part of
God's design as togetherness. In fact, the fundamental work of creating life
which we observe in Genesis 1 is precisely the work of creating uniqueness
and bounded separateness where once only "formlessness" existed. God
establishes differences between sky and earth, land and sea. God marks
distinctions between varieties of plants, animals, and even humans. Life
requires individuals who are differentiated from the whole as much as it
depends on togetherness. Also endorsing this self-defining individuality

force, Paul goes to great lengths to urge the Corinthian believers to preserve their individual identity (2 Cor. 12:14ff). Fitting in with the body
in unity doesn't mean that every part of the body is the same, nor does it
mean that individuals don't need to attend to their own unique role. On
the contrary, if the eye, Paul says, doesn't do the unique work assigned to
an eye, the whole body will suffer. Individuality isn't selfish; it's critically
important to the health of the whole. And it is very difficult to maintain,
especially in the face of an anxious group that automatically exerts pressure for everyone to be the same.

In a relationship where these two forces—togetherness (directing
our energy into the relationship) and individuality (directing our energy
toward self)—are in balance, anxiety is low because people feel safe and
comfortable with both of these needs being adequately met. People perceive that they are "together" enough to feel safe, but they have enough
freedom and independence that they can function as an "individual"
without feeling suffocated.

Shifts in the Balance

However, as circumstances in relationships change, anxiety levels fluc-
tuate, and this dynamic balance between individuality and togetherness
can be thrown off. Two simple, common examples which represent a com-
posite of families who regularly allow me to peek at the emotional process
operating in their homes: A young married couple has enjoyed several
years together as husband and wife, each with a job, friends, and interest
outside of the marriage as well as a comfortable closeness between them
as a couple. Then they have their first baby. The addition of the new child
changes the balance of the marriage so that the wife puts more of her self
into the baby and has less for her husband. In the case of these two busy
professional adults, the necessary reallocation of energy toward the baby,
the greater fatigue induced from adding the role of parent to an already
full life, is a subtle shift, perhaps unrecognizable to anyone outside of the
relationship. However, even this slight change is anxiety-producing for the
husband. The husband describes feeling the need to pursue his wife, pres-
suring her for more attention, in order to reestablish his sense of security
and well-being that was grounded in their original level of togetherness.

A second example brings us back to this same family later in life. By
now, the couple's children are all grown and have moved out of the house.
Soon, both retire from their careers. The wife has always enjoyed her relationship with her husband, but now suddenly without their careers, children, and social activities to moderate the togetherness, she finds herself
suffocated by his constant presence. With the children out of the house and
the husband constantly in the house, she begins to feel like she is "losing
herself." At the same time, she may find that she becomes more and more
critical of her husband, impatient with him. At the emotional level, where

the imbalance in the relationship forces registers as a threat, this fault-finding behavior makes sense as a means of reestablishing a more comfortable distance, pushing him away a bit and reestablishing a more comfortable level of individuality. In both of these examples, a change in the balance of individuality and togetherness forces generates anxiety in the family system to which all members of the system will react. This systemic reaction then produces more anxiety, which heightens individual sensitivity to the individuality-togetherness balance and escalates the reactions.

All of us start life with the balance of these forces tilted all the way toward togetherness. We are physically "one" with our mothers. We are completely dependent on our family to meet all of our needs. Our family shapes how we think, what attitudes we will have, what feelings we will have, and what we will value. We need the approval of others in our family in order to feel secure, because in the immature stage of life we need the others in our family to survive. In this sense, other-dependence can be seen as part of being immature. As we grow and mature, we become less and less dependent on our family to approve of our thinking and "validate" our feelings about things.

Initially, we achieve physical independence at birth when we no longer need the umbilical chord in order to survive, but can breath on our own. The trajectory of growing independence continues on into childhood and adolescence as we begin to manage our own thinking and feeling. We increasingly draw our own unique conclusions about politics, faith, sexuality, and other values. We develop the mature, responsible capacity to define ourselves as separate from our family while still being related to them, and at the same time, allowing other members of our family to define *themselves* differently to us.

Growing Emotional Maturity

In this sense, my ability to think and act for myself without *depending on* others in my family system to validate or approve my thoughts or actions represents more emotional maturity. Each of us ultimately emerges from our family home with some degree of independence and individuality, and with some degree of dependence on others. In other words, as adults we have varying amounts of emotional maturity.

Emotional immaturity—the condition of being *dependent* on others for our well-being, for our emotional, physical, spiritual, or social functioning—makes us vulnerable to those upon whom we depend. The more dependent we are on others, the more vulnerable we are. Vulnerability feels risky and threatening. And any threat, real or imagined, automatically spools up our threat-response system. This is anxiety. As our sense of vulnerability rises, our need to manage and control others increases in an effort to secure our own well-being and reduce anxiety. We see shifts in their levels of approval, attention, or in their expectations of us as *threats* to our well-being which need to be managed. We have difficulty tolerating the ebb and flow of changes that relationships routinely face.

This dependency on others might be expressed at one extreme by people who say, "I can't survive unless you respond the way I want you to," and at the other extreme of, "I can't survive if I do what you want me to" (Kerr and Bowen, 1988). Both of these positions express significant emotional dependence on others, and neither is factually accurate.

The more other-dependence we retain from childhood, the more vulnerable we are to this sense of threat in all subsequent relationships (I can't survive without you! Unless you change, I can never be happy again!), and the more sensitive we are to anxiety in a system. Remember the story about how our congregation wanted to change how we pursued Christian education? The board member who decided "the last thing we want to do is make anyone mad" was expressing a high need for togetherness. He was threatened by the potential loss of any congregation member's approval. The rest of the board, including myself, was moderately sensitive to the "togetherness" need for approval from others. And so we adopted that particular value. Of course, introducing any change without making someone upset is impossible. In our effort to preserve the togetherness of the congregation and avoid loss of approval, we had effectively stymied ourselves. No action could guarantee this result. And the frustration that followed actually produced the very thing we were so eager to avoid: People got mad!

Emotionally Mature Leaders Think for Themselves

Emotional immaturity consigns a person to live in a world governed largely by feelings and relationships, stuck in the togetherness force, rather than enjoying the relative freedom that comes with more emotional maturity which allows one to chart a course based on thoughtful values, goals, and principles. The effort of working towards the emotional maturity which allows an individual to think and feel for him or her self while allowing others to do the same, especially in times of heightened anxiety, is one of the greatest contributions a leader can make to the health of the organization he serves.

Togetherness is both a natural reaction to anxiety and a surefire way to produce more anxiety. The antidote to anxiety in the system is not to do what feels natural, namely moving toward togetherness. When our congregational leadership launched a project to restructure our governance model, we ended up with a series of very anxious and emotionally charged congregational meetings. The perceived threats of change, loss of control, and reckless spending supercharged our congregational system with anxiety. This increase in anxiety turned up the togetherness forces. And people began to form groups based on what each believed about the proposed changes. As we all know, small clusters of people huddled together here and there in the parking lot after a meeting does nothing to actually solve any problems. This herding instinct may offer short-term benefits by calming the anxiety of individuals who find comfort and security in the relationship-dependent approval generated in those well-known parking lot conversations, but this benefit comes with the long-term cost of reinforcing the very relationship-dependent, emotional immaturity that generates anxiety and heightens our sensitivity to it in the first place. Instead, the antidote to anxiety in the system is to become more of a well-defined self. In this case, being a well-defined self meant that I would not feel responsible for the feelings or fears of others. I didn't have to be angry just because someone was angry with me. I would relate to individuals, not to groups. And I would stay focused on my goals (an individuality force attribute) as opposed to fixating on winning a fight (a togetherness force attribute). The result of this effort was that we slowed the change-process down, made some amendments to the proposed structure based on thoughtful input from respected individual leaders, and implemented the new structure with a built-in review schedule for the first two years. No one left the congregation due to this change. But if someone had, I was prepared to let them be responsible for that decision. Emotional immaturity in people who form groups (systems) keeps organizations stuck in the relationship-driven togetherness forces, where everything is sacrificed in the name of preserving the relationship. Change is unlikely in this environment. Emotional maturity in people allows groups to make thoughtful, value-driven, goal-directed decisions. Change, in this case, is possible.

Churches Love Togetherness

Unfortunately, many of the programs in our churches work against this goal. We take great pride in the fact that our church is a "close-knit" group. Churches love their togetherness. And we weave it into our programs wherever and whenever we can: group bonding and team building exercises, small group sharing, efforts to increase closeness and intimacy, and classes to make sure we all agree on doctrinal or ethical issues.

Togetherness isn't bad. It is important for functioning. However, with our programs we subtly and repeatedly instill the expectation that in this group (church, family, staff, etc.), we are all supposed to feel, think, and act as one (Miller, 2008). Individuals become so "fused" with the group that a threat to the group feels like a threat to the individual. Anxiety soars.

What creative, challenging, often life-giving outside-the-box thinking do we miss out on when church members don't share their thinking, restrained by the fear of upsetting the unity? Without deliberate efforts to help leaders and members of churches develop as emotionally mature, well defined individuals, we shouldn't be surprised if everyone in the congregation acts as if they are the same body part—and as Paul suggests in 1 Corinthians 12, what a strange body that would be!

Going Deeper

Emotionally mature leaders are distinct from others while remaining connected to others. Emotionally mature leaders are responsible *for* themselves and *to* others. Emotionally mature leaders learn to detect anxiety inside living systems and respond in productive ways rather than viewing actions as personal attacks.

To learn more about emotional maturity and living systems, we invite you to check out our online resources at http://www.westernsem.edu/journey/ridder.

References and Additional Resources

Gilbert, Roberta, M. *Connecting With Our Children: Guiding Principles for Parents in a Troubled World.* New York: Wiley & Sons, 1999.

Kerr, Michael E., and Murray Bowen. *Family Evaluation: The Role of the Family Unity That Governs Individual Behavior and Development.* New York: Norton, 1988.

McKnight, Ann. "Family Systems with Alcoholism." In *Clinical Applications of Bowen Family Systems Theory*, edited by Peter Titelman, 263–298. New York: Haworth Press, 1998.

Miller, Jeffrey. *The Anxious Organization: Why Smart Companies Do Dumb Things.* Tempe, AZ: Facts on Demand Press, 2008.

Papero, Dan. "What Does a Manager Need to Know about Human Behavior?" (article in handout). Working Systems Inc., 2000.

Stearns, Peter. *Anxious Parents: A History of Modern Childrearing in America.* New York: New York University Press, 2003.

Steinke, Peter. *Congregational Leadership in Anxious Times.* Herndon, VA: The Alban Institute, 2006.

Sternberg, Esther. *The Balance Within: The Science Connecting Health and Emotions.* New York: W.H. Freeman and Company, 2001.

Confessions of an Over-Functioner

I have a terrific leadership team. There is a high level of trust and I feel loved by them. And, I am a classic over-functioner. One result of being an over-functioner is that I get isolated from my family, and then I become angry at church leaders who don't do their part. Of course, because I'm an over-functioner, mostly my leaders don't know the impact of this way of working. So, one day I decided to tell them. That might seem simple to you, but it felt like a highly risky move for me.

One night in a leadership team meeting, I screwed up the courage to raise this topic. I said, "I've been over-functioning—for a long time—and I need your help." It almost felt like an AA meeting. "Hi, I'm Chip and I'm an over-functioner." I told them that the two biggest impacts I could see was that this way of working was putting a huge strain on me and my family—a strain that was not sustainable over time. And, it had me spending work hours on the things that were not high priority. I was just too scattered and spinning too many plates all at the same time.

There—it was out there. My mind was racing and I was pretty anxious. Were they going to fire me? Were they going to see me as being weak? Were they going to hear the implied, "Because I'm over-functioning then you are under-functioning. I even found that in the moment of silence that followed my courageous movement of vulnerability, I wanted to fill the silence by taking care of the discomfort that they must be feeling.

So, I waited—not so patiently. Finally one of the leaders spoke.

"I've seen this for a while. You are a gifted leader who has a hard time saying no. I wonder if you can see that some of us have offered to help along the way, and you won't let us? We want to help."

Another leader said, "This is not something that I've ever heard from you, and I'm not sure how to respond."

It wasn't a straight or easy line, but as I worked to *not* fill the space of my self-disclosure by fixing the problem, our team had some of the most courageous and authentic conversations we've ever had. In the course of the conversations, sometimes we got anxious. Occasionally we said things we wished we had not have said. But, slowly we found our way to a new place.

As a team they worked to redefine my job and to put in place some protective boundaries for me. Some of the things I was doing were delegated. I continue to be a hard worker. But, now I'm working on the more high leverage things that serve the congregation and its mission most effectively.

Ready to Stop Running

I had a crisis moment in the early stages of the Ridder Church Renewal experience that really changed things for me. Up until that point, I had a pattern of relating that I had not been able to see clearly.

The pattern looked like this. I would accept a call to a new church. Early on it was energizing and life-giving to work and serve. However, over time I would have conflict or not be able to achieve what I wanted to achieve. At some point, internally I would be done with these people. Sometimes that would happen within the church. A project I wanted to do would not move ahead, so I would be done with the people involved in that project. I would distance from them and would focus my attention elsewhere. But, ultimately, the larger pattern was that I would leave the church with the illusion that I was just called to the wrong place or these were the wrong people. If I could find the right place and the right people, things would be different.

Before coming to Midland, I had left three congregations.

When I got to Midland, the pattern repeated itself. For the first couple of years, things went well. Then in year three, things began to get dicey. By year five, there was this deep sense of unrest and dissatisfaction, and I was ready to pull up and leave.

During that same time, Tammy had launched her career and was finding success in that. She was making good, deep friendships, and was really settling in for the long haul. Any time I would express my discontent and desire to leave, that conversation produced a lot of upset for her and produced a lot of conflict in our marriage.

What I did not know was that she had confided in one of our elders. She told him that she was not sure if our marriage would survive another move.

That happened just before I attended the Faithwalking retreat in Houston as a part of the Ridder process. I was not prepared for the encounter with God that I had there. One of the sessions in Faithwalking is about the power of being authentic. We were sent to a time of solitude and urged to bring *all of what we know about ourselves to all of what we know of God.*

So, I did that. I put my restlessness in front of God. I told God that I wanted to run. I said that I felt like I had gotten stuck again in a congregation that I didn't fit or that didn't fit me. I was bitter. I said to God, "I am done. I'm leaving. This is not working."

As I sat in that time of solitude and poured out my heart to God, I had the very clear sense that God was speaking personally to me. I heard God say, "You are not going to ever find fruitfulness in your ministry until you commit to a place and a people. Commit to this place and these people, and fruitfulness will come."

That simple but profound exchange changed me. It was the first time that permanence or being settled in a place opened up for me as a real possibility.

That night I called Tammy. I said to her, "I think God might be saying 'stay put and learn what you need to learn.'"

Tammy listened patiently and quietly. Then in the spirit of the authenticity that I had engaged she said, "I'm really shocked to hear you say that. I think it is important for me to tell you that I had already decided that if you did leave, I was not going to go with you." That got my attention in a new way. In my time with God, I was realizing that my pattern of running was a problem. Tammy's comments helped me see the scale and scope of the problem. That was my moment of turning—starting with authenticity with God—and leading into a different level of authenticity with Tammy.

An overlay on this conversation was that I had been doing some work in Family Systems at the Georgetown Center. As I learned about emotional maturity and the power of anxiety, I already had a growing sense that I was contributing to the system that I was in. The experiences in Houston brought that to the center of my radar. There was something empowering about that even if I didn't know what to do with it.

As I began to connect the dots, I could see that often my running was about my sense that things were not working and would never change. I felt stuck. As I began to see myself in the system, I was able to see that staying didn't mean that I was helpless or stuck. I could change. There was something I could do to get a different outcome.

One thing I could see clearly. The anxiety in my pattern of relating to Tammy—and the anxiety in my pattern of relating to the congregation— was contributing significantly to the experience I was having. As I began to focus on my pattern and the anxiety that I was contributing to the system, I began to have a place to focus my energies. I learned to manage my anxiety more effectively. I began to be different in my marriage and in my congregation.

I've been in Midland for nine years and I'm having some of the most fruitful and personally satisfying years of marriage and ministry that I have ever had.

Chapter 10

The Power to Change: From Status Quo to Creative Tension

Nate Pyle

Where is God calling us to go? Where are we now? How will we know when we get there? How will we get from here to there? These are the questions that face every leader.

When God's people have a clear and compelling vision for God's emerging future and when they have a clear and compelling sense of where they are right now, things get tense. More specifically, this process produces creative tension—the kind of energy that empowers change.

Learning to generate and sustain creative tension in order to get people from here to there is a key task of leadership. Learning to manage the anxiety that fills the gap between here and there is also an essential piece of leadership. As we took on this learning, we realized that there were a lot of moving pieces and a lot of ways to become derailed—and therefore, a lot of opportunities to learn on the way to being more effective leaders.

*D*o you have a dream for your congregation? Do you dream of a more impactive youth ministry, a greater presence in your community, a reimagined worship service, or a higher functioning staff? While the dreams differ, the question behind each of these dreams is the same: "What will it take to make this dream a reality?"

You probably know that guiding your congregation to realize God's dreams for them will require mobilizing people and leading change. And you probably have no idea how to do that. Most pastors and many church leaders have been trained to provide pastoral care, prepare sermons, and maybe even exegete scriptural passages in Greek. However, most of us were never taught how to lead a group of people toward a common goal, especially when that involves significant change.

In *Leading Congregational Change*, the authors state that in order for leaders to mobilize people toward a vision, they must master the discipline of "generating and sustaining creative tension" (Herrington et al., 2000, p. 100). When we hold up a compelling vision for the future of our congregation and put it alongside a picture of our current reality, the gap between the two pictures creates tension. This creative tension, which we will later distinguish from emotional tension, creates the necessary energy to move people toward a new vision.

Find a rubber band, place it between your two thumbs, and stretch it out. Can you feel the energy stored in the rubber band? Pluck the rubber band and it oscillates back and forth. You can let one end go and it will snap together. And of course, wrap it around your thumb and forefinger and you can shoot it at an unsuspecting bystander. All this is possible when the rubber band is stretched out. In fact, a rubber band is only useful when it holds tension. The reason is simple: A stretched rubber band is full of energy. In physics, this is known as *potential energy*; the energy in the rubber band has the potential to do something. (I am indebted here to Nancy Ortberg's (2008) discussion of the rubber band as a metaphor for tension.)

The stretched rubber band helps us understand what it means to generate and sustain creative tension. Clearly describing a congregation's current reality while at the same time defining a compelling vision for the future "stretches" the desires of the people and creates potential energy. This potential energy is necessary for change.

It is the leader's responsibility to help a congregation articulate both the current reality and the future vision with enough clarity to create this tension. If there is not enough tension, the congregation will lack motivation to work toward a new vision. If there is too much tension, a congregation will reject change and will hold tighter to the status quo. Effective leaders must be wise with one ear to the congregation and one ear to the Holy Spirit as they work to bring about creative tension.

Jesus was a master at generating creative tension. Most of the Sermon on the Mount is Jesus describing current reality and then holding up a new vision. He began with "You have heard that it was said . . . 'You shall not murder'" (current reality) and then added, "But I say to you that if you are angry with a brother or sister, you will be liable to judgment" (emerging future) (Matt. 5:21). Throughout the sermon, Jesus states current reality and then casts a new vision for the Kingdom of God.

Where We Are Now and Where We Are Going

Current Reality

Current reality is the state of things right now. It is "what is so" in your church (see Figure 10.1). It is the size of your congregation, the number of staff, your location, and the kinds of programs you offer. It is the financial situation, the structure of governance, the attitudes of the people, and the style of worship. Leaders work to describe current reality with as much accuracy and clear-eyed perspective as possible.

Defining current reality may seem straightforward, but it is actually quite difficult. We may distort current reality because of our natural pessimism or optimism. We may fear that telling the truth about how things really are will make us or the church look bad. Looking squarely at our current reality may make us feel hopeless or inadequate, if things are bad. If we are already upset about how things are, we may dismiss any evidence that positive things are happening.

Figure 10.1—Current Reality

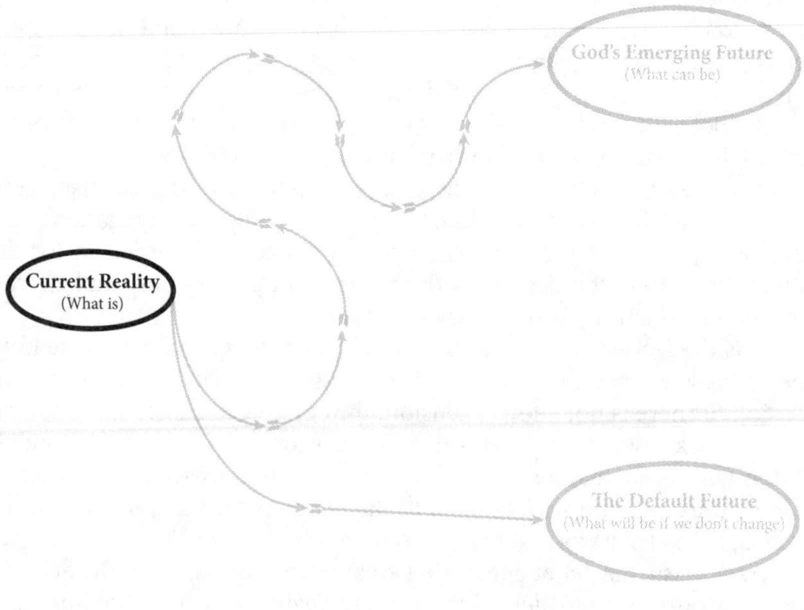

Recently a friend of mine in the church I serve called me up to tell me he and his wife were coming over for dinner. Thankfully, they were bringing the food! After we had caught up and spent time chatting, they got down to the reason for their visit. Our church is in the process of moving from assigning individuals to lead ministries to a more team-based approach. Our friends had come over for dinner to share concerns about how this was being communicated and how slowly the process was moving.

My first inclination was to defend our progress and myself. I wanted them to hear the good things that were happening and the reasons why some things hadn't happened yet. I wanted to paint a very positive picture regarding this new structure. But if I had reacted in these ways, I would have been blinding myself to a fuller picture of reality presented by my friends. I would have seen things as I wanted them to be and would have lost the perspective of others. All of us would have lost any potential energy to continue moving towards our emerging future.

It is tempting for leaders to assume their view of current reality is the right one. It would have been easy to disregard my friends' observations and hold on to my own view of things. The wise leader recognizes his or her own tendency to distort reality and then takes action to gain and maintain a more humble perspective.

There are many ways this can be done. Holding town hall meetings with the congregation brings out the wider voice and experience of the church. Inviting key leaders to share their assessment of reality—and then actually listening to what they have to say—broadens a leader's perspective. Distributing congregational surveys helps uncover the attitudes and morale of the congregation regarding particular areas of ministry or the church as a whole. The knowledge gained from this kind of humble inquiry will help the leader more accurately discern current reality.

God's Emerging Future

After we get a clear picture of what is currently so, the next task in the process of generating and sustaining creative tension, is to discern God's emerging future (see Figure 10.2). This is the vision. It answers the questions: Where are we going? To what are we called? What does God want for us?

While God's emerging future could be contained in the church's mission or vision statement, it could also emerge as we imagine new ways to do children's ministry or serve the poor in our community. It could be as simple as starting a new program or hiring new staff to be able to fulfill the bigger vision, or as big as discerning a completely new mission and vision.

It is the leader's responsibility to help the church discern what the emerging future is, to describe it in compelling ways that create enthusiasm and support, and to help ensure that leaders and congregants share the vision together. We must communicate our vision in a way that is clear, shared, and compelling. This is different than the familiar model where a leader is expected to dictate the vision for the people and then seek compliance to that vision.

When I was being interviewed for my current pastoral position, one person asked, "What is your vision for our church?" The question made me uncomfortable because honestly, I didn't have one. For a couple of years my lack of initial vision bothered me. I chalked it up to the fact that I was coming right out of seminary and was inexperienced. On some occasions, most often when I was frustrated and tired, I thought my inability to articulate a vision from the beginning pointed to an inability to lead. After all, I thought a leader is supposed to go up on the mountain and come back down with a vision.

Sometimes that happens. More often, though, the leader doesn't have to be the sole person responsible for discerning the vision. It is possible for a community of people to come together and through a discovery process, involving honest dialogue and prayer, develop a shared vision of what God's emerging future looks like for them. Under the guidance of the Holy Spirit, a community can develop a shared belief about God's emerging future.

I see now that my response "I don't have one," wasn't a sign of poor leadership. If I had I come to the church with a vision for the church without a knowledge of the people and the context, I likely would have been coming with my own desires and aspirations, not a true picture of God's emerging future for this particular congregation.

Figure 10.2—God's Emerging Future

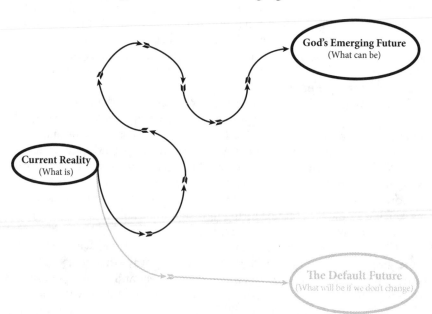

By not having a clear vision, I was more open to looking outside of myself for God's emerging future. Together the congregation and I discovered where God was calling us to go. The leadership recruited people to serve on a vision team in order to begin discerning God's emerging future for the church. As the vision became clearer, the congregation was invited to give input to the work being done through surveys and town-hall-style meetings. Over several months, as we developed a clear picture of God's emerging future, I preached a sermon series on what we believed God to be calling us to. Our small groups discussed the sermons and ideas and, after four weeks of these discussions, we gathered everyone together to celebrate the new direction. This process built consensus in the congregation, not mere compliance. Our picture of God's emerging future was not something I needed to "sell" because they already owned it. Leaders who strategically use their role to guide their congregations to a place of discovering God's emerging future and clearly articulate that future alongside a clear picture of current reality will generate the necessary creative tension to mobilize the people.

Default Future

We have talked about two components of generating and sustaining tension: current reality and God's emerging future. But let's add a third component: the default future. The default future is what will happen if we stay on the path we are on and we do not move toward God's emerging future (see Figure 10.3).

We often think that the default future looks the same as current reality; in other words, things will simply continue as they are. Unfortunately that is not so. For one thing, the world around us is always changing, whether we change or not. Also, our description of current reality will not be perfect. Current reality will always contain imperfections, integrity gaps, things we didn't see and places where what we are doing is not working. Over time, these inconsistencies will work to erode the quality of our current reality.

Once after a sermon, a woman came up to me and said, "I don't believe God wants us to be uncomfortable." We talked about this idea for a while, and what became clear to me was that for her, life was good and she wanted that to continue. Change threatened that status quo and made her uncomfortable. Many congregations feel the same way. Life is good right now. Everything is working well, people are happy, and there are signs of growth. In this situation, the pressure on the leader is to maintain current reality and not promote substantial change.

Often we resist moving toward, or even acknowledging, God's emerging future because we are still attached to the way things were in the past. Maybe we want our Bible study group to stay the way it has always been or we want the children's ministry to look the way it did when we were children. However, our culture is changing at supersonic speeds and if we do not adjust, our congregations will decline and eventually die. Things never stay the same.

Figure 10.3—Default Future

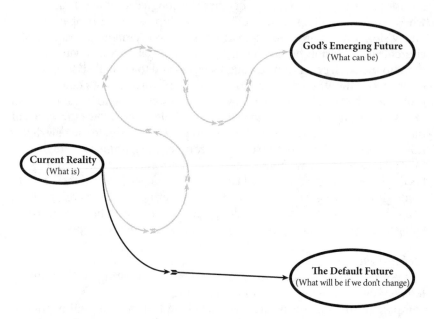

Five years ago our church had over twenty high school students in youth group. For a church our size, it was a large, vibrant group. During the pastoral search process, it was touted as one of the things of which the church was proud. Youth invited their friends, went on mission trips, and were highly involved in many areas of the church. The church wanted and expected the youth ministry to stay the same.

Today, the high school youth group has been combined with both the junior high group and the fifth and sixth graders because numbers are so low. Little has changed in how we do youth ministry here. Why the decline? One reason is that the high school students graduated and we weren't actively working to reach out to kids younger than high school. That was a painful but accurate description of our current reality. Our failure to address the younger students resulted in a default future that was significantly different from our current reality, despite our efforts to do ministry in the same way.

Practice and Reflect

Take a piece of paper and recreate the diagram for generating and sustaining creative tension. Now, think of a situation where you would like to see your life move closer to God's emerging future. This could be at church, in a relationship, or in your personal life. With that situation in mind:

- Describe the current reality of the situation (write it in the diagram).
- Describe the default future of this situation.
- Describe God's emerging future as you currently understand it.

Take a moment and reflect on everything you wrote. What are you present to (emotions, thoughts, the way your body feels, etc.)? Write these things down. We will discuss them later in the chapter.

Tension and Anxiety

As you did the exercise above, especially when you became present to what you felt, you probably felt some tension. In the space between a clearly defined current reality and God's emerging future are both creative tension and emotional tension (see Figure 10.4). Creative tension is not a feeling; it is the energy required to bring about change. However, as we move toward that change, we will likely feel a great deal of emotional tension that threatens to diminish that energy. Emotional tension is the anxiety we feel about change and is expressed in resistance. How a leader manages his or her emotional tension and that of the congregation will determine how the energy of creative tension is used.

Figure 10.4—The Space

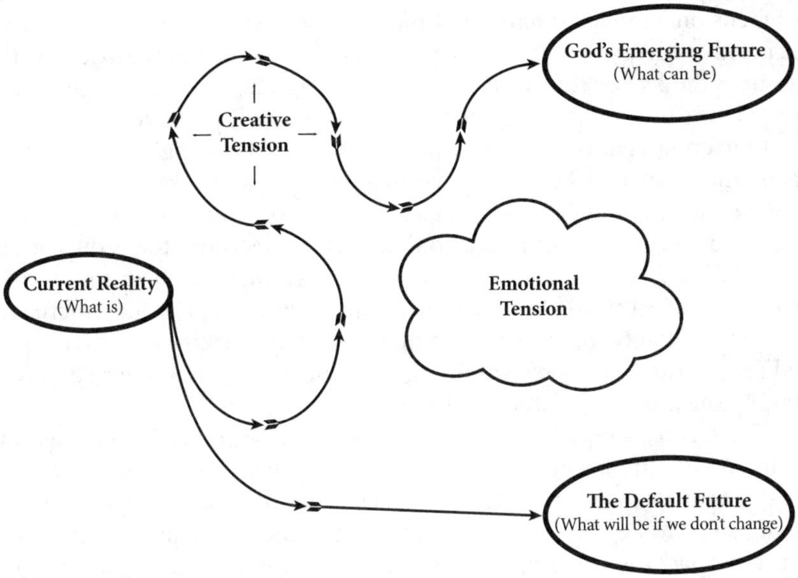

Emotional tension is a form of anxiety, a natural reaction to a perceived threat. For example, if you encounter a mean dog, your adrenaline kicks in and you react instinctively to chase the dog away, run away yourself, or freeze in place. These reactions are known as "fight, flight, or freeze." God has wonderfully wired our bodies so we can quickly respond to danger without having to take time to think about what to do. A situation like this is known as acute anxiety. The anxiety we feel is a direct result of an immediate, life-endangering threat.

There is another kind of anxiety—chronic anxiety. Chronic anxiety is not based upon an immediate, real threat; instead, it is based upon a threat that is imagined or distorted. Many things that feel uncomfortable are not immediate, life-endangering threats. When someone doesn't like me or when they disagree with me about an important decision or when they disapprove of me in some way, I may feel uncomfortable. I may even want to fight, flee, or freeze. But it's important for me to learn that I am not actually in danger and that I can continue to manage my own anxiety and to pay attention to the anxiety of others.

When a congregation begins to look at their current reality and to think about God's emerging future, many people are likely to feel threatened. Emotional tension will rise. Chronic anxiety will light up the system. When that happens, people will react in four predictable ways: conflict, distancing, over-functioning/under-functioning, and projection onto a third person (triangling). Corporately, we can see the effects of anxiety in five predictable ways: a heightened sense of reactivity, a herding instinct, blame displacement, looking for a quick fix, and poor leadership. When you create and generate creative tension, emotional tension in the form of anxiety always accompanies the positive energy necessary for change. Understanding how anxiety works will help the leader deal with two temptations that occur when anxiety is present. The first temptation is to look at current reality with less objectivity.

Our congregation has been hovering around the eighty-percent capacity mark since 1996, and two years ago we began to have some serious conversations about how we would make more room in our sanctuary. As the conversation progressed to the point of decision, the group began to say, "There's more room than what we are saying," "We can squeeze together," "We just need to add chairs to the back or front of the sanctuary." Facing the anxiety that comes with making a major decision leads us to try and relieve the anxiety by modifying current reality, so that we can avoid making the anxiety-producing change.

The second temptation is to compromise our vision of God's emerging future. A church may believe that God's emerging future for them is to care for those in their community struggling with addiction. They may begin taking steps to do that until the reality of the messiness of that vision begins to impact the congregation. This congregational anxiety will tempt the leaders to say, "Well, God really doesn't want us to take all this on," thereby compromising what they initially discerned was God's emerging future.

Think back to the stretched rubber band. Both of these temptations reflect what happens when you move your thumbs closer together, thereby reducing the tension. But when you reduce the tension in the rubber band, the amount of potential energy decreases. The same thing happens when we distort current reality or compromise God's emerging future. We reduce the amount of creative tension needed to bring about change. If the leader continues to clearly describe current reality and does not compromise the vision of God's emerging future, then the only way to reduce the creative tension is to move toward the goal of the emerging future.

It seems so simple, doesn't it? Then why doesn't it happen more? There are a number of reasons. First, this whole process is uncomfortable and painful. Many of us have been taught that a successful leader makes everyone happy and keeps anxiety out of the system. In fact, we may even be tempted to measure our own success by counting how many people we are able to keep satisfied. In this kind of model, tension is not something to be managed, sustained, or heaven-forbid, created. Tension is to be resolved and avoided.

Creating and Sustaining Tension: A Different Response

In good leadership, the opposite is true. In *The Power of Rubber Bands*, Nancy Ortberg says, "As leaders, we constantly need to determine whether something is a problem to be solved or a tension to be managed" (2008, p. 71). For true change to happen, the leader must be willing to create tension and upset the equilibrium that exists.

Stepping Out in Faith

Think about how often this happens for the people of God. God often calls God's people to leave the status quo and to step out in faith, creating both creative and emotional anxiety. God called Noah to build an ark without a rain cloud in sight. Do you think he experienced some anxiety as people said, "I think you are a little off in your discernment of current reality"? Abraham was called to leave everything he knew to go to a place he knew nothing about. I'm sure some people said, "God can't be calling you that far away!" Joshua and Jericho, Gideon and his army of three hundred, David and Goliath, the disciples and their nets, all remind us that when God calls his people to his future, it is rarely to a place of more comfort, but rather, it is often to a place of less comfort. We like our comforts, and so this model will always push up against our natural tendencies to avoid pain and seek comfort. This is what often keeps leaders from creating and sustaining the necessary tension.

Courage Needed

Second, creating and sustaining tension takes courage. Only a courageous leader will intentionally rock the boat. It takes courage to accurately and truthfully describe current reality to people who may not want to see it. For me personally, it takes courage because I have to face directly my fears of failing, of not being competent, and of not being liked. If I don't face these fears, they will dominate what I do or don't do. My actions will be driven not by my pursuit of Christ and God's emerging future, but by my pursuit of protecting myself. I will be the motivation behind what I do, not God.

Our church had been seeing moderate growth for a couple of years. I was very clear that we were soon, if not already, going to be facing a space issue in our worship service. I began talking about this reality and that we would need to go to two services or move our worship into the gym on a regular basis. Sunday morning worship, congregational meetings, and leadership meetings were all places where I talked about this situation. I spoke for nearly two years without taking any concrete actions steps. During one congregational meeting where I was talking about this issue, a woman raised her hand and said, "We've been talking about this for two years. When are we going to do something?" In that moment it became clear that my fear and my desire to be liked was keeping me from making the necessary decisions to help us deal with the present situation. My fear was my motivation. Leaders need courage in order to make the necessary choices in the face of their fears and anxieties.

Don't Forget Patience

Third, creating and sustaining tension requires patience. We live in an impatient world. Less than twenty years ago you had to dial in to connect to the Internet, and that alone took minutes. Today, if I have to wait longer than ten seconds for a page to load on my phone (on my phone!), I get impatient. We want results and we want them now!

Like many pastors, I have read books and attended conferences looking for that one magic program or technique that will transform our church next month or at least by next year. Unfortunately, there are no quick fixes to transformation. Managing the creative tension as we pursue God's emerging future may take months, years, or even decades. Paul writes, "Not that I have already obtained this . . . but I press on . . . straining forward to what lies ahead" (Phil. 3:12–13). For Paul, transformation required constant, intentional, and disciplined pursuit over a lifetime. That is the change that will last, but it requires us to be patient, suspending our desire for immediate results or quick fixes.

Combatting Resignation and Cynicism

As we talk about leading congregational change, we need to acknowledge that people carry a lot of resignation and cynicism. This is true of both pastors and congregations. Countless conferences promised pastors that if they just instituted these particular programs in their church they would see change. Denominations have touted certain leadership techniques that if adhered to by pastors and congregational leaders would facilitate transformation. Many have followed the well-intentioned advice of others only to have seen these "tried and true" methods not work. And so any time a new method or program or technique for change is presented, it is met with an understandable degree of resignation and cynicism. This is also an anxious reaction.

Many a congregation has heard, "Here is the new vision," or "This is what it will be like moving forward," only to experience little to no change. When my church's new vision and mission statement were presented to the congregation, one person stood and said, "I have been here for twenty years and have seen mission statements come and go with no change. We are who we have always been. What's different about this one?" He wasn't alone, not in my congregation and not in yours.

So what turns resignation and cynicism into hope and belief? Integrity— remember Chapter Four? Integrity is *doing what you say you will do, when you said you would do it, in the manner it was meant to be done.*

Any time we fail to be in integrity, we create a gap between what is and that to which we gave our word. Integrity gaps create resignation and cynicism. And, it should be noted, when we give our word to moving toward God's emerging future, we are giving our word to something on which we can't currently deliver. If we can deliver on it right now, then the vision probably isn't big enough! And so, in doing the work of moving toward God's emerging future we will sometimes not know how to do something and we will get stuck. Instead of resigning ourselves to the idea that it is too hard to keep going, we must get in action and learn what we need to know. Or sometimes the emotional tension that exists alongside the creative tension in the system causes the leader's anxiety to rise and the leader backs off from doing what he said he would do, thereby creating an integrity gap. Unless these integrity gaps are closed, resignation and cynicism will stop any progress.

For many leaders, the idea of closing the integrity gaps brings a lot of anxiety. Our fears of looking bad or not looking good, of not having all the answers, or of being perceived as incompetent keep us from being honest about our integrity gaps. Leaders must have the courage to acknowledge their integrity gaps and close them if they desire to see any change in their congregations. Most pastors, if they are willing to take this on, will find that their congregations don't expect them to be perfect. People know perfection isn't attainable. They are looking for a leader who is authentic.

One Monday, I walked into my office to find the deacons' budget proposal for the next year on my desk. Unbeknownst to me, they decided to slash our church administrator's and custodian's salary in an effort to present a budget not requiring us to take money out of savings. In my anxiety, I called the chairman of the deacons on the phone and as close to yelling as I could come without yelling, expressed every problem I saw with their proposal. Later in the day it became clear that my actions and words were not appropriate. I called him back and apologized to him and authentically shared my anxieties and fears. After I shared my fears, he informed me that they were the same fears he had. Together we were able to lead the budget meeting the next night so that it was very productive. Reflecting on that situation I see that my ability to be authentic with him paved the way for a fruitful solution. It wasn't a leadership technique or having the perfect answer. It was simply being authentic.

Balancing Two Kinds of Leadership

Leading a congregation through the process of generating and sustaining creative tension requires leaders to excel at two very different kinds of leadership—operational and adaptive.

Operational Leadership

When we are exercising operational leadership, we are doing the things that will help the system stay the same. Although we may want to incrementally improve on current reality, we are focused on how to keep doing the things we already know how to do and essentially keeping current reality in place. In most congregations, examples of operational leadership are planning worship services, leading Sunday School classes, running the church office, and preparing for the annual stewardship campaign.

Adaptive Leadership

We exercise adaptive leadership when we want to create or manage change. We are focused on doing something unfamiliar and something we don't already know how to do, usually when we have an awareness that traditional solutions won't work and business as usual won't get us where we want to go. Adaptive leadership may look like creating new ways to develop leaders, reaching out to people who are different from our congregation's demographics, or transitioning to a different decision-making process.

Generating and sustaining creative tension requires a delicate balance of both kinds of leadership. Our attention to the operational, allows things to continue to function while things are changing. Our attention to the adaptive, gives us the structure and momentum we need to lead change, and to move toward God's emerging future.

Most of us struggle with getting out of the quicksand of operational tasks and making time and energy for the adaptive ones. Typically, it's easier for us to keep doing what we know how to do—what people expect us to do—than it is for us change course and address the process of change. However, when we fail to attend to the adaptive parts of our leadership, we will stay frustrated by our lack of progress and we will notice that change remains a good intention and not a growing reality.

Successful Adaptive Leaders

Don't Snap the Rubber Band!

Generating and sustaining tension must be done with wisdom. Again, think about the rubber band. If you fail to stretch it far enough, there will not be enough energy to make the rubber band useful. If you stretch it too far, the rubber band snaps. When the distance between current reality and God's emerging future is too great, emotional tension far exceeds the creative tension, and the system will "snap."

Park Community was a congregation that for the last twenty years had been in slow decline. The neighborhood around the church became more ethnically and socioeconomically diverse. Many of the church members moved away to surrounding suburbs, and only came into the neighborhood on Sunday mornings. Over time, the church no longer reflected the community.

After hiring a young and courageous pastor, the church entered into a revisioning process. The vision team objectively identified current reality as well as the default future and proposed two options: 1) close down the church or 2) make serious changes to the church's ministries with a strategic approach to reaching the neighborhood. The changes included in this second option were major: renovating the worship space, remodeling the front of the building to make it more inviting, letting go of one staff person in order to hire another staff person, partnering with the elementary school down the road, and doing prayer walks and door-to-door outreach in the neighborhood, all at the same time. In the end, the leadership chose to adopt the second option. As the changes were implemented, people— including those who voted to make the changes—began leaving the church. Some neighborhood people started attending and the church even saw people come to Jesus, but the vision of God's emerging future was so different from current reality that it actually began to demotivate and create resistance within a portion of the congregation. The rubber band snapped.

As leaders begin to create tension they must ask themselves, "How much tension can the system handle? Is this current vision too much? Do we need to break it into smaller, more manageable pieces? What do I need to be watching for to ensure that enough tension has been created? What do I need to look for to see if too much tension has been created?" Asking these questions will help the leader avoid snapping the rubber band.

Be Willing to Stretch the Rubber Band Again

In 2004, our church completed a million-dollar addition that included a new gathering space, a beautiful kitchen, a full-sized gym, and a youth room. For many in the church, it was a positive milestone in the life of the congregation. When I was being interviewed by the church, I remember consistently hearing how much the congregation pulled together around this purpose. The vision had been cast, they chased after it, and they attained it.

Four years later everyone was asking the question, "Now what?" Our current reality had changed. We were no longer at the same place. We had a new current reality. That meant the gap between current reality and God's emerging future was smaller. And a smaller gap meant less tension —and less tension meant less energy. In order to sustain creative tension, the leader must help the church continue seeking after God's emerging future.

After a substantial shift in a congregation's current reality, it may be tempting to not enter into the process all over again. However, in order for a church to continue to grow, we must sustain the creative tension. Robert Quinn (1996) highlights the necessity of this when he says that institutions are either experiencing slow death or deep change. When we stop changing, we begin to die.

In order for churches to keep experiencing growth and transformation, leaders must master the art of not only generating creative tension, but also sustaining it over time. When our efforts are seen as successful, we may become lazy and complacent. If we are not successful, we may become discouraged and resigned. Either way, we may resist sustaining the creative tension that drives change. When we fail to discern what the next step in God's emerging future is, routine takes over, creativity and energy ebbs, and slow death begins to define the church. Effective leaders continually practice the discipline of generating and sustaining tension.

Measure Progress

Many of us resist the idea of measuring success in the church. It seems too secular and unspiritual. After all, we deal with people and spiritual matters, so how can we measure success? Success may be the wrong word, and in the context of church, success is difficult to define. But if there is clarity about God's emerging future, then *progress* toward that future can be measured. While it's true there is much a church does that cannot be measured, it is also true there is much a church does that can (and should) be measured. In order for a church to know if it is moving toward God's emerging future, it must work to measure its progress. If we measure nothing, we cannot have a clear picture of current reality, and without a clear picture of current reality, we cannot know where we stand in relation to God's emerging future. To help us measure our progress toward this future, leaders must measure outcomes, outputs, processes, and inputs (see Figure 10.5).

Figure 10.5—Measuring Progress

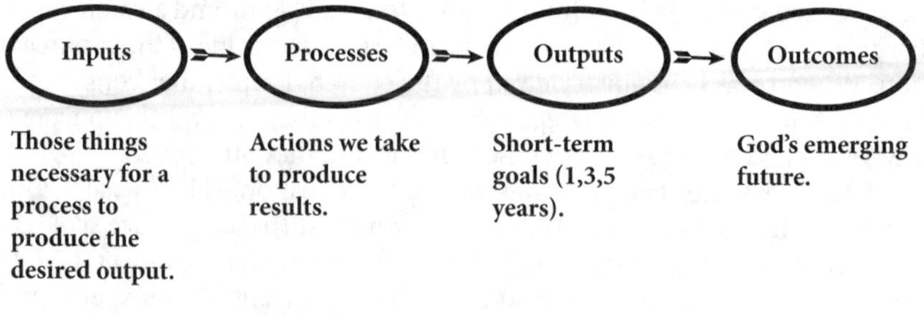

Inputs	Processes	Outputs	Outcomes
Those things necessary for a process to produce the desired output.	Actions we take to produce results.	Short-term goals (1,3,5 years).	God's emerging future.

Outcomes. Measuring progress begins by being clear about God's emerging future, the desired outcome. My congregation's desired outcome is that we would develop disciples of Jesus who impact the world. This outcome has two parts we want to measure: developing disciples and impact. However, directly measuring them is difficult. How do you measure if disciples are being developed? How do you measure impact in the world?

Outputs. To measure progress toward the desired outcome, the leader must define specific outputs—those results that indicate whether a desired outcome is being achieved. I will use our church's desired outcome of developing disciples as an example. We are measuring stories of transformed lives, participation in community groups, participation in obedience and missional-focused discipleship, and financial giving as outputs—evidence of progress. Tracking these outputs allows us to discern current reality in relationship to God's emerging future.

Just as important as *what* we measure is *how* we measure. In the example of above, how we measure financial giving seems straightforward. However, it may be more important to measure whether the number of people who are giving is increasing rather than measuring if the total income is increasing. For us, measuring the number of people who give provides a better picture of how we are doing when it comes to developing disciples rather than measuring the overall budget. Measuring stories of transformed lives is more difficult, but that doesn't make it any less important. Currently, our ability to tell stories is our measurement. Are there new stories of changed lives? Are people telling their stories in small groups and during the worship service? Do leaders have stories from their ministries from the last six months? Asking these types of questions helps us to measure progress toward the preferred future.

Processes. Measuring outputs like participation in community groups or financial giving also gives us a picture of the current processes of the church. Processes are the actions taken to produce results—the events, programs, classes, and structures of the church. Processes are developed based upon a set of beliefs we have about the outputs and outcomes they will produce. Clearly stating outputs and rigorously measuring them allows the leader to see whether or not the current processes are producing the desired output. If not, the leader must ask, "Is this the right process, or is something missing?"

Inputs. For processes to work, they must have the necessary inputs. Inputs are very tangible. People, money, facilities, and marketing are all examples of inputs and are necessary to the success of a process. A great process will fail without the right inputs. For example, you can develop a wonderful worship service (a process), but without the right facility (an input), you risk your process failing.

Perhaps an example using all these terms will be helpful in seeing how they relate to one another. Our church measures three inputs during our Sunday morning worship service: members, regular attendees, and visitors.

While we have a number of visitors every week, our assimilation rate (an output indicating we are achieving our desired outcome of developing disciples of Jesus who impact the world) seemed lower than we would have liked it to be. So two years ago we did a complete overhaul of how we greet visitors and follow up with them. The new process helped some with assimilation, but not as much as we would have liked. In other words, our assimilation rate, our output, wasn't what we desired it to be. We then looked back over our process (how we greet visitors) and our inputs. As we looked at the input of visitors, we realized there were actually three different types of visitors coming to our church: first-time visitors, regular visitors, and people who were members of other churches but with us for just one morning. We now see that our assimilation rate compared to first-time visitors is acceptable, but we would like to see our first-time visitor input increased. This insight has led us to look at our current outreach strategy. Measuring outcomes, outputs, processes, and inputs has helped us be more accurate in measuring our progress toward God's emerging future.

Making It Personal

While the discipline of generating and sustaining tension works at the congregational level, it also applies personally. Peter Senge (1990) presents this idea in *The Fifth Discipline*, using the language of "personal mastery." Generating and sustaining tension is a way for a person to work toward achieving their purpose in life.

I have a whiteboard on the wall in my office, and cannot tell you how many times I have drawn the diagram of generating and sustaining tension in counseling sessions. Whether it is helping people get clear about a habit they wanted to get rid of, a marriage that was rocky, or hope they had for their children, the principle of generating and sustaining tension helps motivate people into action toward achieving God's emerging future for their life.

As a pastor, my first instinct is to put off using this principle in my personal life until after I have used it in my congregation. However, generating and sustaining tension in my congregation forces me to generate and sustain tension in my personal life. The leader cannot do one without doing the other. The reason is simple: In trying to move the congregation the pastor will experience anxiety, need more courage, and/or not know what to do next. The leader must engage in the work of personal transformation in order to lead congregational transformation. In order to stay in action, the pastor will need to honestly assess current reality and God's emerging future in relation to themselves so that they may continue to effectively lead their congregation.

I am not a risk-taker. I want to be perceived as one, but I rarely make a decision unless I know I can handle it. After I shared this with a mentor, he looked at me and said a little sardonically, "Isn't that a safe way to live?" In other words, how can I ever work toward God's emerging future if I am only doing those things I know I can do within my own power? If I am afraid of risk, how well am I going to lead? Am I going to lead at all? No, I will manage, but I won't lead. In order for me to lead effectively, I have to be willing to generate and sustain tension in my personal life so I can do the same in my congregational setting. Personal transformation leads to congregational transformation.

Peter Senge ends his chapter on personal mastery with the following: "The core leadership strategy is simple: be a model. Commit yourself to your own personal mastery. Talking about personal mastery may open people's minds somewhat, but actions always speak louder than words. There's nothing more powerful you can do to encourage others in their quest for personal mastery than to be serious in your own quest" (1990, p. 162). While we would change the language of "personal mastery" to "God's emerging future," Senge is absolutely right. If you want to see others move toward God's emerging future, model it for them. If you want to see your congregation move toward God's emerging future, then begin to move toward your own. True transformation will take place at the intersection of your ongoing transformation and the congregation's.

Going Deeper

Generating and sustaining creative tension is difficult but necessary for deep and lasting change. Effective leaders recognize the importance of helping congregations articulate "what is so" (current reality) as they seek to discern a vision for God's emerging future.

To learn more about generating and sustaining creative tension, check out our online resources at http://www.westernsem.edu/journey/ridder.

References and Additional Resources

Barna, George. *Think Like Jesus*. Brentwood, TN: Integrity Publishers, 2003.

Heifetz, Ronald, Marty Linsky, and Alexander Grashow. *The Practice of Adaptive Leadership: Tools and Tactics for Changing Your Organization and the World*. Boston: Harvard Business Press, 2009.

Herrington, Jim, Mike Bonem, and James H. Furr. *Leading Congregational Change: A Practical Guide for the Transformational Journey*. San Francisco: Jossey-Bass, 2000.

Ortberg, Nancy. *Unleashing the Power of Rubber Bands*. Carol Stream, IL: Tyndale, 2008.

Quinn, Robert E. 1996. *Deep Change: Discovering the Leader Within*. San Francisco: Jossey-Bass, 1996.

Senge, Peter M. 1990. *The Fifth Discipline: The Art & Practice of the Learning Organization*. New York: Doubleday, 1990.

Chapter 11

High-Performance Teams: From Completing Tasks to Solving Big Problems

John Sparks

The world is full of lone rangers, well-meaning Christians who get ideas and then get busy trying to implement their ideas—alone. Sometimes that works, and we're grateful for the work of individuals who get busy and make things happen.

But when the stakes are high, we need each other. Research clearly shows that in most cases we can produce more together than any one person can alone. You may know the old saying, "To go fast, go alone. To go far, go together." Often, we do not go far because we do not know how to go together.

Because we are committed to working together in community, we had to learn how to pursue the vision God had given us collectively. We learned to form teams that could function as disciplined and loving learning communities as we learned together how to live differently, how to do church differently, and how to pursue mission differently. We had to learn to stay organized around a common purpose. We had to learn new skills and practice them—together.

S everal years ago, I sat with a group of pastors in the Ridder Church Renewal process listening to a presentation based on the book *The Wisdom of Teams* (Katzenbach and Smith, 2003). The timing of this presentation could not be more perfect. My church had recently identified three churchwide goals through the work we did around current reality and God's emerging future. One of the goals was to develop a clear process for discipleship. Following the presentation, I began to imagine a team forming around this goal and decided without delay that the creation of a churchwide discipleship process was the perfect job for a *high-performance team*, a team designed to solve big problems. This is the story of what I have learned and experienced through the deployment of high-performance teams, teams that are capable of producing remarkable results.

With one seminar and a book on the subject, I launched a team that eventually took on the name IT (Inspirited and Transformed). The IT Team was to be a grand experiment that I hoped to learn from while at the same time achieving high performance. Along the way, we made a number of mistakes, but we learned about teams and ourselves, had some fun, and made measurable progress in developing and implementing Apprenticeship Training Teams for our church. I am so very grateful for each member of the IT Team and for their willingness to build the bridge of teaming while we walked on it.[1]

In Chapter 10, we discussed generating and sustaining creative tension as a way to think about moving a church from its current reality to God's emerging future. High-performance teams are teams that have the real potential to transform. I hope our story and experience inspires you to take a serious look at teams as a potent tool to move your church toward what God has in mind for your church and your community.

I remember a day when almost every church called a working group a committee. At some point a certain amount of cynicism grew up around committees and there was a push to make them more relational—and perhaps, more attractive to join. In the hopes of seeing different results, the name "team" replaced "committee," and for a while, calling every working group in a church a team became an ecclesiastical fad. We went from an Adult Ministry Committee to an Adult Ministry Team. However, in most cases, the nature of the group of people who gathered monthly did not change and neither did the results. The thinking behind high-performance teams is not a matter of a name change that produces better working relationships and feelings. Rather, it is a different way of thinking and being—a different way of working together—that can produce greater fruitfulness.

---

1.   "Building the bridge as you walk on it," a concept from *Deep Change* (Quinn, 1996, pp. 83–88).

The Nature and Disciplines of Teams

By definition, a high-performance team has great potential to produce extraordinary outcomes due to its nature and disciplines. In recent years, there have been a number of books written for corporate America on the subject of teams. These books are in response to some of the significant challenges facing business in the twenty-first century. Challenges include the fast rate of change and the very real threat of market share loss.[2] In many ways, the church is facing similar challenges ministering in a rapidly changing world and ample evidence that we are losing our influence and impact in our neighborhoods, cities, and workplaces.[3] With such similarities, the current interest in and research of productive teams can serve as a helpful guide for the church today. From the perspective of business, we can learn from teams that have worked well through the trials of cultural turmoil while experiencing significant productivity; and when we consider such high-performance teams, we learn that they possess a unique nature and commitment to particular disciplines.

The Nature of Real Teams

In light of how easily churches can apply the title of "team" to any working group, we need to define clearly what we mean by teams. Teams that I call "real teams" share three characteristics. First, real teams outperform individual effort (MacMillan, 2001). Unlike committees and work groups that function more like individuals who happen to meet from time to time without clear purposes or common goals, real teams have the capacity to produce more than individuals can, especially when there is a significant goal or challenge at stake (Katzenbach and Smith, 2003; Quinn, 1996). We agree with Katzenbach and Smith, "When teams work, they represent the best proven way to convert embryonic visions and values into consistent action patterns because they rely on people working together" (2003, p. 19).

This idea of team faces some resistance. One of the cultural challenges we face is American rugged individualism. From our movies to our literature, we tell stories about lone wolves, solo heroes, and law enforcement that never needs backup. In some ways, teams seem anti-American, and yet, such stories are not limited to those who live in the United States. In Exodus 18, Moses faced the challenge of a changing situation and poor results (MacMillan, 2001). You recall that Moses was attempting to act as the lone judge for all of Israel. This produced a situation where the people

---

2.   John P. Kotter's articles and books are one example of the work that is addressing the challenges facing businesses today. His book, *Leading Change* (1996), while a business book, eerily raises many of the challenges facing the church in the twenty-first century.

3.   You can find a helpful and thorough source of data to substantiate this claim at: http://www.thearda.com.

were frustrated and Moses was burning out. Moses was a great leader, but he could not continue as a solo judge. Fortunately, Moses' father-in-law, Jethro, approached him with an idea of creating a team of judges. The result of this team was that they were able to do more than Moses could. Jethro's team approach addressed the need for change and the need for different results. The team of judges met the people's needs, frustration went down, and Moses no longer had to live under the crushing demands of the people as the one and only judge of Israel.

The second characteristic of real teams is that they can't be spoken into existence—they have to be made. The truth about teams is that no group of people who come together to form a team instantly and automatically become a real or highly productive team. Taking on the name "team" or simply engaging in teamwork does not make a team. Calling a group of people meeting monthly to work on adult Christian Education a team, when in actuality there is very little working together, doesn't make them a team. Teams are born and they grow into maturity, or not, according to how they give themselves to specific team disciplines (MacMillan, 2001). Every committee or board starts their working relationship with one another as a potential team. Real teams are those who not only decide to take on team disciplines, but are rigorously practicing them. High-performance teams are those few teams that are mastering team disciplines and in so doing produce extraordinary results (Katzenbach and Smith, 2003).

We are not advocating that high-performance teams take over every area of the church. Teams are not better than work groups or committees. Teams, committees, boards, and work groups are all tools in the toolbox of organizational leadership. Real teams are the right tool when the challenge is big and the need for productivity high. Boards, committees, working groups are good for managing, reporting, deciding, coordinating, and planning. You would no more convert every committee in your church into a team than you would use a hammer for every construction need. One of the benefits of learning the skill of high performance teams is that leaders can rightly discern when it is wise to deploy teams and when it is wise to use other working groups.

A third unique aspect of the nature of real teams has to do with how productive teams see and conduct themselves, or how they "be." Real teams think of themselves and act like learning communities. A learning community is "a set of significant relationships among people who are mutually committed to the transformational journey and who provide a source of objectivity, accountability, and wisdom for one another" (Herrington et al., 2003, p. 170). Said another way, a learning community is a small group of people who are continuously improving their capacity to get results that all members of the team truly desire.[4] Part of the "transfor-

---

4. This is a simpler definition that Jim Herrington uses today in teaching about building teams.

mational journey" has to do with how team members and the entire team change over time (being) and how the entire team transforms a portion of the world around them (doing).

Team members learn about themselves first and what it means to function well as a member of a real team. They learn to practice and master authenticity, integrity, and how to manage anxiety. Real teams learn about their purpose and goals. They are gathering information, learning new skills, and discovering novel and formerly unknown solutions. In his book on the art and practice of the learning organization, Peter Senge states "learning expands a group's capacity to achieve its desired results" (1990, p. 236). Furthermore, Senge observes, "When teams are truly learning, not only are they producing extraordinary results, but the individual members are growing more rapidly than could have occurred otherwise" (1990, p. 9). The nature of real teams is that they consist of lifelong learners who readily admit that they do not know everything and are hungry for other ideas and opinions (Herrington et al., 2000).

Team Disciplines

A distinctive mark of a real team is the rigorous commitment to disciplines, which, if practiced to the point of mastery, directly contribute to high levels of productivity (Katzenbach and Smith, 2003). Senge defines "discipline" in this context as:

> a body of theory and technique that must be studied and mastered to be put into practice. A discipline (from the Latin *disciplina*, to learn) is a developmental path for acquiring certain skills or competencies. As with any discipline, from playing piano to electrical engineering, some people have an innate gift, but anyone can develop proficiency through practice (1990, p. 10).

This kind of learning requires intentional and regular practice for mastery to take place. Team disciplines are about people deliberately learning how to be different with one another in the face of pressures that usually accompany a performance challenge. From their research of teams and non-teams, Katzenbach and Smith have identified six disciplines that produce real teams with the potential for high performance (2003).

Real Teams Are Small

The research reveals that the number of people that make up a real team ranges from two to twenty-five. The majority of the teams studied had less than ten members. This particular discipline does not carry the same weight as the other five, but it does offer a practical guideline for establishing the size of a team.

Many of us understand the implications of this discipline. Working with a large number of people on a constructive level is far more difficult than working with a small number. A small number can greatly enhance efficiency, community, and communication that the logistics and personal dynamics of a large number of people can make more difficult, if not impossible. For example, scheduling is much easier with a smaller than larger number of people. With fewer obstacles, small teams can arrange and rearrange their calendars. Meetings can be moved or added much easier with fewer than many team members. As a member of the IT Team put it, "a small number allows us to be nimble." Relationally, a small number allows authentic relationships to build more quickly and deeply. On a communication level, there is ample space for everyone to speak and participate. The discipline of small number does not imply that there are only a few working on the team's purpose and goals. There may be in fact dozens of people that are involved in the overall effort, but the core of the team is small.

As you think about the deployment of real teams in your church, how many people do you think should make up your team? How would you determine that number? The next discipline of real teams can help provide some answers to these questions.

Team Members Have Complementary Skills

Who should be on the team? First, there must be some understanding around what the team is going to be doing in terms of its common purpose and performance goals. With basic purpose and goals in mind, team creators recruit potential team members according to skills that complement each other and the work around common purpose and performance goals. Second, as a team grows in its clarity of purpose and goals, the team recruits additional team members according to needed skills, which were not present at the creation of the team. As a learning community, real teams identify new skills and acquire them in order to accomplish their purpose. This means that they may recruit additional team members later in the process or it may mean that some on the team will learn new skills. A well-formed team should include technical expertise, problem-solving, decision-making skills, and interpersonal skills.

For some group leaders, this discipline requires a new way of thinking. Church committees and work groups often consist of the willing, stakeholders, elected, like-minded, or other characteristics that have little to do with the purpose and goals that brought the group into existence. Pastors can have a default way of being, recruiting potential team members based on church politics, "movers and shakers," and/or "yes-people" who are safe, predictable, and pastor-pleasers.

I did not fully grasp this discipline with my first team effort. I formed my team around people I knew and had a passion for biblical discipleship in the local church, which is not a bad thing, but I did not recruit people with a variety of skills. In fact, through the DiSC® personality survey,[5] I discovered that the majority of the team shared my personality type. The team represented only two out of the four personality types. However the truth of real teams is, according to MacMillan's research, "The more different a team is, the smarter it can be" (2001, p. 37). Furthermore, we did not recruit additional people with needed skills later in our process when lack of skills became apparent. We just could not overcome old thinking patterns that said, "Once you form a group, the group is closed and you make no changes." The result of our old way of thinking was to hinder our team's performance. In our case, I think a greater variety of personality types would likely have produced greater results. With a few other skilled people, we would likely not have burdened team members with work they were not equipped to do, and we would likely have had produced a better product in some cases.

Practice and Reflect

Is there a significant project, new area of ministry, or challenge that you are facing in your ministry? Are you beginning to see where a real team could be fruitful? What are some of the skills that this team will need in order to accomplish its primary task? Consider making a list. Are there people that you can name right now who could bring some of the skills that this team will need? How will you ensure that you recruit a diverse group of people?

Real Teams Have a Common Purpose

Perhaps the most significant work that a team can do that leads to high performance is the work of establishing a common purpose (Kotter, 1996). A common purpose is an inspiring challenge that has the capability of motivating a team to high performance. Clearly defining a team's primary task is vital. MacMillan writes, "A clear, common, compelling task that is important to the individual team members is the single biggest factor in team success" (2001, p. 44).

The *Tallahassee Democrat* newspaper had a costly problem in customer service due to the poor quality and errors in the advertisements printed in the paper. A team emerged to address this problem and took on the name the ELITE Team. The primary task of The ELITE Team was to "eliminate all errors" (Katzenbach and Smith 2003, pp. 67–69). The ELITE Team's common purpose was to take on the enormous challenge of eliminating all errors from all of its printed advertisements. In this same way, real teams come to agree on a common purpose, which has a powerful

---

5. The DiSC behavior profile is a tool that helps people describe their preferred behavior patterns in a way that allows others to understand and learn to communicate more effectively with them. For more information on the DiSC behavior profile, go to http://www.discprofile.com.

galvanizing effect on them. A clearly defined and deeply shared purpose inspires a team, promotes responsibility, provides rich meaning and direction, and creates an identity that is bigger than any one person on the team. In fact, if there is no common purpose of this type, there is no team (MacMillan, 2001).

The work of discerning and reaching agreement on a common purpose is no small thing. This vital labor "develops direction, momentum, and commitment by working to shape a meaningful purpose" (Katzenbach and Smith, 2003, p. 49). Rushing this effort is never a goal of real teams: "The best teams invest a tremendous amount of time and effort exploring, shaping, and agreeing on a purpose that belongs to them both collectively and individually" (2003, p. 50). Teams who rush this process or do not create a compelling common purpose will not see the kind of fruitfulness that is possible when teams develop a clear and shared task or objective. Groups that do not develop a common purpose remain pseudo or potential teams.

Creating a common purpose requires some new ways of being. First, in our fast food, instant gratification culture, there may be some pressure to arrive quickly at a common purpose because it feels better to "do something" rather than just talk. Team members may express impatience or frustration when the team continues to work on their common purpose into the eighth or tenth meeting. They may not understand why you are suggesting day or overnight retreats in order to work on this and other team disciplines. Spending time on the subject of team purpose can be an uphill battle in a culture that cherishes instant answers and prepackaged programming, but stand firm in the face of resistance. Rushing through the creation of a common purpose will harm the team and its ability to be fruitful. Second, with a diverse group of people where everyone has a say, establishing a team purpose will probably not come without some conflict. This is another reason why team members need to learn new ways of being and why the discipline of developing a common purpose is more than simply making a decision. Team facilitators will need to work carefully with their team on what a common purpose is and how the team will arrive at their purpose[6] Third, real teams must keep their common purpose before them with constant review. While this may appear obvious, groups often drift away from their intended purpose rarely making their purpose a part of their agenda to review on a regular basis. Leaders of real teams have a role to play in this, but each member of the team must learn that one of her or his responsibilities is to hold the team accountable to its purpose. Real teams work hard at creating *their* common purpose and they keep working hard on *their* common purpose throughout their time together.

---

6.   *The Performance Factor* has some helpful suggestions for team leaders at the end of each chapter (MacMillan, 2001).

In my early efforts with building teams, I learned firsthand how challenging the creating of a common purpose can be. Pastors will find the main challenge is not in discerning the right purpose or making the decision. The main challenge is in all the ways that we "be" when we come together to make a decision like this. When people come together, there are a multitude of mental models and experiences operating in and behind the scenes. For some on a team there is some resignation and cynicism around past efforts or similar goals, while others have learned to be passive. Each team member likely has different assumptions about how meetings should run, the role of the pastor, or what it means to do real work between meetings. In addition, team members will have different ways of coping with anxiety, dealing with conflict, and addressing integrity breakdowns. All these things and more are what people bring to a team, and all these things are stirred up when you sit down and ask, "What are we here for?" Teams make a devastating mistake when they do not confront ways of being that threaten the team's common purpose.[7]

Practice and Reflect

Think of some common purposes a team might rally around for something new or needed at your church. Practice writing several draft common purposes for that area. After developing a list of three to five, which seem clearest and most compelling to you? Invite three other people to read your drafts. To which purposes are they drawn?

Real Teams Have Performance Goals

Performance goals go hand in hand with common purpose by defining a team's work-product. Specific and measurable goals are the necessary steps that will enable a team to do the work necessary to accomplish their common purpose. If the common purpose of a real team is to climb a God-sized mountain, then performance goals are the crucial steps that will enable the team to make progress up the mountain. Creating compelling goals help teams stay focused on getting results.

The IT Team's common purpose was to develop a clear process for discipleship. For us to achieve our purpose we discerned that we had to work toward three performance goals. First, we had to create a new and inspiring mindset. We wanted to communicate and demonstrate that our discipleship process was an amazing opportunity and represented a new way of thinking about apprenticeship to Jesus. Second, we had to create a new and inspiring framework for the process. We needed new wine skins for our new wine so that we could experience different results (MacMillan,

---

7. A very good book that illustrates the negative and positive ways of team being is *The Five Dysfunctions of a Team* (Lencioni, 2002). I highly recommend this book as a part of a team's learning and growing.

2001). Third, with a new and inspiring mindset and framework, we recognized that we were going to have to provide training. We had to develop training content and opportunities for the congregation, church leadership, apprenticeship training team facilitators, and the ongoing leadership team, if we were going to achieve our purpose. Focusing on these goals kept the IT Team moving toward fulfilling its common purpose and made it possible to experience high performance. Thus, real teams work to identify, develop, and accomplish performance goals. These performance goals should be S.M.A.R.T. Goals (Specific, Measurable, Attainable, Realistic, Time-based). Teams with fuzzy goals will struggle to accomplish them and will fail to gain much ground on their common purpose.

Practice and Reflect

Recall your most compelling common purpose and practice developing one to three S.M.A.R.T. Goals based on that purpose. Consider sharing them with someone and ask them to give you some feedback. Are they clear and compelling? Are they specific, measurable, attainable, realistic, and time-based? Note what you learn from this practice and consider re-working your goals based on what you learn from the feedback.

Real Teams Commit to a Common Approach

The fifth practice of real teams is the discipline to commit to a common approach. How will the team work together to accomplish its purpose and goals? Thoroughly answering this question, and practicing and reflecting on new habits at each and every meeting is an essential mark of a real team. Team members, not a solo leader, clearly define how the team will function and work together according to their common approach. Teams that rigorously embrace this discipline have the capability to experience the power of transformation because new practices and patterns determined by the team signal the expectation and opportunity for new ways of being.

Of all the real team disciplines, I think the discipline of developing a common approach gave the IT Team the best way of becoming a different kind of team. We spent many hours in the first days of our existence defining how we would be together. We talked about authenticity, what it meant for us to be reliant on the Holy Spirit, and the unique practices we would take on during our meetings, like a time for solitude and silence. We defined how often we would meet, when our meetings would begin and end, and the length of time we would stay on the team. We also had conversations around my role as facilitator of the team and how that differed from my role as pastor. Each conversation gave us ways to practice and drew us closer to becoming a real team.

One of the "must-dos" for the discipline of common approach is to understand and practice that everyone on a real team does a fair share of real work. This means that each team member takes on assignments and does work outside of meetings. The availability of e-mail, conference calls, and Facebook provide a variety of possibilities for work in between meetings. Steve, a member of the IT Team, shares his experience when he writes, "When discussing the real work that teams do, I would emphasize the work done outside of the meetings and the communication among members mostly by e-mail. I think the real-time feedback while work is in progress greatly increases efficiency, improves the creative quality, and promotes solidarity of the team."

However, I recall a meeting where I saw firsthand what could happen when real work is not part of a team's way of being. Following a less than energetic and full participation IT meeting, I reflected with a few others why the team's energy and participation appeared to be so low. After some reflection, I realized that I had put myself in a position of doing most of the work for that meeting, while the rest of team had little to no meaningful work to do. The team took a passive stance in the meeting because they had no active involvement with the purpose and goals of the team and so there was nothing for them to do at the meeting but to sit and listen to me. When situations like this happen, and they will, a team's common approach serves as a wonderful corrective. Over time, and with good work done around a common approach, real teams learn that meetings are not limited to commenting, reviewing, and deciding.

On one particular occasion, I knew that the IT Team had made progress in their commitment to a common approach. Early in our time together, we had a member resign by e-mail, in part over some frustration with our process to develop a common approach. Our team decided that as a learning community we needed to put ourselves in a place where we could learn whatever we needed to learn from this individual and to provide a safe place for an authentic conversation (being a learning community with authenticity is one of our common approaches). We asked the person who resigned if she would be willing to meet with us and she agreed. Everyone on the team worked on preparing for the meeting, we each had a part to play, and everybody on the team was mindful that we were doing something different. The meeting turned out to be a wonderful learning opportunity with high levels of authenticity and provided a way for the individual to finish well with no shame or condemnation. We look back on this meeting as one of our most transformational moments in our efforts to become a real team. Without our common approach, I think we would have let the e-mail resignation stand as an agenda item at the next meeting with a motion to approve and accept.

Practice and Reflect

If you were to form a team today, what would you want to include in your common approach? Make a list of some practical, behavioral, and spiritual items that you might like to see a team commit. How do you understand the concept that on a real team everyone does real work? How is this "must-do" similar or dissimilar to other groups you have experienced?

Real Teams Practice Mutual Accountability

The discipline of mutual accountability is another defining characteristic of real teams. The word accountability, like team, has a multitude of meanings. MacMillan defines this discipline in the following way: "To be accountable is to be answerable. It's an implied obligation to give an account of one's actions, progress, or results" (2001, p. 148). Within real teams, everyone is answerable to everyone on the team. Unlike many committees and work groups, real teams work hard at developing mutual accountability. Within a committee or work group there is usually a hierarchical line of accountability that connects from group members up to a pastor or ministry leader, but real teams look more like a spider web where every string or thread connects each member to every other member of the team. This web of accountability holds together by integrity, which has to do with the promises we make to ourselves and other team members. Real teams practice holding one another accountable because they understand that without mutual accountability, the team will not likely succeed. For example, imagine a team where Joshua reports at the next team meeting that he did not do the work assigned to him. In a work group or committee, a pastor or ministry leader might hold Joshua accountable, but rarely would a member of the group consider that they too should hold Joshua accountable for the work he is not doing. This is due in part to the assumption that only the person at the top of the leadership hierarchy is responsible for success or failure. In a real team, there is so much passion and personal ownership around the purpose and goals, team members will address Joshua's lack of performance, with grace and truth, because so much is at stake. Team members will also offer Joshua the help he may need to be successful with his tasks so that the entire team will be successful. They will not allow him to fail because if he fails, the team fails. This kind of accountability is rare and a major reason why so many teams fail to be highly productive (Lencioni, 2002).

From my perspective, mutual accountability is perhaps one of the most difficult disciplines to take on. Pastors tend to have a way of being that can work against this discipline. A variety of mental models like *sola pastora* (the pastor alone), reluctance to trust ourselves to others, and the avoidance of confrontation all work against the practice of mutual accountability (Roxburgh and Romanuk, 2006).[8] Although the practice of mutual accountability feels risky, the discipline is another essential characteristic of real teams that are moving toward high performance.

---

8.   See also Lencioni, 2002; MacMillan, 2001.

Practice and Reflect

What are you aware of as you reflect on the discipline of mutual accountability? What stirs you up? Where do you feel resistance? What would need to change in you in order to practice mutual accountability on a team?

When to Deploy Teams

When should teams be deployed? What are the conditions that indicate the need for teams? When it is better to use a committee or work group?

Big Challenges

Teams deploy when there is a specific performance objective that necessitates a collective effort, shared leadership, diverse skills, viewpoints, and experiences (Katzenbach and Smith, 2003). In the church, the deployment of teams is often in response to a God-sized vision (Herrington et al., 2000). Imagine a situation where a church is facing something new and/or challenging that touches a number of people in a variety of ministry areas. If the performance challenge is too large or new for an existing committee or work group to achieve, then it is likely that a team should be deployed. For example, recall the birth of the ELITE Team and their response to poor customer service that was having a negative impact on the paper's bottom line. The performance objective of eliminating all errors within their advertisements required a team approach due to the size, scope, and newness of the effort. The deployment of a team in this example was the best choice, which is clear from hindsight because of paper's eventual achievement of a consistent accuracy rate of above ninety-nine percent and almost no loss of business due to errors—a very high-performance team.

Operational or Adaptive Leadership Needed?

Beyond the size and scope of the vision, leaders need to understand what kind of leadership is required to accomplish the goal. In general, committees and work groups represent the best leadership to address operational leadership. Operational leadership is the work pastors and church leadership do around the day-to-day needs of running a local church, such as the weekly worship services, staff meetings, budgets, and weekday programming. Many church staff meetings function as a work group. The senior pastor, youth pastor, children's director, and worship leader come together to align calendars, report on progress in their area of ministry, discuss the benefits of having an outdoor service over the Labor Day weekend, and other operational matters (Herrington et al., 2000). The meeting shares information that will help each individual in their area of ministry, but the purpose of the meeting is not to work as a team around a common purpose and goals (Katzenbach and Smith, 2003).[9] If the focus

---

9. I am not saying that a pastoral staff should or should not become a real team.

of the work is on the side of operational leadership, then a committee or work group may be the best tool in the leadership toolbox for the job.

Most churches understand the need for operational leadership. In fact, many pastors would admit that they spend the majority of their working hours on operational matters. However, if a congregation is to move toward God's emerging future, church leaders will need to also become adaptive leaders. Adaptive leadership is the work leaders do around what is new. Healthy congregations give time and energy to both operational and adaptive leadership.

In Chapter 10, we introduced to you to the idea of creative tension. Generating and sustaining creative tension requires ongoing operational leadership because as a church moves towards God's emerging future, there will be ongoing day-to-day operational needs. This practice also requires adaptive leadership (see Figure 11.1).

Figure 11.1—Operational and Adaptive Leadership

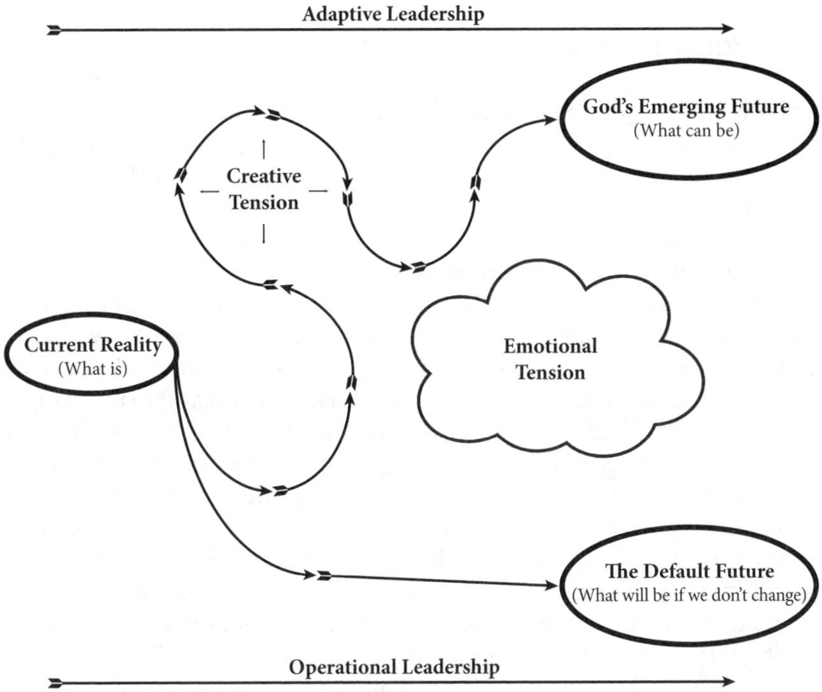

Part of what generates and sustains tension is the gap between a church's current reality and God's emerging future. The work of closing the gap is adaptive leadership and one of the tools of adaptive leadership is the deployment of teams.

In the case of my church, we discerned three churchwide goals through our current reality that we believed would move us toward what we sensed was God's emerging future. Believing that God was calling us to grow in our capacity to make disciples that make disciples, we identified three large goals: (1) develop a clear process for discipleship; (2) clarify and communicate our values around worship and their impact on worship leadership and two different worship services; and (3) strengthen evangelism by engaging visitors and teaching the congregation about their unique calling using a curriculum known as "Purposeful Living." We recognized this work as adaptive leadership and we created three teams to accomplish our goals, while our boards and committees were responsible for operational leadership. Not all of our teams became real teams, but the ones that did produced results that significantly closed the gap between our current reality and God's emerging future.

The greatest challenge for me as a pastor has not been in deciding when to deploy a team, but in being able to engage fully in team disciplines once the team starts to function.

High-Performance Teams and Pastors

In order to take full advantage of what teams have to offer, pastors and others who serve on teams must learn to be different themselves. This is the first work of becoming a real team. In particular, pastors need to grow in the disciplines of mutual accountability, integrity, real work, and managing healthy conflict.

The Challenges of Mutual Accountability

There are risks involved when a leader makes herself accountable in a public setting. Accountability can seem counterintuitive. Why share a God-sized purpose and goals and then choose to be accountable for them by others? Pastors, like most people, want to look good and resist the idea of this discipline because they are uncomfortable with the possibility of failure and learning in a public setting. Pastors and church leaders also find mutual accountability difficult because of their mental models of leadership. Upper management usually holds others accountable, but they do not expect or invite others to hold them accountable as leaders. This indeed may be the case in some settings and there is nothing wrong or bad with this arrangement. However, real teams function with mutual accountability. Pastors and team members must take responsibility for their own learning and seek to practice and master the disciplines of real teams as the ultimate way to be mutually accountable to each other.

Practicing Integrity

Another area where pastors and team members can struggle relates to integrity. In the early stages of a team's development, people do not always do what they said they would do. Team members may come to a meeting without doing their work, choose to ignore a team value like authenticity, or repeatedly show up to meetings late. Some pastors find it difficult to hold people accountable for what they have given their word to because they say, or act out, "these are just volunteers so I can't hold them accountable." The same is true for "volunteers." Volunteers can refuse to hold pastors and church leaders accountable because they are the "experts," "paid professionals," or simply the fact that they are "in charge." On an evening when I let myself become overwhelmed by the demands of the day, I showed up at an IT Team meeting confessing that I was not prepared to the degree that I would like. At some point in my distracted mind, I got the idea that we end our meetings at 8:00 p.m. Our commitment to our common approach states that we start and end our meetings on time. This is one of the many things that we are all responsible to each other. The problem on this evening was that our agreed ending time was 8:30 p.m. However, as I closed the meeting, no one on the team questioned why I was ending the meeting thirty minutes early. To my surprise, I discovered my mistake after I got home. At our next meeting, I asked the team what was going on inside of them when I suddenly ended the meeting thirty minutes early. For most, it seemed to have caught them by surprise and they chose to let the situation go. Others gave me the benefit of the doubt, thinking that I had to get somewhere else. I suspect at that moment, consciously or unconsciously, we slipped into an old habit where the pastor gets to be in charge and everyone else falls in line. Any member of the IT Team should have taken responsibility and held me accountable for ending a meeting early, but at that moment, we did not practice mutual accountability, authenticity, or integrity.

Everyone Does Real Work
Pastors are used to managing people and ministries by holding others accountable for work, but in a real team, everybody does real work in between meetings, including the pastor and other leaders on the team. If pastors do not take on an equal amount of the work, they will miss out on the rich learning and partnership that is only possible when everyone does real work that directly contributes to the team's common purpose and performance goals.

Managing Healthy Conflict
A final growth area is in the discipline of managing conflict. Real teams have healthy and productive conflict. This is due to the nature of teams where a big purpose, along with compelling performance goals, is naturally going to generate conflicting ideas. Such conflict can be productive as Senge rightly observes, "The free flow of conflicting ideas is critical for the creative thinking, for discovering new solutions no one individual would have come

to on his own" (1990, p. 232). In this way, real teams learn how to be different in the face of conflict by learning to make differences of opinion healthy and constructive. Patrick Lencioni describes the differences and similarities between productive conflict and destructive conflict:

> It is important to distinguish productive ideological conflict from destructive fighting and interpersonal politics. Ideological conflict is limited to concepts and ideas, and avoids personality-focused, mean-spirited attacks. However, it can have many of the same external qualities of interpersonal conflict—passion, emotion, and frustration—so much so that an outside observer might easily mistake it for unproductive discord (2002, p. 202).

Pastors need not fear productive conflict, but they must learn how to respond to destructive conflict along with the rest of the team. In the face of conflict, real teams are learning how to listen, manage defensiveness, and welcome ideas that are not their own (Senge, 1990).

I remember a conversation on the IT Team about measuring results. Two of us on the team were very committed to the idea that we can and must measure the fruitfulness of our Apprenticeship Training Teams. Most of the team agreed with the two. However, one of our team members showed courage and disagreed. For a moment, there was a sense of awkwardness because in our way of thinking, nice churchgoing people do not disagree with one another; after all, we were a team! Fortunately, we were able to practice some of what we had been learning about conflict. The two who were for measuring results were able to put themselves in a place to listen carefully to the objection and were able to manage their defensiveness, even though they were passionate about their own idea. The one who objected was able to say what he needed to say without caving into the majority. Through this productive conflict, new insights surfaced and all involved knew that we had arrived at a better understanding and practice of measuring results. This outcome would have never have happened if the team sought to avoid or suppress conflict. This too seems counterintuitive, but real teams invite, welcome, and engage in healthy conflict and pastors lead and model the way.

High-Performance Teams and The Way Forward

A healthy church dedicates some of its time and resources to the on-going work of adaptive leadership. One of the most effective adaptive leadership tools available to pastors and church leaders is the use of real teams. Real teams are a productive way to move the work of adaptive leadership into concrete action. Pastors and church leaders will need to create teams of learning communities that will take on the new and challenging missional work of the church in today's world. This enterprise will require the mastery of many of the values and skills found in this book. Healthy pastors and church leaders take on adaptive leadership because they have a vision of God's emerging future.

Perhaps while you were reading this chapter you may have thought that this chapter feels less about personal and congregational transformation and more like a chapter on how to run an organization. I believe that the work of developing real teams is very much a work of spiritual transformation. In the church, we have operational, adaptive, and character work to do. The work of personal transformation around my Christlike character development (personal transformation) undergirds my operational and adaptive work (see Figure 11.2). I must do the character work in order to increase my capacity in both my operational and adaptive leadership work. However, if I grow my character so that I have more integrity and am more authentic, courageous, and loving but do not get the adaptive work done, my congregation will not move forward missionally into God's emerging future. Thus, real teams are an essential part of the transformative work that God has in mind for you and your church.

Figure 11.2—Transformational Leadership

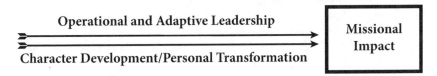

Practice and Reflect

I have an elder in my church who likes to say at the end of sermons and meetings, "So what?" Now that we have reached the end of this chapter on high-performance teams, I want to invite you to reflect on what you have read, and to allow God to say whatever he would like to say. Take twenty minutes to consider the following questions. First, what has this chapter stirred up in terms of new dreams that God might be calling your congregation to live in to that will make a missional impact on your community? Do you see how the formation of a team could help you move in that direction? Second, as you continue to reflect, are you or the congregation experiencing any sense that you are stuck or stopped? Perhaps you and the leaders of your church have had some good ideas of what God is calling you to do in the recent past, but you have never been able to get into action in a way that would move the people of God toward that calling. Could the deployment of a team be a way to get unstuck? Third: The ultimate "so what" has to do with the end game, which is mission. Can you see how the skill of developing real teams with the potential for high performance can directly contribute to missional impact, impact to change you, your church, and the community you serve?

Going Deeper

Real teams play an important role in providing the type of leadership needed to take a church from its current reality to God's emerging future. Committees work best for completing tasks related to the ongoing operation of the church. Real teams take on bigger challenges and engage in specific disciplines to increase their effectiveness. To learn more about real teams, check out our online resources at http://www.westernsem.edu/journey/ridder.

References and Additional Resources

Herrington, Jim, Mike Bonem, and James H. Furr. *Leading Congregational Change: A Practical Guide for the Transformational Journey.* San Francisco: Jossey-Bass, 2000.

Herrington, Jim, R. Robert Creech, and Trisha Taylor. *The Leader's Journey: Accepting the Call to Personal and Congregational Transformation.* San Francisco: Jossey-Bass, 2003.

Katzenbach, Jon R. and Douglas K. Smith. *The Wisdom of Teams: Creating the High-Performance Organization.* New York: HarperCollins, 2006.

Kotter, John P. *Leading Change.* Boston: Harvard Business Press, 1996.

Lencioni, Patrick. *The Five Dysfunctions of a Team: A Leadership Fable.* San Francisco: Jossey-Bass, 2002.

MacMillan, Pat. *The Performance Factor: Unlocking the Secrets of Teamwork.* Nashville: Broadman and Holman, 2001.

Quinn, Robert E. *Deep Change: Discovering the Leader Within.* San Francisco: Jossey-Bass, 1996.

Roxburgh, Alan J. and Fred Romanuk. *The Missional Leader.* San Francisco: Jossey-Bass, 2006.

Senge, Peter M. *The Fifth Discipline: The Art & Practice of the Learning Organization.* New York: Doubleday, 1990.

Chapter 12

Understanding Your Congregation as a System: From Reacting to Systems Thinking

Nate Pyle

The human body is a collection of complex and interdependent subsystems that must all work together to create health and vitality. In the same way, a congregational system is comprised of subsystems, each with many moving parts that are all interacting at the same time. Leading such a complex system to change requires that leaders can keep their eye on the parts and also see the connections between them.

We learned that seeing the congregation as a body helped us with that task. We identified the components of the system and developed ways to see what was happening in each component over time. We also learned to target our change efforts to the deepest levels, those of mental models, systems and structures, instead of looking for quick fixes and shallow modifications. The result—increased congregational health and vitality—is what we wanted to see all along.

*T*he human body has always amazed me. It is a collection of systems and structures that can be analyzed and studied individually, but at the same time are intimately connected. It's difficult to study one system without looking at another. For example, if you were to examine the process of bringing oxygen into the body, you might be tempted to just study the respiratory system. But you'd find that the respiratory system is dependent on the circulatory system and the muscular system, and the muscular system is dependent on the nervous system, and the nervous system is dependent on the skeletal system. Everything is connected!

Maybe you have gone to the doctor suffering from stomach pains. During the visit, the doctor then began to ask you a series of questions about work, family, exercise, and sleep patterns, making you wonder if this quack read the chart saying you came in because of your stomach. After you humor the doctor by answering his questions, he says the reason for your stomach problems is your stress level. Why? Because everything is connected!

The human body is an elegant example of an organizational system with many subsystems. A "system is a set of things—people, cells, molecules or whatever—interconnected in such a way that they produce their own pattern of behavior over time" (Meadows, 2008, p. 2). The circulatory system has cells, organs, veins, and blood that are interconnected in such a way that they have a pattern of behavior: they move blood.

The church, with its people, programs and structures, is also a system. Leaders who want to see transformation in their churches must learn to see the church as a system of interconnected pieces that have a pattern of behavior.

That pattern of behavior is largely determined by the structure of the system itself. Think of a Slinky® (Meadows, 2008). Hold the Slinky® between your two hands, one hand on top, the other supporting the Slinky® from below. Now, take away your bottom hand. The lower end of the Slinky® drops and begins to oscillate up and down like a yo-yo. What makes the Slinky® move the way it does? Is it your hands? Of course not. If you were to hold a balloon in your hand, it wouldn't behave the same way as the Slinky®. The behavior of the Slinky® is found in the structure of the Slinky®. So it is with systems. The structure of the system, to a large extent, determines its behavior. In other words, *the system is designed to get the results it is getting.*

Practice and Reflect

Pause for a moment and think about the implications of that statement as it pertains to your church. *The system is designed to get the result it is getting.*

How is your church doing at assimilating people into the life of the congregation? *The system is getting the results it is designed to get.*

What kind of disciples are you producing? *The system is getting the results it is designed to get.*

Are you burning out volunteers? *The system is getting the results it is designed to get.*

Are your congregants bored and apathetic? *The system is getting the results it is designed to get.*

Take a moment and list the results you would like to see from your church. After you have a good list, make a list of the results your church is actually getting. Get very present to the differences you see. Notice what is happening in this space. You are generating and sustaining tension. You are probably present to some integrity gaps within the system. Anxiety is present.

Hear this: There is no shame, judgment, or condemnation on you as a leader for these results. No one deliberately creates systems that get results different from what we desire. No one wants to continually get undesired results. In fact, there has undoubtedly been extensive effort to change the results! Too often our effort for change focuses on a small part of the system or on a presenting symptom. Without looking at the whole system and at how the interaction of the parts may be producing the symptom, progress toward the desired result will be minimal.

Biblical Examples of Systems

Both the Old and New Testaments contain very explicit examples related to systems. In Chapter 11, we find Moses overextended by the need the Israelites had for him to moderate their conflicts. People would stand around waiting for him to judge from "morning till evening." The system wasn't working. Jethro, Moses' father-in-law, saw this clearly and said, "What you are doing is not good. You and these people who come to you will only wear yourselves out" (Ex. 18:17–18, NIV). Moses then followed the advice of Jethro, changing the system so the burden was lifted off him and the people's disputes were solved more quickly.

In the New Testament, shortly after Pentecost and the explosive growth of the church, we see a conflict arise between Grecian Jews and the Hebraic Jews over the distribution of food. The apostles realized the system for distributing the food wasn't working. Something needed to be done, so they changed the system by appointing seven people to be responsible for this important task.

Jesus alluded to this by saying that you cannot put new wine in old wineskins. Why not? Because new wine will cause the old wineskins to break. Getting new results requires not just new wine but new wineskins as well. To transform churches we need to transform their systems.

Layers of the Church System

In *Leading Congregational Change*, the authors speak of four "layers" to congregational systems: events, trends, structures, and mental models. Each layer is interconnected with the other layers (see Figure 12.1). The discussion that follows draws on the concepts articulated in *Leading Congregational Change* (Herrington et al., 2000):

Figure 12.1—Four Layers of the Church System

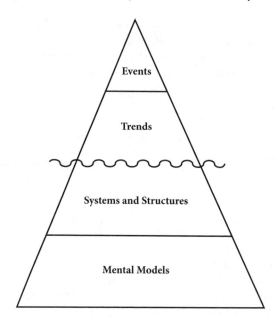

Events

Often, when people speak of change within a congregational setting, they are often referring to a change in *events*. Events are anything a church does. Worship, youth ministry, vacation Bible school, service projects, and fellowship outings are all examples of events. Of all a church does, events are the most visible. They are also what make a church's mission become a reality. Because events are so closely tied to the lived life of the congregation and to its mission, leaders are most often drawn to events when they are leading change.

Trends

Trends give a picture of the congregation at a particular point of time. Is worship attendance increasing or decreasing? Is giving up or down? How many people are participating in discipleship opportunities? Trends are often quantitative, but can also include things like morale, attitudes, and relational and spiritual vitality. Some trends are measured in weeks, others in months, and still others in years.

To get clarity about the system, trends may need to be measured over multiple time periods. Our congregation has been experiencing steady growth over the last two years. We wanted to know how to best accommodate that growth so we plotted the Sunday morning worship attendance over the last eighteen months. The growth became very clear. We then plotted the average monthly worship attendance over the last sixteen years. What we saw was our congregation's attendance had gone through many periods of increase only to give way to a period of decrease. Systems thinking taught us to look for other factors impacting the trend of growth. We began to think about our space. Plotting a straight line at eighty percent of our sanctuary capacity allowed us to see how that trend was related to that line. Attendance would increase until it got above the eighty-percent mark for a period of time and then would slowly drop off, only to increase years later. Identifying this trend allowed us to generate and sustain enough creative tension that we were able to move the congregation towards substantial change in our congregational system.

We moved worship out of the original sanctuary into our gym and we hired a part-time pastor of outreach and community. Conversations among the leadership shifted from, "What can we do to meet the needs of our people?" to "What can we do to meet the needs of those we are trying to reach?" Suddenly, it became very clear that our system was opening up to create room for people who were currently not a part of our congregation.

Structure

Churches have a way of doing life together. There is a way budgeting is done, leadership is elected, expectations are expressed, and pastoral authority is approached. These ways of doing life are the church's *structure*. Do not think of structure simply as the organizational hierarchy. Structure also refers to the way the church thinks and acts. Is there a strong emphasis on everyone agreeing? Are budget meetings filled with conflict? Is there something in the church's history that people don't talk about?

As our church moved our worship from the original sanctuary to our multipurpose room, we had one week where a lot of volunteer work was needed with construction. We created sign-up forms in the narthex for people to sign up to help. We encouraged people to sign up through the website. We communicated this need in multiple ways for three weeks. The Sunday before the work week, six people had signed up to help for the entire week. We were hoping for six to eight a night, and we had six total. Needless to say, even though people assured me help would show up, my anxiety was high heading into the work week. However, almost twenty people showed up every night! This is what people told me would happen. Why? Because this is part of the structure of our church. People don't sign up, but they will show up to help.

Another example of my church's structure related to the service of elders and deacons. Our leadership structure stated that elders and deacons could serve a two-year term and were then required to take a one-year break from leadership. This meant that every year, fifty percent of our leadership team turned over. Continuity was a missing aspect to our church leadership. Difficult conversations were started, and before they were over, a new group of people came on to our leadership requiring the conversations to start all over. Two years ago our congregation changed this structure by allowing elders and deacons to serve a second consecutive term. As I write, we are entering our third year of this new system and have seen a drastic improvement in the leadership of our church. First, the relational vitality among the leadership is greatly improved. Secondly, difficult conversations are seeing their conclusion, resulting in renewed clarity and focus around mission. Finally, there is an increased ownership of the mission and vision of the church by the leadership because for some of them, they have been praying and thinking about the mission and vision for four years. Changing the structure of leadership is one of the reasons our church is changing.

Mental Models

Mental models are the assumptions we have about how the world we live in works and what it means to take effective action in that world. As we've mentioned before, when you have a headache, you know to take an aspirin to alleviate your pain. You do what you do because of the mental model you have. Our mental models shape what we do in the world. Mental models impact every area of our lives, including church.

The greatest transformation in our churches will occur when we change the collective mental model about church. When I arrived at my church it was clear the congregation took pride in their enjoyment of one another. I would often hear people talk about how much they valued knowing everyone in the congregation. It was a shared mental model the congregation had about itself: We are a church where everybody knows everybody. It didn't take me long to figure out this wasn't true. However, the fact that the church collectively believed it was true made it difficult to talk about any change that challenged this deeply held belief. This mental model ruled out any possibility of going to a second worship service because "then we wouldn't know everyone." The prospect of growth created anxiety because if too much growth happened then everyone wouldn't be able to know everyone. However, it was already true that people didn't know everyone. I began to challenge the mental model by talking about people in the church I knew not everyone was familiar with. I had them come up front and share their stories; I referred to them in sermons; and in conversations, I asked longtime members if they had met some of the new people. Slowly the mental model was challenged. When it came time to move out of our sanctuary to accommodate the growth we were experiencing, the congregation was not only amicable, but excited and inviting their neighbors to join us.

Deep transformation is possible when we do the hard work of thinking about the church as a system. When we get below events and trends and into structures and mental models, we will have the greatest change impact. We will also create the greatest anxiety. Changing an event creates some anxiety. Changing a mental model creates an immense amount of anxiety.

The Leader's Personal Responsibility

A leader working for deep transformation must take responsibility for their personal transformation so they can handle the anxiety they will face. When a leader is less reactive and more emotionally mature, he resists the urge to cast blame on people and will begin to see the system as the source of its own problems. This takes a new way of seeing and thinking. But this new way can give us the courage and wisdom to restructure the system for different results.

The leadership of our church began to assess how the church was doing in terms of our mission. A survey was sent out to the congregation to invite them into the conversation and to get their input on what was working and what needed work. The first question of the survey asked people what they saw as the strengths of the church. The top three responses were Preaching, Worship, and Relationships. The second question on the survey asked what they saw as the weaknesses of the church. The top four weakness (two got the same number of votes) were Discipleship, Outreach, Leadership Development, and . . . Relationships. The congregation perceived relationships as both a strength and a weakness. How could this be?

Using what I was learning about systems thinking, I began to ask myself what else could be going on below the surface. I began to wonder about our growth and how that might affect relationships, so I counted the number of people who attended the church on a regular basis who had been there longer than me. Then I counted those who attended regularly who had come to the church after me. (We had a lot of fun at our congregational meeting referring to these two groups as the pre-Natel's and post-Natel's!) The counting revealed that sixty percent of the people who regularly attended our church had been at the church longer than I had, meaning forty percent had come since I started pastoring the church. I then looked at the surveys again. The result was eye-opening. Of those who took the survey, sixty percent reported that relationships were a strength while forty percent saw relationships as a weakness! After some follow-up conversations, it became clear that those who recently began attending our church were having a hard time building relationships at church. The hard pill to swallow was that the system was designed to get these results! Rather than blaming the long-term members of the church for their unwillingness to reach out to new people, we have had to evaluate our system of assimilation and community building.

This example reveals the interconnectedness of everything discussed in this book. When faced with discouraging information, I kept my anxiety low by asking questions about the system rather than letting my anxiety rule me. Had I allowed my anxiety about the situation take over, I would have felt like a failure who would soon experience rejection. By keeping my anxiety low, I was able to think more clearly and stay away from defensive routines. Thinking in a systems approach also helped me avoid blaming others. Because I approached the problem by thinking rather than blaming, the proposed changes to assimilation and community building strategies have been well received.

The leader's ability to change the system is predicated on his or her emotional maturity. The more a leader responds to anxiety out of anxiety, the less the leader will be able to lead change. The most important preliminary work a leader can do before leading change is the work of increasing her emotional capacity. This is the work of personal transformation, which is absolutely necessary for congregational transformation.

Recognizing the Church as a System

Systems are easy to see in the human body. They are also easy to see in business. Much of the work of studying organizational systems has been done in the business world. With concerns like shipping delays and consumer demand, it is easy to see how everything is interrelated in a business system.

Church, however, is a different beast. There are three reasons that systems are more difficult to recognize in the church. One, we don't spend a lot of time building systems. That doesn't mean they don't exist. It just means we don't intentionally build them. Churches tend to be more organic, responding to the needs around them—or equally likely, just doing what they have always done. But don't be fooled, churches are systems! Think about this: Large churches often have very detailed systems for how they plan to move someone from being a first-time visitor to becoming a member. The process is clearly laid out and publicized often. It is easy to identify this process as a system. Not all churches are like this. Until recently, our church's membership plan was that it had no membership plan. We just hoped visitors would come, would stick around, and then when we had enough people who were interested we would offer a membership class. That doesn't sound like a system, but guess what? That was our system. And the system got the results it was designed to get!

The second reason systems tend to be more difficult to identify in a church is that we quantify less. In the business world it is easy to identify delays in an inventory system because there is so much that is quantified: orders, production rate, workers needed, shipping times, etc. All these areas can be specifically measured, which allows you to see if and where there is a delay. But in a church, what do you measure outside of attendance and cash? Again, this doesn't mean that churches are not systems, only that it can be difficult to see them that way.

The third reason systems are not readily identified in churches is probably the most straightforward: We simply aren't looking for them. We need to start. The health of our churches depends on our ability to think systemically about them. When talking about the church, the Bible paints a picture of deep interconnectedness. In 1 Corinthians, Paul says the church is like a body. There are hands, feet, and eyes, and all are necessary and all are different. Each part is doing what it was made to do, and working together in common mission, each is dependent on the other and each affects the others in the work they do (or the work they don't do). Church, if it is anything, is a place where what seems to be unconnected is in fact profoundly connected.

Hidden Subsystems in the Church

The idea of organizational systems was introduced using the human body as an example of how systems work. This isn't the first time a parallel between the church and the body has been drawn. In 1 Corinthians 12, Paul makes the same connection. The most common exegesis of this passage is about every person having gifts to be used in the church, and that no one gift is more important than another gift. For this reason, an "eye cannot say to the hand, 'I don't need you!'" (1 Cor. 12:21, NIV).

Let's apply that same exegetical point to the idea of subsystems within a church. Can a small groups program say to the worship program, "We don't need you"? Should a children's ministry say to a hospitality team, "We don't need you"? Of course not. Just as the individuals in a church are necessary for the church to be the church, so is each subsystem necessary.

The human body is made up of many subsystems that are easy to recognize. It is much more difficult to recognize all the subsystems of a church. Often we think about the different ministries such as the system of the worship ministries or children's ministry. These are easy to recognize. But many systems are not so easily identified. Examining the visible systems while failing to examine the more hidden systems is like checking a person's health by looking only at height, weight, and resting heartbeat. It gives you a picture, but it is a very limited one.

In *Leading Congregational Change*, the authors lay out a model to encourage church leaders to shift their focus away from visible aspects of the congregation's life such as worship, Bible study, leadership training, facility maintenance, and finances to vital components of congregational life that are largely unseen. While "invisible," these subsystems of a congregation play a vital role shaping the life and mental model of themselves (Herrington et al., 2000).

This congregational body-life model helps us see the following congregational subsystems:

- Mission and vision
- Boundaries
- Context
- Heritage
- Leadership
- Ministry
- Feedback

Mission and vision. The *mission and vision* of the church shapes how it will conduct itself in the world. The church, universal and local, has been given the mandate to participate in the *missio dei.* How a church fulfills that mandate is uniquely expressed in its mission and vision. Mission expresses what the church is doing; vision explains how the church will do it. Please note: It is one thing to have a mission and vision—it is another thing to be faithful to do the work that accomplishes the mission and vision.

Boundaries. Every church has *boundaries* in which it exists. The physical boundaries, like location and the buildings' structures, are easy to identify. There are also strategic and spiritual boundaries. Denominational affiliation, as well as having a distinct identity, creates boundaries between churches. A church's expectations for members and non-members create boundaries between these two groups. Spiritually, we believe there is a boundary between the light and the dark. We, as the church, have a responsibility to push the boundary of darkness back by being light in the world.

Context. Each local church finds itself in a unique *context.* The context includes the community itself, the demographics, the relationships between churches and pastors, school systems, and education level of the community. Context is important because each church, as a part of its being, interacts within its context differently. If a church is comprised of people over fifty years old but is in a context of young families, it becomes clear there is a systemic challenge in how the church lives in its context.

Heritage. Whether a church is six months old or sixty years old, every church has a *heritage.* Heritage consists of more than just the major dates in the history of the congregation. It is every aspect of the congregation. For example, when the church I pastor began, they changed the time of worship on the Sunday of the Indianapolis 500 so that people could attend church and then go to the race. When the church was starting out, this made complete sense. But this decision created a culture of church being secondary, something people would add to life if they had room for church. We have since acknowledged this and repented of it. Heritage can also include events, circumstances, pastors, and previous controversies. Anything that has contributed to the life of the congregation is a part of its heritage.

Leadership. This book is about our stories of personal transformation leading to congregational transformation. Facilitating that transformation happens from the *leadership* subsystem. In order for change to happen, leaders need to be identified and equipped, systems and structures need to be developed, and space for learning needs to be created. We are not promoting a CEO model of leadership where change is dictated. In the CEO model, change will happen, but it may not be transformation. Transformation occurs not when what we do changes, but when who we are changes. Leaders who facilitate transformation are those who have been transformed.

Ministry. Generally when people think of the church, all they think of is the *ministry* subsystem. They see the programs the church offers— Sunday school classes, benevolence, and worship. They see committee work and fellowship, pastoral care and church administration. Ministry is a complex subsystem of a wide variety of moving parts. Often when attempting to solve a challenge that the congregation is facing, leaders look to the ministry subsystem and only this system. Frequently the challenges that show up in the ministry subsystem come from other subsystems.

A young pastor came to a church in Houston that had been struggling to reach people for a dozen years. He was an effective leader and there was a lot of hope surrounding his arrival. Three years later, despite a ton of energy, new programs, and a massive marketing program, the hope was quashed and resignation reigned.

As this young pastor sought the wise counsel of an older neighboring pastor, he began to look outside of the ministry subsystem. He interviewed a number of the long-time leaders and discovered that nearly twenty years earlier, the pastor of the church had an affair with the church secretary.

In an effort to spare both the pastor and the congregation further pain, the deacons fired the pastor, announced his departure the following Sunday, and agreed among themselves that they would simply put this behind them and move on. Twenty years later, the deep distrust between congregational leaders and congregational members was a part of the culture, and that deep distrust undermined every leadership initiative.

With the encouragement of the older pastor, this younger pastor found the man who had the affair twenty years earlier. He had spent those twenty years filled with shame and regret. The young pastor took a couple of deacons with him, and a painful and powerful conversation unfolded. Forgiveness was asked for and given on both sides.

While it didn't happen immediately, over a couple of years following this event, mysteriously and powerfully, the trust between congregational leaders and congregational members began to change. The problem was not in the ministry subsystem. It was in the heritage subsystem. The problem just reared its ugly head as a symptom in the ministry subsystem.

Feedback. The final component of the congregational bodylife model is *feedback.* Feedback is how the church measures its progress. How does the church voice its concern or criticize? Are there avenues for this? Feedback is always happening, whether it is solicited or not. Congregations instinctively let leaders know how they feel. The leader can either listen to the feedback or try and ignore it. Seeing feedback as an essential subsystem of the larger system allows the leader to harness its power in transformation.

Understanding what is happening in the subsystems of the church can help church leaders understand what is happening in the overall system of the church. This comprehensive approach will help leaders design more effective strategies for dealing with change.

Everything Is Connected

Thinking in systems can be overwhelming. Once you begin to see systems, you see them everywhere. The interconnectedness can be paralyzing. For years our church has had a potluck brunch after the worship service on the second Sunday of the month. In the late '90s it was one of the events of the church that provided vitality and growth. However, since I have arrived at the church, there has been a steady decline in attendance. When I brought up the possibility that brunch had run its course, I was met with enthusiastic resistance. Why was this event such a sacred cow? Systems thinking helped us see that brunch wasn't just an event. This event was connected to structure, mental models, heritage, and ministry. To make changes to brunch, I had to acknowledge the interconnectedness. Think back to the pyramid (events, trends, structures, mental models). I started to track the attendance of brunch looking for the trend. The tracking confirmed my thoughts. Fewer people were attending brunch. I then asked people why brunch existed. This question helped me (and them) to see the ministry it provided as well as the mental model behind it. Two reasons emerged: fellowship and assimilation. People saw brunch as a place where they could fellowship with the entire congregation (never mind that only a third of the congregation was attending), and a place to invite visitors (again, never mind the rarity with which that happened). Seeing the mental model allowed me to ask the right questions: Is brunch fulfilling these purposes? Could we be more effective doing something else? Why do you think so many people aren't coming? Through these conversations, the mental model was not only exposed, but also started to shift. Deep change was now a possibility.

Structure Is the Key to Transformation

Remember, *a system is designed to get the results that it is getting.* Without deep change to the systems and structures of the organization, transformation is nearly impossible. We say this again because it is so counterintuitive to our current way of thinking.

Both pastors and churches struggle with a "grass is greener on the other side" complex. Pastors think another congregation will be easier to change. Churches think another pastor will bring about revitalization and growth. Thinking in systems allows us to see that changing pastors will do little to change the congregation. Peter Senge says, "Different people in the same structure tend to produce qualitatively similar results . . . more often than we realize, systems cause their own crises, not external forces or individuals' mistakes" (2006, p. 40). When we realize that the system creates its own results, we can refrain from misplacing blame on individuals. I recently worked with a church that had a history of pastors who experienced burnout. Each pastor received a disproportionate amount of blame for not moving the congregation toward health. The church's issue didn't lie with the pastors *per se*, but the issue was endemic to the system of the church. Changing pastors wasn't going to move the church in a new direction; changing the system might.

Think back to the example of the apostles and the system of distributing food to the widows. Do you think that if the church fired the apostles and got different ones the problem would go away? For all his tendencies to "act first-think later," was Peter the problem? Of course not! We would never say that. But we do say this with pastors, elders, ministry leaders, and congregants all the time. Systems thinking is revolutionary because it forces us to think beyond blaming the person to see that the system is designed to get the results it is getting. Not only does systems thinking allow us to get to the root of the problem, but it also allows us to extend grace and compassion to those in leadership. We might just see that they are not to blame, but rather are victims of a dysfunctional system.

Leaders must examine the systemic structure to explain the results and behaviors they are observing. Peter Senge (2006) designed an illustration (see Figure 12.2) to help explain how structure impacts results and behavior:

Figure 12.2—Structure Impacts Change

Let's look at "Events," at the bottom of the diagram. Event explanations are strictly reactive. They are "who did what" or "who didn't do what" type of explanations. While there may be some truth to these explanations, they are overly simplistic and fail to account for the complexity of the system. However, event explanations are the most common. For example, a church that has a difficulty finding volunteers for their nursery may explain the situation by blaming the church members for not being willing to serve. This is an event explanation and is reactive.

Reacting to events can be counterproductive. What may seem like a solution to an immediate situation may actually exacerbate the problem and not be a solution at all.

Patterns of behavior explanations go a bit deeper by looking at trends over a longer period of time. Using volunteers for nursery as an example, the church may see that every three or four months the number of volunteers in the nursery shrinks. They may also notice that every time the pastor makes an announcement regarding need, they get more volunteers. Rather than blaming the congregation for not being willing to serve, now we can see that they may just need a reminder about the need for nursery volunteers. The pattern of behavior is that people respond to the prompting of the pastor to step up and fulfill a need.

Structural explanations are the "least common and most powerful" (Senge, 2006, p. 52), focusing on the question, "Why does this pattern of behavior exist?" In the case of the nursery volunteers, there are many possible explanations. The volunteers may not feel adequately trained. They may feel unappreciated. They may not understand how they are contributing to the mission of the church. There may be a systemic problem when it comes to membership and the expectation of members. It may also be an assimilation problem of not helping visitors get plugged into different aspects of congregational life.

Since the structure of the system generates behavior, change to the structure will produce the greatest amount of change to the behavior of the system. In order to change the structure, leaders must change their thinking. The hopes leaders have for improvement is directly tied to how they think. If "event thinking" dominates the leader and leadership of the church, then changing the behavior becomes nearly impossible. Leaders must learn to think structurally where behavior and results are generated.

Going Deeper
Learning to understand the congregation as a system helps church leaders move from reacting to addressing the church's structure where deep and lasting change can happen. To learn more about congregations as systems, check out our online resources at http://www.westernsem.edu/journey/ridder.

References and Additional Resources

Herrington, Jim, Mike Bonem, and James H. Furr. *Leading Congregational Change: A Practical Guide for the Transformational Journey*. San Francisco: Jossey-Bass, 2000.

Meadows, Donella. *Thinking in Systems*. White River Junction, VT: Chelsea Green Publishing, 2008.

Senge, Peter J. *The Fifth Discipline: The Art & Practice of the Learning Organization*. Rev. ed. New York: Doubleday/Currency. 2006.

A Different Kind of Conversation

Mark came to our church shortly after I became the pastor. His family had recently moved into the neighborhood of our building. They were drawn to the church by the biblical teaching and the warm reception they received.

Mark got involved quickly and began to exert influence over the congregation for two primary reasons: First, God has granted him leadership gifts. He is the kind of guy who can influence a room by his very presence. Second, Mark is a devout follower of Jesus who knows his Bible very well. This quickly earned the respect of many of the long-time members.

However, all was not right. Over time, it became apparent that Mark was strongly opinionated, and the way in which he expressed those opinions could sometimes shut down an entire room full of people. (Remember, he is a strong leader who can influence a whole room by his very presence.) He never meant any harm, but his approach was intimidating and counterproductive. Mark was not aware of it, but despite his best intentions, his very way of being was working against both his desires and God's potential. Other people in the various groups and meetings of which Mark was a part were hesitant to address the issue with him. In our congregation, as with many others, there is a culture of being nice at the expense of being honest. I learned of their concerns when they expressed their anxiety to me instead of speaking directly to Mark.

As we engaged this Ridder material, and as I was challenged to understand that I am the number one obstacle to the deep change that God desires, I reflected about my role in this dysfunctional system. It became apparent that I needed to sit down with Mark—not because I needed to function for others, but because I myself had witnessed the ill effects of his way of being, and yet had never addressed the issue. I, too, had chosen to be nice at the expense of being honest; my choice directly affected the whole system. My silence represented both a lack of responsibility and a lack of love for Mark and for our congregation.

In my heart, I was blaming Mark and failing to take personal responsibility for not loving him enough to be honest. The reality is that Mark meant absolutely no harm and was simply unaware of the effect he had on the people around him. It became very clear that my role was to "hold up a mirror" in the most loving way possible. As the Scriptures say, I was to admonish him with all wisdom . . . to speak the truth in love (Col. 3:16; Eph. 4:15). I was to be both kind and candid, both respectful and honest. For a long time, I foolishly believed I had to choose between the two. In the spirit of kindness, I would avoid the conversation and perpetuate the problem. In the spirit of honesty, I would deliver a harsh dose of the truth and demoralize a person. I was determined to be different in this situation, and as a consequence, experience a different result.

After much prayer to summon both courage and compassion, I met with Mark for lunch. I genuinely affirmed his many gifts, including knowledge and leadership. Then, filled with the grace of God, I lovingly and directly shared with him what I saw: that his way of being was getting in the way of even greater influence. I did my best to paint a vivid picture of his leadership potential, which could only be realized if his inspired thoughts were conveyed in a more gracious way. I emphasized that he did not need less truth; he just needed more grace.

At first, Mark was both stunned and hurt. He immediately called several friends from his former town to see if they concurred. They verified some of my observations, and Mark slowly—and at first, it seemed, begrudgingly—took a deep look at himself.

Starting at the very next meeting, I saw change. Mark continued to share his opinion, but he began to use a different approach; he shared in an inviting and life-giving way. His contributions generated conversation instead of shutting it down. The change was amazing to witness, and I made sure to tell him so after the meeting. Ever since then, I have noticed Mark being very careful to process his thoughts without sharing the first thing that comes to mind. The net effect is that we move further into faithful discipleship and mission because what was true of Mark before is still true of Mark: He is a solid leader who genuinely loves Jesus and wants to see the world love Jesus too. The difference is that now he is more effective both in conveying his thoughts and also in compelling others to come with him.

Many people, both within the congregation and without, would argue that Mark was the obstacle to healthy change. When taking a systems approach, however, it becomes plain that every person plays a role and blame is the abnegation of that responsibility. Whereas, taking responsibility for my role led to real change. A series of small but significant acts like this one can lead to larger systemic reformation.

Part 4
Additional Tools for the Journey: Equipping Ourselves for More Effective Leadership

There were surprises along the way. While we were learning what we set out to learn, we discovered that there were other skills and perspectives that we hadn't anticipated and that turned out to be crucial in our learning process.

In Part Four, we want to share what we had to learn and begin to master in order to practice all the other skills in this book competently. These tools come last, but in a sense they are foundational and support everything else we learned.

Chapter 13

Recognizing the Vows That Block Us: Learning to Respond Thoughtfully

Michael DeRuyter

> *The problem is that we often focus on changing the sinful behaviour through self-discipline. But if we ignore the underlying idolatries and lies which shape our hearts, then rules for behaviour will not work (Colossians 2:20–23).*
>
> —Tim Chester, *Delighting in the Trinity*

We wondered, along with the apostle Paul, why we do the very things we hate. Why does that happen? Why do we do the opposite of what we really want to do? Why do our hearts want to follow Jesus but then our actions sabotage that desire?

We believe that one reason is rooted in our past experiences, especially the ones that made us feel unsafe and afraid. As we make decisions about who we need to be in the world to keep ourselves safe, we move further and further away from being the person God created and calls us to be.

We are learning to reverse that process by identifying those decisions and, in repentance, making new ones that God can use to draw us to him. We are experiencing transformation we never dreamed was possible, and we are expectant about how God will continue to lead us into freedom.

*W*atching my daughter's game at our local soccer complex, my attention was drawn to a disturbance on the sideline of the field behind us. It appeared that a parent-coach had pulled one of his players off the field in the middle of play and had begun to scream at the little girl. His red face inches away from hers, he screamed about all of her failures as a player. Oblivious to the stunned onlookers, he was berating the young athlete for evidently failing to block a kick. In a moment it was over. Like a ship's crew caught in a sudden squall, the episode passed before anyone nearby could muster an intervening response other than to deal with the messy aftermath.

It is doubtful that the coach chose to volunteer his time teaching young girls how to play soccer in order to publicly berate them. It's also unlikely that the coach woke up on that particular Saturday morning and decided that this was the day he would fly into a rage because of a petty provocation. One important reality we acknowledge in this soccer field scenario is that an adult screaming at a child is not a valued practice which most of us, including that specific coach, would affirm. Indeed, simply reading the account of his tantrum will anger many. Our collective and immediate rejection of this behavior indicates the presence of the opposite value. We value protecting and nurturing children. Yet the incident happened in spite of this powerfully held value.

A second reality underscored by this incident is that the coach's angry outburst was not an isolated, unique behavior. In fact, in addition to provoking some angry feelings, reading the short account of this experience likely triggered memories of similar encounters that you have personally witnessed. Parents and coaches rage at children on playing fields (and in homes) every day. Both of these two realities are true. Both the value and the behavior are real.

Doing the Very Thing We Hate

This isn't surprising news to us, because unfortunately, we have all stood in the coach's shoes. Having stood there, we agree with Paul's self-assessment in Romans 7 admitting that, in varying degrees, human beings consistently act in ways that violate their own cherished values and convictions. This sort of violation is part of my own life to such an extent that I must often confess along with Paul that, "I don't really understand myself. . . . I want to do what is right, but I don't do it. Instead, I do what I hate" (Rom. 7:15, NLT). Our guiding beliefs and our actual behaviors often end up as strangers.

Hardly limited to outrageous or embarrassing or even recognized breaches, this estrangement evidences itself whenever we fail to keep a confidence, return a promised phone call, or to meet with God in prayer. Likewise, our values and behaviors are alienated from each other when we consistently overeat, surf for pornography, or grab the spotlight. Perhaps the value-violating behavior in your life is largely invisible to the world, existing instead as a subtle yet constant inner voice of blaming and criticizing, judging and dismissing the people around you.

How does one account for this sort of failure wherein we know the right things to do, we desire the good, and yet our lives demonstrate behaviors and decisions that are inconsistent (and even in conflict) with the right and the good? Specifically, how do our dreams and visions for outbreaks of *shalom* in our communities fail to yield the practical fruit of wholeness and justice in and through our lives? What undermines our commitment to integrity and authenticity, courage and love so that we end up with broken promises and hidden failures, living fearful, self-serving and self-protecting lives? How is it that so many of us get stuck here, and more importantly, how do we get unstuck?

We might be tempted to suggest that people sometimes just get caught up in the emotion of the moment. We can all relate to the experience of having our passions run away with us. There is no doubt that emotions and passions are powerful forces in our lives. Yet, this answer simply begs the question: What is it about a particular moment that generates such an emotional tempest capable of overwhelming a person's intentions and values?

How Vows Get Created

We can gain some insight into where these emotions come from if we flip the script and look at the story of the coach and the soccer player from the perspective of the little girl. Of course we don't know what was actually transpiring in her heart and mind, but we can well imagine, given that most of us have stood in her shoes as well.

From her place on the sideline at the soccer complex that day, what might the little girl have seen? Perhaps more importantly, what might she not have seen? In our imagination, we can suppose that the unknown and unseen facts of the situation include the detail that the coach had been up all night with his own sick child. We can add to that the devastating and unfair job review by his team leader before he left work on Friday. Finally, we can imagine a frustrating losing streak for his soccer team that the other coaches have been teasing him about for weeks.

While there is absolutely no excuse for his destructive words and actions, it is also the case that actions take place in a context. The features of this context play a role in the events that transpired.

Therefore, in the coach's story (for our purposes of imagining without specific information), the context includes all of these facts contributing to a moment of explosive anger being displaced onto a convenient scapegoat. Furthermore, we can imagine that the wet, slippery soccer ball was kicked on a trajectory and with a stubborn spin that together would have made it extremely difficult for even far more experienced players to block.

The little girl doesn't have access to all of these facts. She doesn't see the full context. She is simply caught in the withering barrage of raging words. Her most immediate reality is overwhelming shame. Swamped in this shame, no longer imaginary, but clearly visible to all in her tears and red cheeks and ragged breathing, she automatically begins to construct a context to explain and understand what is happening. She sees her failure and her fault. She is letting down her team. Her coach is rejecting her. She feels alone. She is a unique disappointment and failure. She knows these things the way she knows when she is hungry or thirsty or tired, without thought or attention or reflection. A deep, visceral, primal conviction emerges unbidden from within: I will never allow myself to experience this terrible feeling of worthlessness again.

Imagine now a course through life for this little girl that automatically and habitually attempts to fulfill this vow to her ten-year-old self. Avoiding the shame of failure and worthlessness becomes a self-evident guiding truth in her life. She becomes an expert at reading the needs and expectations of others and reflexively adjusts to meet those needs. She establishes intimacy and security in relationships by always fulfilling those expectations. As a high school student, no matter how often she promises herself that she will set better boundaries on her time and schedule and learn to say no, she finds that she is constantly overextended. As a young adult, her hypersensitivity to the expectations of others in her life leaves little room for failure or mistake.

So even though she sings "Amazing Grace" on Sunday mornings, she becomes a harsh taskmaster towards her colleagues and family, holding them to the same rigorous standards to which she holds herself. In middle age, increasing fatigue and depression mean that she simply avoids relationships with people who have expectations that she cannot manage with her depleted energy reserves. She begins to isolate herself even from God; God's expectations are utterly unmanageable in her view, hence the humiliating failure, which leads to shame, is virtually certain. While she promises herself she wants a deeper, more intimate prayer life, and reads books about prayer and goes to prayer retreats, she never prays. She never overcomes the fear of potential failure before God while her ever-present vow to avoid shame operates quietly in the background of her soul.

Our imaginary story is vastly oversimplified. It is certainly not my intention to say that the coach caused these potential, imaginary outcomes, or that he is responsible for the girl's choices in life. What I do intend to suggest is that the vows we make to ourselves when we are wounded, rejected, shamed, overprotected, or abused, continue to register an impact long after the initial moment of hurt and in ways that we may not immediately recognize. Specifically, these vows show up as places of habitual disobedience in one's life of discipleship. Lack of progress toward maturity in Christ, routinely unmet goals, regularly broken promises to self and others and God, and frequent failures to live out our professed values, are all likely symptoms of one or more operational vows. Often the vows are unrecognized, deeply submerged beneath time, assumptions, and accommodations, but nevertheless they powerfully influence our lives in unintended ways. The remainder of this chapter will examine how this is so and what we can do about it.

We Long for Connection

According to Genesis 1 and 2, human beings have characteristics of both "from above-ness" and "from below-ness." We are both breath and dirt. From above, we share with God a basic, powerful orientation toward meaningful, intimate relationships that reflect the relational nature of our triune God. We are designed to be connected to one another in authentic and loving ways, and we long to fulfill that design (Bolsinger, 2004). As creatures made from the dirt, this longing is embodied in physical and physiological processes. These processes are designed by God with a self-protective, self-preserving bias in order to help keep us safe. Further, these original design characteristics have been distorted by the loss of our primary intimacy with God himself (Gen. 3).

The result of this is that we move through life with distorted, but powerful, longings for connection. We hunger for intimacy and security and purpose. We reach out to others to fulfill these needs. Little girls seek approval from their soccer coaches and fathers. Little boys crave the attention and warmth of their mothers. Children seek the safety of belonging in their families. Yet, doing so from within our distorted and broken world means that we expect too much of others to meet our needs, and we receive too little from them in return. The brokenness of the other meets our own brokenness, and we are repeatedly wounded by rejection, anger, humiliation, or overprotection and worry.[1] We experience our failure to get our needs met as a painful wound and overwhelming threat. As our sense of pain and threat mounts, "brain and body chemistry become altered. Behavior and even anatomy may change" (Gilbert, 1999, p. 23).

When we are confronted with a painful or threatening experience, our from-below, dirt-derived but God-designed physiology begins to do some predictable things, all of which are ultimately aimed at alleviating the pain and surviving the threat.

First of all, as we assess the pain or threat, there is an emotional arousal. Virtually every aspect of our physical body is impacted by the cascade of chemicals that we experience as a feeling (Pert, 1997). The brain itself is altered, and the perceptual apparatus responsible for our sensory inputs begin to filter and sift incoming signals in slightly different ways. In

---

1. In *Connecting with Our Children*, Dr. Roberta Gilbert suggests that worrying about one's child is a hostile act (1999, p. 81).

other words, in a complex reciprocity, our perception of an event elicits an emotional response, which in turn actually changes how we perceive the event, which in turn further excites our emotional response. For instance, our emotionally heightened state will help determine which details are noticed and which are missed; it may adjust which senses are heightened and which are dulled. Further, input signals which make it through this emotionally tuned perceptual screen are matched with other existing memories, assumptions, and experiences. The result is that a meaning is formed to make sense of the sensory inputs. This is what it means to have a mind and to be a self. Put another way, "You construct your understanding of the world and your place in it through the lens of your own story" (Thompson, 2010). Human beings are meaning-makers.

How We Make Meaning

This idea was made stunningly clear to me one afternoon when I received two visits from two individuals who were seeking pastoral input for concerns that they had about a child. The first visit was from the child's mother. She expressed deep concern about how her child was "out of control." She didn't understand why the child was struggling like this, especially in light of her unique ability to give her child all the love and attention that her own mother never bothered to gave to her. Asked to elaborate on this point, she went on with great detail and strong emotion to prove to me that her own mother was "never there" for her.

Later that day, I was surprised by a second visitor to my office. This was the child's grandmother, who lived out of state and whom I had never before met. Her concern was that her daughter was not "there for" her grandchild the way she thought she should be. This failure was baffling to her, because she felt she had set such a good example of how a mother should always prioritize her children. In fact, she was "always" a part of her daughter's life, and gave her "everything" she needed. Neither mother nor daughter ever knew of the other's visit to my office.

Two women were looking at the same period of history, and constructing not just different but absolutely opposite meanings about what had happened, yet with enough similarity in how they were processing this history that they both independently sought me out on the same day.

We are constantly dealing with the meanings that we construct, which are based on our emotionally shaped perceptions of a situation, far more than the objective facts of a situation. The meanings we make will register their impact on how we see the world, how we operate in the world, and how we protect ourselves in the world. Rejection by someone I ask out on a date means I am ugly or unlovable. Betrayal by a best friend comes to mean no one can be trusted. A parent's divorce means I am a burden. Incidentally, sometimes the most powerful meanings get created around positive experiences. One of my earliest vows is connected to the positive experience of my family's praise and affection after I brought home a good report card. While this was certainly not the only occasion for such expressions, I loved the feelings generated by my success, and vowed that I would always be successful. As I discovered the implausibility of that vow, I modified my aim to always appear successful. The appearance of success produced the same rewards. We make meaning out of our experiences, both positive and negative. These meanings register their presence in our life story as they take their place as part of the lens that helps us filter and interpret other new experiences. This emerging and developing filter will lead us to be biased as we confirm through new experiences the meaning we have already made from earlier ones.

What is more, the emotional valance and intensity of an experience will impact the way that a particular event and its meaning is encoded into our memory for retrieval (Thompson, 2010). The emotion attached with the memory can be triggered by contexts or events that are similar, but not necessarily identical to the original. The ordeal of listening to your parents' blistering fights about money every evening for months until they end up in divorce is an experience that will be filtered, processed, and filed in your memory banks in such a way that years later when your spouse brings up a budget, you are gripped with fear and respond as if she is a threat. Some recent research in marriage and family therapy suggests that as much as eighty percent of the emotional conflict between couples is "rooted in events that pre-date the couple knowing each other. . . . Much of the conflict is not so much a direct outgrowth of a current event as something that flows from the parts of their minds that are remembering" (72).

In neuroscience, Hebb's Law states that "neurons that fire together, wire together." Thoughts, feelings, perceptions, indeed all mental processes, depend on neurons firing in our brain. Certain discrete pathways for neurons get established with repeated uses. We call this learning. With practice, tying one's shoes and working an algebra problem both become easier as neuronal pathways are laid down, repeated, and established. With repeated use comes increased use: A trail through the woods becomes a path, the path becomes a lane, the lane a road, the road a highway.

For our brains, this means that the more powerful an experience happens to be, or the more repetitions of that experience we undergo, the more likely it is that the neuronal pathway responsible for the mental process associated with that experience will grow from being a foot path to a interstate highway—a habitual part of one's life.

When it comes to riding a bike this is good news. The neuronal circuits know just what to do, firing away without my conscious effort so that muscles and balance work to produce the right result, a pleasant bike ride. Even after a long winter of no bike riding, the superhighway of neurons in my brain remains intact, and I can hop on my bike and ride on the first spring day. We may come to say that bike riding has become second nature, and indeed it has. When it comes to driving a car, this can be unsettling. Not long ago, I left home headed for the grocery store and moments later pulled into the church parking lot. The familiar roadways followed by the neurons through my brain were more real in determining my destination than the actual road in front of my car. In life's most important relationships, the existence of these habituated neuronal pathways can be profoundly challenging.

For instance, imagine that every time you told your father that you felt sadness, he told you that "real men don't cry." If you did shed a tear, the result was a shame-inducing reproach from your father. With each repeated pairing of your sadness with your father's response, the more powerfully engrained into your memory circuits will be the emotion of guilt or shame along with the feeling of sadness. A child faced with this painful and frightening threat that his father's approval and love might be jeopardized if father sees him crying may quickly learn how to squash the impulse to express sorrow, thereby removing the threat.

Here, then, is the constructed circuit. Sorrow means shame, which means loss of relationship, which means squelch the tears, cover up the sadness, and remove the painful threat. This is how a vow is formed, repeated, and rehearsed: In order to secure my father's approval, when I am sad, I won't cry. In time, this is no longer a decision based on the facts of the situation. There doesn't even need to be a thoughtful decision to "keep our vow." In this case, hiding one's tears is as automatic as riding a bike or driving to a familiar destination.

In a world distorted by sin and dislocated from God, our "from-above" longing for intimacy collides with the best "from-below" efforts of our mind to protect us from pain. This results in neither our intimacy nor our pain-avoidance goals being met. No wonder Paul holds out the renewal of our minds as the gateway to transformation (Rom. 12:2).

The final contribution offered by a "from below" perspective on the human creation is the fascinating discovery of neuroscientist Benjamin Libet. Libet was able to show in an ingenious experiment that a person's behavioral response begins .5 seconds before the person is aware of it. This is true for both stimulus responses and volitional responses (Papero, 2012). For example, put your hands together in your lap. Whenever you want, lift one of your hands above your head. What Libet discovered is that the decision to lift your hand is already made a half of a second before you realize you made it.

Evidently, we are wired with an autopilot. Indeed, as the psalmist says, we are "fearfully and wonderfully made." We are designed to handle complexity, as we process decisions even faster than we can become aware of them in some cases. Yet our autopilot mechanism can only follow the mental circuits we have already laid down. Our automatic responses are limited and confined by the meanings and emotions and vows that we have rehearsed and confirmed over and over. My brain had already made the decision to take me to the church before I was aware I had decided to go to the store. Changing the destination requires a conscious decision to override the autopilot.

The soccer coach yelling at his young player that Saturday will not likely change his behavior by force of will alone. There are deep needs and longings for security, purpose, and intimacy present in his life, and the imprint of his Creator's breath. These needs and longings are a legitimate part of what it means to be a human. However, in order to meet these legitimate needs in legitimate ways,[2] he must contend with the very real physiological constraints that come with his creaturely brain: an autopilot, scores of hardwired neuronal pathways, and a bias towards accepting emotionally charged, perceptually-limited, constructed meanings as if they are objective facts. This means that he must contend with the vows that have emerged over the years of facing a painful and threatening world. We turn now to the question of how to recognize these vows.

Recognizing Our Vows

In a similar fashion as we did with the young soccer player, I would invite you to engage your imagination once again. This time, instead of imagining our way forward from the moment of the wound on into her adulthood in order to discover the ongoing impact of her implicit vow, we will work our way backward in the coach's life from the present day moment of rage to an earlier wound. As I have suggested, the fact that his behavior cuts against the grain of his own deeply held values, purpose, and intentions for his life indicates that there is a vow lodged in the neuronal pathways of his mind. This vow is deeply embedded, strengthened through repeated experiences, and is waiting to be uncovered and identified.

As the coach reflects on the incident that evening, an image from his own history appears in his mind. In a flash, he is standing outside under a large oak tree on his second grade playground. Standing alone, the last to be chosen for a kickball team, his classmates are pointing at him and laughing. His stomach clenches as he remembers, connecting with the rage he felt surging through him that long-ago morning—rage at his mocking classmates, rage at his own athletic weakness, rage at his helplessness and shame. In a blink, the image shifts. He is seated at his desk and a spelling test is handed back. Again he feels rage as he sees the failing score scribbled in red ink across the top. The memory shifts yet again, and now he is opening the door to his house, home from school, and looking forward to the security and comfort of his mother after a painful day. As

---

2. "Legitimate" here means that the need is actually met through God-designed means: genuine love, worship of God, appreciation of his gifts and truth rather than the usual substitutions such as food, lust, approval of others, or busyness. See Romans 1.

he pulls open the screen door, the family's beloved golden retriever comes bounding out. He hears his mother's accusing shout, "Don't let that dog get out!" The young retriever is too excited, too powerful for his little arms to hold the dog back. The dog escapes through his grasp and runs down the street. In his memory, the soccer coach watches a slow-motion replay of his pursuit, futilely willing his young legs to pump faster. From around the corner, he hears the sound of a car's horn, the screech of rubber on asphalt, and then, a dull thump.

Again, he curses his weakness . . . rages at his failure . . . seethes under self-blame. Three times he has constructed the meaning that he is a weak failure. Three times rage has accompanied the experience of weakness and failure. Mental circuits are laid down and strengthened, forging a bond between the emotion of rage and the perception of weakness. A longing to avoid these painful relations with others resonates in his soul. A vow forms: I will never be defeated by weakness. I will embrace the strength of my rage instead.

Granted, we have just assigned to this coach the worst conceivable day. These imaginary events are compressed into a single day to illustrate how the process of identifying vows at work in our lives begins with the practice of visiting our two or three clearest memories of times when we were hurt, embarrassed, shamed, deeply afraid, or grieved. These are the moments when conditions are ripe for a vow to form.

Practice and Reflect

Since reading a chapter about vows is not the same thing as actually doing the work to identify one's own vows and the impact that they have, we want to encourage you to take some time as you conclude this chapter and actually do the hard work of unearthing vows that you have made. To do this, begin by identifying two or three places of hurt in your life's story. To identify these places, begin with a prayer that invites God to show you what he might want you to see. Ask for the courage to visit memories that may be painful. Consider times of transition in your family: births, deaths, moves, divorce. Are there vivid memories of more mundane experiences that stand as signposts to painful patterns or repeated hurts from childhood? You don't have to pick the "right" memory in order for this to be a useful exercise. Simply begin with the memory that God reveals to you. As you visit the details of this memory, in narrative form describe how old you were, the setting, and what happened. Build in as many details as possible. As a second step, share one or more of these experiences with a friend, coach, or pastor. What further learning or insight emerges as you write about your experience? What else do you become aware of as you share your story with another?[3] Hold

---

3.   This exercise is from the Faithwalking 201 Notebook (Herrington et al., 2013, p. 26).

this reflective work up before God as a way to gently open your heart to "see" a vow that has emerged in your life. In the aftermath of the painful event that you have recalled, did you promise yourself, or act is if you had promised yourself, that you would not be hurt in that way again? If so, how did you act on that promise?

In real life, the exercise of visiting these memories might look like this story from Chad:

My parents were divorced when I was nine months old. My mom got full custody and I ended up seeing my dad for about five hours every other Sunday. He would pick me up from church and drive the half hour to his house. We would spend the afternoon together and then he would drive the half-hour back home. I grew up never knowing anything different than this, so it was just the rhythm of my life.

One day I did not want to go. I don't remember why really, but I remember feeling some incredible anxiety as I thought about telling him I didn't want to go. I told my mom that I didn't want to go. She said that was fine, but I had to call him. So, on a Saturday afternoon I stood in our kitchen and called my dad. I was seven years old. As I see this story from my dad's point of view now, I imagine a guy who only saw his son every other week for about five hours who was being told by that son that the son didn't want to see him. Today I can imagine that made him pretty anxious—maybe even desperate. In that anxiety and desperation, my dad fought with me. He tried to persuade me to come—he was practically begging. When I hung up the phone, I cried. I bawled. I didn't want to disappoint him, but I didn't give in. I stood my ground, and he finally relented.

We got off the phone and some of you might be thinking, "Hey, what a confidence builder! He stood up to his dad and asked for what he needed." That isn't what I was thinking though. I made meaning out of that event, and the meaning I gave it was: "That was too hard. I will never do that again if I can help it. I must avoid pain at all costs."

Now I played football, so I didn't avoid all pain, but as I grew into different stages of life I avoided emotional pain at all costs. I didn't want to disappoint anyone because I didn't want to feel the pain of their disappointment. I became pretty good at avoiding emotional pain. I was pretty good at not letting anyone get too close or know the real me so that I wouldn't have to feel the emotional pain of rejection.

This came to a head my freshman year of college. I don't remember a lot about that year. I went to the University of Michigan and though I was a full-time student, I only went to class about half the time. I had been admitted into an accelerated pre-med track but I really ended up majoring in Coors Light and minoring in Sega Genesis. I also spent a lot of time watching TV. For some reason I got hooked on Cheers reruns and Star Trek: The Next Generation.

One day while watching TV, I saw a commercial that had a huge impact on me. The commercial was shot in black and white. In it there was a man wearing a large overcoat running in the rain in a city—his arms are wrapped around his chest and the whole scene is in slow motion. As he reaches a place of safety out of the pouring rain, he takes one hand and opens his coat, and you see a smiling infant son looking up at him. It was a commercial for some clothing store or cologne I think. But at that moment all sorts of pain started flooding into me. In that moment, I realized that I had never experienced my dad's protection in that way. We had never played catch—ever. How could he abandon a newborn son? How could he only come to my games when it was convenient for him? As those thoughts raced through my head—all of that pain—could no longer be avoided. In order to numb myself from that pain, I turned to alcohol and drugs. This led to a deep, out of control spiral into depression. I eventually stopped that self-destructive pattern with the help of a counselor and my pastor, and the authentic community of grace and truth I found in my friend Vince. However, I was still the king of pain-avoidance.

I see it in my life even today. There have been places in this process that I haven't wanted to go: with my wife, with my family, with my church, with myself, and with God. I had made a vow that I would avoid emotional pain at all costs and I am still capable of living into that vow today.

So, where is God in all of this? God was there, but God did not do what you might think. God did not rescue me from my pain and magically take it all way. What God did was empower me to see my vow and the impact that it has had in my relationships. God helped me to see and know the truth. God also grew my courage. God helped me lean into my pain and work through it. There was some suffering in that, and in that suffering, I learned obedience. I know that in pain I grow closer to God. I'm becoming more courageous, and I'll share a secret with you: most of the time what I think will be too painful to face, doesn't turn out that way.

Identifying and recognizing the painful experiences of our life can be easy in some cases. One woman who was undertaking the important

work of identifying vows that had formed in her life around painful epi-
sodes in her youth was able to pinpoint an experience very quickly:

> *When I was sixteen, my father took his life. Dad was one of those*
> *very rare individuals who was able to hide his depression success-*
> *fully until he decided to die. It was only in the aftermath of his death*
> *that we were able to uncover what he had hidden so well, his de-*
> *pression, his deep pain, and his belief that we would be better off*
> *without him.*
>
> *In the wake of the devastation and the rebuilding of our lives,*
> *I determined that fathers are not to be trusted. My vow was that*
> *I would never trust anyone in the role of father again. What this*
> *meant for me was that no one would be allowed to fill the role of*
> *a father-figure in my life, but it also meant that I would not accept*
> *God in the role of Father either.*

Others will need a lot more time, prayerful reflection, and careful listening to God's Spirit in order to identify their vows. This will be especially
true for those who were raised by high-functioning parents and who have
no obvious trauma in their past. Even in these circumstances, you were
hurt—at home, by peers, or by others in your life, and in those hurts, you
made a vow about how you had to "be" in the world in order to be safe as
a child. In these less extreme circumstances, learning to see the connection between a painful experience in your past, the attending vow that
was formed, and the impact of that vow in your present life can be more
challenging.

At a recent prayer retreat with members of our congregation, one
eighty-year-old man participated in a session on identifying vows. He expressed afterwards that although he had participated in other inner-heal-
ing and prayer retreats over the years, he had never been able to identify a
place of on-going brokenness that still needed to be brought before God's
gracious presence, until this retreat. He had finally been able to identify
the impact of a childhood wound and the way that wound continued to
impact his functioning in his family.

A second way to identify a vow is to "back into it." Instead of beginning with the memory of an early wound, begin with the ongoing impact. Identify a place of ongoing disobedience in your life. Describe some
way of functioning in your life that is designed to protect yourself, even
withhold yourself, from God, or your spouse, or some other person with
whom you have an important relationship (Herrington et al, 2013). Think
of some part of your life that isn't "working." Sometimes we describe this
as a place of being "stopped."

We get stopped or disempowered in conversations or experiences all
of the time. Noticing these places when they occur is a critical skill when

it comes to identifying the vows that are at work in our lives. For example, did you get stopped as you attempted to have a conversation with someone about the painful experience you wrote about in the exercise above? How have you gotten stopped in your effort to implement other real-world exercises suggested in this book? What is it that got in the way of your best intentions? You will recall that many of our behaviors (including lack of action) are the result of our functioning autopilot, those self-protective, pain-avoiding, long-established neuronal pathways working to keep us safe from harm as we perceive it.

This autopilot will function on our behalf based on the meaning we make of a perceived threat or challenge in any given circumstance. If you failed to engage the suggested conversation exercise, even after promising yourself that you would, your autopilot, self-preserving, pain-avoiding mind intervened as soon as your perception of the task registered as a risk (and maybe even before you were consciously aware that a risk had been perceived and avoided).

So then thinking back, what was the risk that you perceived? As you examine this behavior, (in)decision, or moment of inaction in your life, ask yourself what meanings you have made that fix this behavior in place in your life. When did you decide that some particular behavior or conversation, such as self-disclosure for instance, was risky? What can you say about where and when you first made this meaning? What lengths do you go to in order to avoid certain unpleasant feelings that may be generated by the contemplated action or conversation? As you reflect on your experience in this fashion, you will begin to approach the vows that are at work in your life.

Identifying the origin of meanings that you habitually and routinely construct about your experiences can lead to the identification of a vow. One pastor has described the experience of identifying a self-made meaning and "interrogating" it:

> *Apparently, I didn't know I had an issue with failure until I was sitting in the middle of a situation where I had interpreted that I had failed. And the meaning I was suddenly adding was "You failure. No one is going to stand by you when you are discovered as a failure." And so I was going around in circles, afraid to talk to anyone in leadership.*
>
> *Then one day I was listening to Deuteronomy 22 and hearing how Moses told the Israelites that there were things God had not opened their eyes to yet, and God spoke right to me. "Andy, you are worried that no one will stand by you in your struggles. In reality, I will never leave you nor forsake you. You have encountered something new, and you are learning. Where is the other voice coming from?"*

It was at that time that I realized my need for accomplishment had become a powerful enough voice that it spun a story that devalued my wife, my family, my friends, my church leadership, and my community. Ever since then, I have been interrogating that story whenever it pops up and trying to write a new narrative of grace.

As you reflect on experiences or conversations where you get stuck, as you interrogate the meanings that you make, there are some predictable categories of meaning that you will tend to identify.

1. We get stopped when we make our circumstances mean that we are Victims. Whatever problems we face are not our fault.
2. We get stopped when we make our circumstances mean that we are Helpless. Not only is the challenge or problem not our fault, but we utterly lack the resources to change things.
3. We get stopped when we make the meaning that others are Villains. This seductive meaning dehumanizes others as we blame them for our problems (Patterson et al, 2002).

Which of these meanings is most routinely descriptive of your experiences? If you don't know, ask the three people closest to you! When do you fall back on this meaning? What are your earliest recollections of a time when you made that meaning? Is there a vow that emerges into view?

The purpose in this chapter is not to deepen our experience of shame and guilt about the meanings we make or the vows we take. Rather, our goal is to recognize that all human beings respond to painful wounds in ways that are designed to promote healing and protection from further pain. The vows that we make are one such mechanism. A vow about never again touching a hot stove will serve one well for an entire life. A vow that says we cannot trust father-figures or that we can never show weakness will end up creating more problems than are solved.

Whether you begin with a painful memory or with a present-day expression of your autopilot "way of being," the goal is to express the vow in a single sentence and with as much clarity as possible. Getting clarity about our vows is essential but not sufficient to bring about change.

Making New Vows

Seeing, understanding, and owning one's vows is hard work, but it is not the final step. Once you can recognize how a meaning has been assigned to a life experience and describe the self-protecting vow that has been made, you can begin to see what was once an automatic and invisible part of your life. The second step is to take this new insight before God and acknowledge that this vow has had an impact on how you see the world, what you believe to be true about yourself and others, and to what degree you trust God. Because a vow emerges from a scarred mind situated in a marred and broken world, the self-protective reflex behind the vow means that these beliefs are not in line with what God says is true (Herrington et al., 2013). Therefore, in order to put the vow in the past, I need to repent of the cherished belief that was actually moving me away from God's truth about myself, others, or the world.

Having identified the vow and repented of the impact the vow has had on my life, the next step is to replace the old vow with a new one. This is the New Testament model for transformation: taking off the old (through repentance) and putting on the new (through faith). The new vow that I take is based on the truth that God has spoken in Scripture. For instance, instead of a vow that says, "I have to be perfect in order to be loved," I might vow instead to "Always rest assured in the God who loves me unconditionally." This new vow gives me the freedom to see struggles and imperfections as opportunities for continued growth and learning instead of preludes to rejection.

Practice and Reflect

There is great power in sharing our vows. Earlier we practiced sharing our old, wound-based vows with another person in order to gain perspective and clarity. Now, we want to encourage you to share your new, Scripture-based vow with another person, or group of people, in order to gain strength and support. As you share your new vow, begin by telling the story of your old vow. Describe the moment when it was formed, the distorted lens that it created, the faulty perspectives on your self, others, and God that resulted. Share specifically about what you had come to believe about yourself, God, or others that was false according to God's Word. Tell about and how you brought that distortion before God with a prayer of repentance. And then name the new vow that you have made—deliberately and purposefully based on God's Word—to replace that old vow. In order to share clearly, work ahead of time to refine the "wording" of your vows, old and new, so that they can be shared in a sentence or two.

Holding on to a new vow will take time and practice. You are literally re-wiring neuronal pathways in your brain as you learn to deliberately approach old, challenging situations with a new vow. Over time, the new vow will become more and more second nature. In the meantime while you are doing the practice of developing that new, second nature way of being, having a community of trusted people to encourage you, express grace to you, reflect with you about progress and setback, is one of the most important determinants of genuine transformation. Without community, transformation won't happen. Period.

When you find yourself getting stuck in your progress toward the new vow, go through the steps again and again. There may be additional vows to see, or more clarity to develop. What is the nature of the setback? What does getting stuck indicate about the presence of a yet-unidentified vow? It may be that you need to repent again and reaffirm the truth of your new vow from God's perspective. You may need to confront the dusty old vow-driven impulse to hide from others the failures and setbacks that you experience as you try to live with your new vow.

This past summer, I returned from a lengthy vacation and was about to preach again for the first time in a month. My routines were rusty. And as the congregation sang the song just prior to the sermon, I reached down to the battery pack on my belt to switch on the wireless microphone. Only it wasn't there. I had completely forgotten to get "wired" for sound prior to the service that morning. And my old vow came rushing back. My first thought was, "Is there a way that I can preach without a microphone and not look bad? Can I make this look intentional?" When I realized that there was no way to pull that off, I decided to run for it. I dashed out of the service, sprinted to my office, removed my sport coat and installed the microphone, and slipped back in to the sanctuary while the congregation sang the last verse of their song. After the service that morning, I realized it would be important for my own ongoing transformation to tell some trusted friends about the way this old vow had come roaring back. I don't always see it, but when I do, I need to name it. Keep telling the unfolding, dynamic story of your journey in conversations, and make sure to include in those stories the signs of new life and shalom that are evident as God does his transforming work.

Going Deeper

Pursuing the goal of transformation in our lives means gaining clear understanding about how we were *formed* in the first place. We are shaped and formed by early life experiences, both good and bad, as we orient ourselves toward pleasure and away from pain. We make promises, or vows, to ourselves that are designed to meet our childhood needs and protect us from harm. When these vows continue to operate in our adult lives, they actually become counterproductive, standing in the way of our obedience to God and the life he designs for us to live. You can find additional resources about vows at http://www.westernsem.edu/journey/ridder.

References and Additional Resources

Bolsinger, Tod E. *It Takes a Church to Raise a Christian*. Grand Rapids: Brazos Press, 2004.

Damasio, Antonio. *Self Comes to Mind: Constructing the Conscious Brain*. New York: Pantheon Books, 2010.

Gilbert, Roberta, M.D. *Connecting With Our Children*. New York: John Wiley & Sons, 1999.

Herrington, Jim, Steve Capper, and Trisha Taylor. *Faithwalking Notebook 201.* 2013.

Papero, Daniel. Lecture, Georgetown Family Center Postgraduate Program, June 7, 2012.

Patterson, Kerry, Joseph Grenny, Ron McMillan, and Al Switzler. *Crucial Conversations: Tools for Talking When Stakes Are High.* New York: McGraw-Hill, 2002.

Pert, Candace, B. Ph.D. *Molecules of Emotion: Why You Feel the Way You Feel.* New York: Scribner, 1997.

Thompson, Curt M.D. *Anatomy of the Soul: Surprising Connections between Neuroscience and Spiritual Practices That Can Transform Your Life and Relationships.* Carol Stream, IL: Tyndale, 2010.

Chapter 14
Can We Talk?
From Discussion to Dialogue

Trisha Taylor

> *We cannot and should not try to make our lives more authentic by dramatic gestures. Rather, we must learn to engage in everyday tasks as common as learning to speak the truth and—perhaps, even more demanding—to hear the truth through the time-consuming work of patient conversation.*
> —Rowan Williams, former Archbishop of Canterbury

As systems struggle to change, progress happens at the speed of conversation. When we avoid talking about the hard subjects or when we use conversation to manipulate or dominate others, we move further away from our goals. When we learn the skills of effective dialogue, though, we are able to make things happen—like consensus, inspiration, problem-solving, and real change.

We cannot overstate the importance of guiding people to talk about the important issues that are before us and to talk about them in authentic and loving ways. We had to learn to facilitate dialogue, and we often learned the hard way, through hard practice about hard topics. We also learned that the better we got at dialogue, the more real change we saw in ourselves and in our congregations.

*I*n congregations and in relationships, deep change happens at the speed of dialogue. Whether we need to change systems and structures or whether we need to change hearts and minds, we can only move as fast as our conversations. Leaders lead through communication.

Think for a moment about how leaders influence how communication happens. To a large extent, leaders determine what will be talked about publicly and what won't, how the subject will be addressed, who will be invited into the conversation, and what the tone of the conversation will be. When we engage these processes with skill and maturity, we get closer to the desired outcomes. We all know what happens when we don't manage communication well—when conversations deteriorate or never happen at all, when emotions flare out of control, when people are marginalized or silenced, when relational messes are not cleaned up.

Communication by itself is not enough to facilitate healthy change. Sometimes the urge to talk things through is just an expression of our anxiety or our reaction to the anxiety of others. Sometimes we need to talk but lack the maturity or a strategy to do it well. Sometimes our nonverbal communication drowns out everything we are trying to say out loud.

We are learning that mastering a particular kind of conversation—dialogue—changes everything. We started by distinguishing dialogue from discussion. Without splitting too many linguistic hairs, it helps to think about the origins of both words. Discussion comes from the Latin word *discussus,* which connotes the idea of using conversation to "shake or to strike," the same Latin root being found in the words "percussion" and "concussion." When I approach a discussion, I am usually trying to make my point and to get you to see things my way. Even if I do it as nicely and as politely as my southern Christian upbringing taught me to, I am still, in the end, trying to win with my words.

Dialogue, on the other hand, comes from the Greek word *dialogos,* which connotes the idea of allowing meaning to flow through a conversation. It is where we get the idea of "talking through" an issue. When I engage in dialogue, I am most interested in an exchange of ideas and perspectives in which the conversation is not something we inflict on each other, but is something we share. Even when dialogue is intense or passionate, we both come away understanding more than we did when we started.

When we engage in dialogue, we have one goal: mutual understanding. Of course, we hope that the mutual understanding will facilitate all kinds of things—solving problems, building relationships, resolving disagreements. But in the moment that we are in the conversation, we can have only one goal—to understand and to be understood.

In fact, this is the bottom line: I must learn to talk so that I can be understood and listen so that I can understand.

Listening to Understand

Let's start with listening. There are few acts as loving and compassion-ate as the gift of deep listening. Deep listening is much more than polite-ness. When we listen deeply, we are not just quiet, patiently waiting for our turn to talk. Actually, we are doing something very profound.

Deep listening is the ability to pay close attention to the thoughts and feelings of another person, holding them in the space between us with calmness and without judgment. When we listen deeply, we listen to the words that are used and we listen for the meanings that are underneath and behind the words—we listen to what is spoken and to what is unspo-ken.

When we listen deeply to another person, we are conveying respect and care all at once. We are saying, "I care enough about you to hear what you have to say, to know how you see things. I respect you enough to be-lieve that you may see something I don't see." Maybe one reason we often don't listen well is that we don't truly respect or care enough. Listening tends to help us expand both our caring and our respect.

In *The Fifth Discipline*, Peter Senge (1990) describes active reflection and inquiry as skills we can use to surface mental models. And, we can also be intentional about developing those two skills to help us become better listeners. When we actively reflect or inquire, we take a position of humility, the posture of a learner, acknowledging that we don't know everything. Active reflection happens when we reflect back to a person what we think we heard them say, and we double-check both the words and the meaning with them before we proceed with the conversation.

Inquiry is the skill of asking questions to draw out meaning to enhance understanding. The best listeners are the ones who can ask the questions to help people say what they were previously unable or unwilling to put into words. People often poke fun at Barbara Walters and her off-kilter questions to celebrities and world leaders, such as the oft-mocked "If you were a tree, what kind of tree would you be?" However, her genius at draw-ing people out and getting answers to questions that no one else thought to ask is indisputable.

I often have the experience of not really knowing what I think about something until someone asks a wise question that draws it out. Several years ago, my husband and I moved to a different city where I was unable to find a job. Up to that point, I had always joined the staff of an already-existing ministry. This time, though, I was starting to think about going out on my own. About halfway through one particularly whiny conver-sation, my dear friend Janet let a long silence form and then asked me quietly, "What are you afraid of?" I rattled off a few easy answers, such as not being able to pay the bills and not knowing if I would enjoy work-ing on my own. She let the silence linger a little while longer and then asked again, "What are you afraid of?" Suddenly, I was aware of a rush of dread and could name the fear of failure that was keeping me stuck in dithering and indecision. Then, from what seemed like nowhere, I heard myself say, "I guess I have two choices: I can settle or I can risk." Instantly, I knew which choice I wanted to make. My friend Janet has mastered the art of inquiry.

I believe that listening is an act of discipleship, a part of following Jesus. Here's what I mean: Jesus instructs me to love my neighbor as I love myself (Matt. 22:39). Well, I already know what I think, what I feel, and what makes sense to me. I love my neighbor as I love myself when I also invest in knowing what he thinks, what he feels, what makes sense to him. While holding on to my own perspective, I lovingly take the perspective of another person, my neighbor.

Practice and Reflect

Reflect on the idea that deep listening is a way that you can love others as you love yourself. In your journal, prayerfully answer these questions:

- Am I more likely to engage in discussion or dialogue? However polite I may be, do I tend to approach conversations trying to get others to see things my way or do what I want? How often do I approach difficult or important conversations with the single goal of mutual understanding?
- How often do I invest in loving others by listening to see things from their point of view?
- How often do people leave a conversation with me feeling cared for and respected? Does the way I listen convey care and respect?

Now test your impressions in a real-life setting. Pay close attention to your approach to three conversations and then reflect on these questions. Write your answers in your journal as soon after the conversations as you can.

- Did I give my full attention to the conversation?
- Did I talk too much? Did I interrupt?
- Did I "listen to understand" without immediately interjecting my own opinion?
- Did I reflect my listening back to the other person in a way that helped that person feel understood?
- Did I ask questions that helped to move the conversation to a deeper level?

Talking to Be Understood

Once we've learned to listen when others talk—and in that order—then we must learn to talk so that others can listen. If the goal is mutual understanding, then it is my responsibility to say what is so for me in the clearest and most understandable way possible. This starts with a healthy dose of courage and humility: the courage to say what I mean and to mean what I say and the humility to let go of trying to manage others' opinions of me.

Dialogue requires that I learn to "say what is so" for me, clearly and directly, even when that makes me feel vulnerable and exposed. When we feel vulnerable, we often hide behind various forms of conversational armor to help us feel less exposed and more in control. On one end of the continuum, we may go on the offense with sarcasm, one-upping, debating, correcting, and judging. On the other end of the continuum, we play defense by hinting, hiding, and pretending. In both cases, we are probably not even very aware of what we are doing or why.

Of course, there are some forms of communicating that are never helpful—yelling, contempt, stonewalling. All of these hinder our attempts at dialogue and stand in the way of mutual understanding, and we must intentionally lay them down. This is why mastering the art of dialogue is one of the most courageous things we can do.

Because people are different and situations vary, it helps to learn to say what is so for us in several different ways. As a basic skill, we can learn to define ourselves clearly and courageously by saying as directly as possible: This is who I am, this is how I feel, this is what I want, and this is what I'm going to do. This kind of direct approach helps people to understand what we are saying without having to guess and most people appreciate it.

However, there are other ways that we can make ourselves understood on a deeper level. One way we can connect on a more emotional level is to tell a story from our own experience that helps another person to understand not only what we think, but what has shaped us to think that way.

One of the pastors in the Ridder process, Edie Lenz, has served as pastor to two churches. In her first pastorate, she led the congregation through the process of closing the church's doors. In the second, her current pastorate, she has led her congregation through a merger with another congregation that was facing closure. Edie says, "When the process of the merger started, there was a lot of skepticism about me. I'm young and I'm female, and there was some doubt about whether I could lead both congregations through such a painful change. One day, the vice president of the consistory came to my office and told me as much; he said, 'I had no confidence that you could handle this. But when I heard you tell the story of closing the first church you served, for me, that changed everything. I realized that we could trust that you understood how hard this is and you would meet us where we were. We saw that you were loving people who were hurting and not just trying to get what you could out of it.'" By sharing her story, Edie went farther in gaining trust than any number of sermons or explanations could have accomplished.

The View from the Balcony

There is one more skill that leaders can learn that will enhance the potential for dialogue more than you can imagine. When one person in the conversation is able to focus on both the *content* of the conversation (what we are talking about, our issues) and the *process* of the conversation (how we are talking about it, what is going on in and between us) and to give words to both those things, the quality of the dialogue increases beyond measure.

This means that even as we are deeply engaged in dialogue with another person, we are able to detach ourselves enough to take a "balcony view"—in other words, to take a vantage point that will allow us to watch what is happening in the conversation even as we are participating in it (Heifetz and Linsky, 2002). From this vantage point, we are able to stop and ask, "How are we communicating? What is the pace of the conversation? What am I saying and how am I saying it? What is the other person saying and how is she saying it? What is likely to happen if we keep communicating this way?"

Being able to then stop talking about the content of the conversation and shift the focus to the process of the conversation is a high-level skill. I might stop and say, "I'm noticing that the longer we talk, the more agitated we're getting. I know that my heart rate is way up and I'm feeling more intense than I want to. Do you mind if we take a break?" Or I might say, "I love the way you're asking me questions about this—it's really helping me think through things. Thanks for that." Or, "I've noticed that each of us is just restating our position over and over and I'm not sure that's helpful. I'd like to tell you what I'm hearing and see if I've got it right. Would you do the same with me? Then maybe we can start to problem-solve." The ability to focus on both *what* we are talking about and *how* we are talking about it is a valuable skill that is worth cultivating.

Practice and Reflect

What kinds of conversational armor do you put on to protect yourself when you feel vulnerable? Consider whether you employ sarcasm, debating, one-upping, judging, hinting, hiding and pretending, or destructive patterns like contempt and stonewalling. If you really want to know the answer, ask a few people who are close to you, especially people you work with or live with. Write their answers in your journal for future reflection and thank them for sharing their observations.

Learning to take a "balcony view," takes intentional practice. As you engage in conversation today, practice fully engaging the conversation while at the same time detaching from it enough to see the details of the conversation as they unfold in real time. Share your observations with the person you are talking with.

Crucial Conversations

There are two different kinds of conversations that we must master if we are going to make a real difference in the systems we lead. One is the crucial conversation and the other is the transformation conversation.

In the Ridder Church Renewal process, we have found *Crucial Conversations: Tools for Talking When Stakes Are High* by Kerry Patterson and colleagues to be an important resource. All of the pastors and their leadership teams have used the wisdom in *Crucial Conversations* to guide them through the difficult conversations that must accompany change. The following discussion of crucial conversations relies heavily on the information articulated in that text.

A crucial conversation is one in which people have differing opinions, the stakes are high, and people have strong feelings about the matter at hand. That sounds like almost every important conversation that congregations have—or should have. We can avoid these kinds of conversations (and many of us do), we can have them and handle them badly (many of us have experience with that, too), or we can learn to have crucial conversations and handle them well. The success of our influence and leadership depends on us choosing the latter (Patterson et al, 2002).

We begin the process of crucial conversations by looking at ourselves—our motivations and our goals. By focusing on ourselves first, we avoid the trap of trying to use dialogue as a blunt instrument to get other people to change. We take the time to get clear about what is the core of the issue and what do we really want to have happen—for ourselves, for the other person, and for the relationship.

We are very careful in this early stage to identify and to avoid the "sucker's choice," where the issue is framed as an either-or choice where neither choice is ideal (Patterson et al., 2002). For example, I often hear people defend themselves when they have lost their temper by saying, "Well, I don't want to be a doormat and just roll over," as if being hostile and being a doormat are the only two options. In church, a sucker's choice is created when the chair of the worship committee says, "We've got to figure out whether our worship services are going to please the young people or the older people." I once attended a church business meeting in which one person said, "We can either keep these neighborhood kids out of our building or just let the building be destroyed." People nodded as though these were our only two choices.

We can avoid this trap by always generating multiple options, not allowing ourselves to be backed into a corner where there are only two choices. I had a colleague once who would stroke his beard thoughtfully and offer a third choice, "Well, we could always stand on our chairs and sing the National Anthem." It always made me laugh and remember that there are never just two solutions to any problem.

By definition, crucial conversations are risky and make us feel vulnerable. That is why people who are masters of dialogue are also masters of making things safe. They have learned to watch the process to insure that no one in the conversation is being bullied, coerced, judged, or blamed. They have learned how to slow things down to help people express mutual respect and care. They know how to spotlight the shared purposes—the things all sides want in common—instead of only focusing on differences. When emotions run too hot, they know how to cool things off and make them safe again. Everyone in a crucial conversation is responsible for keeping things safe and leaders can help to make sure that happens (Patterson et al., 2002).

As we engage in more and more crucial conversations, we learn that we are often not emotionally stirred up about the issue itself but about the story we are telling ourselves about it. In any dialogue, there are the facts, the stories we tell ourselves about those facts, and the feelings that those stories create. Of course, we often believe that our stories are the facts and that our feelings are too, and that's when we get off track (Patterson et al., 2002).

When a musician in her church became angry about new changes in the worship schedule, Pastor Jess Shults initially assumed she had a power struggle on her hands. The young drummer was sending her angry text messages asking why changes were made, why he had not been consulted, and wondering why the church had hired him in the first place. However, through the process of inquiry, Jess realized that the musician was not upset about the facts themselves—that he was no longer on the worship schedule every week—but about the meaning that he had made about the facts: that he had done something wrong and was being displaced. Jess listened as he told stories about how he had previous experiences in other churches that had left him hurt and a little suspicious, and she heard his fear that his faithful ministry didn't matter. Once the drummer realized, through a series of crucial conversations, that he hadn't done anything wrong and that the changes were designed to allow another drummer with no ties to church or to faith to participate in the worship music, his feelings about the schedule completely changed and he returned to his ministry with renewed enthusiasm.

Crucial conversations eventually lead us to a place of getting into action about the issue at hand. We have to decide what the next steps are, who will do them and what kind of accountability there will be. In very complex or emotionally charged situations, it may take many crucial conversations to reach that point. There are two ways we often get off track. One is to move too quickly to a plan of action. Until people believe that their points of view have been heard and respected, any move toward major action will doom the effort to failure. However, we also get off track when we fail to move toward action at all. When people talk and talk but nothing ever happens, the change process gets stalled and momentum lags.

Years ago, I found myself sitting around a conference table with five or six co-workers and a newly hired consultant, talking about the strategic plan for our nonprofit organization. The bad news was that we had gathered around this same table time many times in the past few years to brainstorm and share ideas. Meanwhile, nothing had changed. As the consultant asked his questions, designed to help us talk about our ideas for the ministry, I threw a small tantrum. "I know you're new to this, but we've been having this conversation for years and nothing has changed. There is nothing new here and nothing is going to change." He acknowledged my frustration and kept asking his questions. Not long afterward, nothing had changed and the ministry closed its doors.

Looking back, I deeply wish I had committed to be part of the solution instead of just pointing out the problem. I wish I had taken the time to sum up the ideas that had been expressed, and then had started asking questions about how we wanted to move forward, which could have helped keep us on track until we had identified next steps and action plans. Instead, I allowed my frustration about the constant talking and failure to act to sabotage our efforts.

Although the purpose of dialogue is to foster mutual understanding, it also gets us to the point that we are ready to decide and to act. A leader will help the participants in the conversation to first decide how they will decide. Are we going to vote? Is a leader or a committee going to make the final decision with input from the whole group? Are we going to work until we reach consensus? How much time do we have to make a decision? How will we know when we are ready to act? If people don't know how decisions are going to be made, they are likely to feel blindsided or even betrayed when the time comes for action (Patterson et al., 2002).

At this point in a crucial conversation, some participants may be tired and ready to be finished. Others may be resisting a decision if they fear it will not go their way. Others may be feeling content that their feelings have been addressed and feel content to finish without an action. However, at some point—after hours, weeks, or even years of conversation—it is time to decide: What will we do? Who will do it? When will it be finished? How will we follow up? What is the process of evaluation and making adjustments? It is a leader's job to pay attention to this process and to make sure that it gets completed.

Practice and Reflect

A crucial conversation is one in which there are differing opinions, the stakes are high, and people have strong feelings about the matter at hand. We have three choices when we see a crucial conversation loom-ing—we can avoid it, have the conversation and handle it badly, or have the conversation and handle it well. How are you currently addressing the crucial conversations that are facing you?

Think about a situation you are currently facing that will likely require a crucial conversation to move forward. Stop a moment and consider:

- What outcome do you really want? What do you want for your-self? For the other person? For your relationship?
- What sucker's choice is threatening your best thinking and cre-ative problem-solving? Take a moment to generate as many other choices as you can, even if they seem unlikely or silly. You can start with singing the national anthem!
- How are you going to keep these conversations safe, so that people can freely express their thinking and feeling in productive ways?
- What stories are you telling yourself about the problem you face? What stories are you telling about the motives of the other people involved? Do your stories often make you out to be the victim of other people's villainy? What other stories can you tell?
- Is it time to stop talking and act? How will you know? Have all the people in the conversation agreed on how decisions will be made?

Transformation Conversations

The second kind of conversation that we must master if we want to lead change is the transformation conversation. We have transformation conversations when we are talking clearly, authentically, and passionately about how we are pursuing transformation and how God is working in our lives. Although we are definitely trying to bring energy and passion to our conversations, a transformation conversation is not a "pep talk," in which we are just trying to get other people excited or motivated. In the church I attended as a teenager, the youth leaders encouraged us to say, "Praise the Lord!" more often and constantly interject "what Jesus is doing in my life" into otherwise ordinary conversation as a way of evangelizing. That's not what I mean here. And although we hope that people will see new possibilities for their own lives, a transformation conversation is not a sales pitch in which we are trying to sell someone something, even if the thing we might be selling is the change they so badly need.

Instead, a transformation conversation is a powerful practice for keep-ing change alive in our own lives and communicating our vision for change to others. When we talk about what we are pursuing, what God is doing, and where we are seeing hope and change, we remind ourselves of all these things in powerful ways. Talking about it makes it real. Talking about it holds the vision in front of us, working against the powerful pull toward inertia and status quo. These transformation conversations connect us more deeply to the dream we have for our lives. They also have the potential to leave others feeling energized about new possibilities or curious about what might be possible in their own lives or inspired about the changes they see in us. Transformation conversations are also a way for us to move to a shared vision. As each of us share clearly, authentically, and passionately about our desires for the future, we can create a common vision that we can all pursue.

My friends and colleagues Brett and Kellie Hurst are masters at trans-formation conversations. Every time they talk about their vision for mar-riage ministry and the real life stories of transformed relationships, includ-ing their own, I am left feeling inspired and motivated, with all kinds of creative juices flowing. When they talk about what they can see in the future of marriage ministry, I can also see what they see. I need to hear them talk about their passionate love for their ministry every now and then just to keep myself on track with my own commitment to similar work.

To master transformation conversations, we must learn to be clear. I shared earlier about the transition in my life from one city to another when things didn't seem to be working out the way I expected. During that confusing time, I visited with another minister in my new city, hop-ing he could help me figure out the lay of the land. At the beginning of our conversation, he leaned back in his chair and folded his hands behind his head. "So, Trisha. Why did God bring you to Austin?" I babbled for a while and finally, in embarrassment, just stopped talking. However, the question became a powerful one and a week later, I had crafted a four-sentence answer. Preparing to answer that question in the future helped me get clear about what I knew about God's leading in my life and kept me focused when I got confused.

We must also learn to be authentic. Authenticity is what distinguish-es transformation conversations from the fake-happy evangelistic tech-niques I learned as a teenager. When we are authentic, we talk about our successes and our failures, the places we see progress and the places we are stuck. We take off our masks and our vulnerability draws people toward us and allows us to feel honest about our lives.

Transformation conversations are also passionate conversations. This doesn't mean that we have to talk loudly, stand too closely to people, and wave our arms around. It does mean being energetic and life-giving in the way we use our words. Think about how children naturally engage in these kinds of conversations, as they share what they are learning with abandon, honesty and enthusiasm. Sadly, many of them will learn to exchange their passion for "playing it cool."

Learning to be clear, authentic, and passionate is not just about learning techniques to make us more effective communicators. This kind of learning requires that we confront ourselves and all the things that keep us from clarity, authenticity and passion. We learned in the previous chapter about the vows we make to keep ourselves emotionally safe. We may have vows about not sharing ourselves authentically or about not showing that we care. We may use vagueness as a way to hide in conversation. Transformation conversations challenge us to confront ourselves and our vows.

Although I experience the power of transformation conversations on a regular basis, I still find them very difficult to initiate. As a young teenager, I had a series of painful experiences with friends that taught me that passion and enthusiasm were embarrassing and definitely not cool. Later, as a female professional working mostly with men, I learned to dial back anything that hinted at emotionality or talking about myself, believing that it was more acceptable to keep things superficial, not disclose too much, and not get emotional in public. Learning the skill of transformation conversations has not been enough for me. I have also had to confront my autopilot—that voice in my head that says, "Be cool. No one cares what you have to say. Don't reveal too much. Don't be too emotional."

Practice and Reflect

Can you think of the last time you had a transformation conversation? Typically, when you talk about your life, are you clear, authentic, and passionate? If not, what stops you?

Think of a way to practice sharing something God is doing in your life (maybe even through this book) with another person in a way that is energizing and life-giving for both of you. Who will you share with? What will you say? How will you say it? Give your word to intentionally initiating at least one transformation conversation and once you have done that, write your reflections about it in your journal.

Dialogue and the Core Values

At its core, our commitment to dialogue is a commitment to our core values: authenticity, integrity, courage and love.

When we engage in dialogue, we bring our authentic selves to the conversation and say what is so for us. We say what we believe, where we are confused, what we want, what we feel, and what is going on with us even in the middle of the dialogue. Because discretion is also important, being authentic doesn't mean that we always say everything that we could say. It does mean that what we say is genuine and that we bring our true selves to our conversation.

Integrity keeps our conversations meaningful. When Jesus reminds us to "let our yes be yes and our no be no," he is not just giving us rules about swearing oaths. He is reminding us that our conversations should be places of wholeness, not places of duplicity or manipulation. If we have integrity, our conversations will not be full of empty promises that we know we are unlikely to keep: "I'll pray for you," "I'll call you later," "I'd love to volunteer for that" can be ways of looking good to others while selling out our own integrity. Instead, our conversations can be places where we clean up messes and make deep commitments.

It takes courage to engage in dialogue, especially in the midst of conflict and change. When we are brave enough to be vulnerable, to define ourselves clearly, to listen deeply to another person, our courage moves us and our relationships to a new level. Superficial and manipulative conversation often originates from the fear of bringing our true selves to our dialogue.

The apostle Paul reminds us, "And above all, put on love." In dialogue, love is both the means and the end. We love enough to care about the outcome of the conversation as much for the other person as for ourselves. We are careful not to use words to dominate or bully or try to win. In love, we work to understand and to be understood; in love, we tackle the crucial conversations, moving past our comfort level to give the relationship a fighting chance; in love, we use words to keep our transformation alive and create possibilities in the lives of others.

Going Deeper

When we practice the art of dialogue, everything changes. Our words become a means of grace and a source of power. We can cast vision, manage disagreements, make things safe, and keep change moving forward. And remember, deep change happens at the speed of conversation. Let's make our conversations count.

References and Additional Resources

Heifetz, Ronald and Marty Linsky. *Leadership on the Line: Staying Alive through the Dangers of Leading.* Boston, MA: Harvard Business School Publishing, 2002.

Patterson, Kerry, Joseph Grenny, Ron McMillan, and Al Switzler. *Crucial Conversations: Tools for Talking When Stakes Are High.* New York: McGraw-Hill, 2002.

Senge, Peter. *The Fifth Discipline: The Art and Practice of the Learning Organization.* New York, NY: Doubleday, 1990.

Chapter 15
From Good Intentions to Measurable Accountability

Jim Herrington

Loving and empowering accountability acts as scaffolding, providing the structure and support we need as we are learning new ways of living. Meaningful accountability goes far beyond the legalistic, anemic check-ins that many of us are familiar with. When we enter into accountability, we have help in taking responsibility for ourselves, honoring our word, learning new skills, and moving toward missional living.

Congregations, too, can benefit from accountability to help avoid usual pitfalls and approach the change process with courage and consistency. When congregations get stuck, a coach can help them find ways around the obstacles and challenge them to approach problems differently. When we add accountability to the process of deep change, we are no longer left only to ourselves and what we know—we now also have access to a process that supports our transformation.

*T*hroughout this book we have been holding Jesus up as the most fully differentiated, emotionally mature human being to ever live. Despite pressure from the enemy, his family, religious leaders, and his friends, Jesus stayed calm and clear-headed, and never wavered from his mission. He had an intimate relationship with God and only did those things that he saw God doing. There was something about the nature of Jesus's inner life that made it possible for him to always hear God's voice and then fully obey. Obeying was not always easy, but Jesus always did it.

Was Jesus's capacity to obey unique and beyond our ability? It is my belief that Jesus *learned* obedience (Luke 2:52: Heb. 5:8), and that it is possible for us to learn obedience as well. Said in another way, it is possible for us to close the gaps that exist between the behaviors to which God calls us and our current practices. In fact, in the Ridder Church Renewal process, we believe that it is both possible and necessary to close those gaps. If we are to join God in achieving God's mission in the world, we must increasingly be conformed to the image of Christ. The apostle Paul admonishes us clearly: "Do not conform to the pattern of this world, but be transformed by the renewing of your mind. Then you will be able to test and approve what God's will is—his good, pleasing and perfect will" (Rom. 12:2, NIV).

As Drew Poppleton described in Chapter 3, we believe that personal transformation precedes congregational transformation. So what is an individual to do when they don't or can't follow Jesus's lead in always hearing and obeying the voice of God? In this chapter we write about the importance of accountability in the journey of personal and congregational transformation.

Many of us don't have an empowering relationship with accountability. On the one hand, we have had bad experiences with accountability in which we were shamed or condemned for not reaching our goals or living into our guiding principles. On the other hand, none of us is immune to the sin of sloth, otherwise known as laziness. Life is challenging enough already, and the cost of growth that comes with accountability is often more than we want to take on. You are encouraged to be aware of both of these concerns as you read and reflect upon the nature of personal accountability and congregational accountability.

Personal Accountability

Jesus had the capacity within himself, based on his relationship with God, to be consistently faithful to his mission. He was able to be and to do all to which God called him. I believe that should be the goal of every follower of Christ. Imagine a congregation that is full of people with the capacity to consistently both hear and obey God.

If we follow Jesus's example, the source of authority in our lives should come from within us, where as a result of an intimate relationship with God, we hear God's call to take on character traits consistent with the fruit of the Spirit described in Galatians 5:22–23, and to take certain actions such as being on a reconciling mission with God in the places where we spend most of our day.

What is a Christ-follower to do when he can't discern God's calling— or having discerned it, is powerless to get into faithful and fruitful action? In the journey of personal transformation, when I can't do what God is calling me to do, I need someone outside of myself to hold me accountable. This is a humbling reality, and pride often stands in the way of getting into action to seek the accountability needed.

Asking for accountability does not mean we enter into a relationship where we allow someone to order us around or tell us what to do, giving up our free will and our ability to think for ourselves. It means that we choose to enter into a trusting relationship with a more experienced follower of Jesus who can pray for us, share his or her experience, and offer wise counsel and encouragement. In the relationship of accountability, the one who is being held accountable is ultimately responsible for what he or she chooses to take on.

The goal is for the outside accountability to help me grow the spiritual muscles in my inner self so that eventually the source of accountability moves *from* the person to whom I am being accountable *to* within me where I consistently listen to and obey the voice of God.

My Own Story

By the time I became a young adult, I had learned to use anger as a tool to protect myself. When I felt vulnerable or threatened, I would get angry. The more intense the threat, the more anger I expressed.

I was twenty-five years old and serving on the staff of a mid-sized congregation in Fort Worth, Texas. I was one of four staff members who served with the senior pastor and on the particular day that I'm describing, our senior pastor had called a Saturday morning staff meeting. I don't remember all of what led up to my outburst, but I remember clearly that my anger boiled up in me to the point of rage. I rose to my feet and shoved the round table where we were seated. Coffee went flying everywhere. I stuck my index finger right in the face of the senior pastor and yelled, "You can stick this job where the sun doesn't shine. I'm going home." I know it's not pretty, but it is what actually happened.

I left the meeting and went home. For the rest of the day and through the night, I was filled with anxiety. What had I done? Why had I done it? What were the consequences going to be? I was certain that on Monday I would be fired. On Sunday I went to church because I got paid to be there. The congregation was large enough that I was able to avoid any personal conversations with the senior pastor. Sunday night was even worse. I knew that on Monday I would have to face him. He would fire me. It was another fitfully sleepless night.

Monday morning I screwed up my courage and headed to the office. The pastor met me at the door. As I walked in he said, "You know, we have to talk about what happened on Saturday."

"I know," I said. "Let's get it over with."

He asked me to come into his office where we sat down. I braced myself for the firing, and he said, "You know Jim, you are one of the finest young pastors I have ever had the privilege of working with."

I was totally disoriented. I was expecting judgment and I was getting grace. It took me a minute to gain my sense of equilibrium so that I could hear what he was saying.

"You are a really gifted young man, but there are some things going on inside of you that if you don't get them worked out, you will never live into your full potential." He went on, "You must get some accountability from an outside person to help you learn the source of your anger so you can learn to overcome it. I've taken the liberty of setting that up for you. If you want to continue to work here, you must do what I'm asking. I want to introduce you to Joe Cross. I've asked him to see if he can help."

I didn't know Joe and didn't have a clue how he could help, but I went to meet him the next day filled with gratitude at this unexpected turn of events. Joe was a pastor of another church about two miles down the road from the one I served. At the start of our first meeting he said, "You've got to promise me that you will not act out your anger like you did last Saturday at the staff meeting ever again." Then he smiled and said, "And when you break that promise, you have to agree to tell me that you broke it."

I promised and agreed.

And for the next two years, Joe met me every Tuesday afternoon for a couple of hours. We talked about my anger. I told him the story of my childhood and adolescence. I confessed to him other outbursts of rage that were a part of my young adult story. He helped me see how some childhood wounds had turned into negative vows. He listened deeply every time we were together.

I broke my promise several times in those two years, and as I had agreed, every time I confessed those experiences to Joe. He was always forgiving and never shamed me. He thanked me and said, "We've still got work to do." Sometimes we would just talk. He gave me things to read. He had me go back to people at whom I had gotten angry and repent to them for what I had done. He didn't seem to have a formula, but he always had me in action.

I did not notice the change at first—it was almost imperceptible. The wounds in me were being healed. It wasn't that I quit getting angry, but I did notice that increasingly, I was able to contain the anger. Often after an episode where I had successfully contained the anger, I would meet Joe on Tuesday and tell him what had happened. He would celebrate with me and there was this growing sense that I was being changed.

Over time, I moved from needing Joe for my accountability to having the internal resources that flowed from my relationship with God to obey Paul's admonition to be angry and not sin (Eph. 4:26). I will forever be grateful for the loving accountability that I got from Joe. It changed the trajectory of my life.

Toni's Story

Toni is a friend who participated in the Faithwalking experience in Houston. While she was in Faithwalking, she found a renewed sense of vitality in what Faithwalking calls *the spiritual workout.*

The spiritual workout is more than a daily quiet time. At the beginning of the Faithwalking journey, participants are asked to identify several spiritual disciplines that they will practice throughout the twenty-four-week experience. Some are daily disciplines like reading the Bible, meditating, or studying contemporary Christian literature. Some are weekly disciplines like a one-day fast or participating in a corporate worship experience. Some are occasional disciplines like a quarterly retreat of silence and solitude.

In the first session of Faithwalking 201, each participant gives his or her commitment toward doing this spiritual workout for the duration of the process. When Toni finished her Faithwalking 201 course, by her own testimony, she had been transformed in several ways. When asked what made the most difference, she said, "It was the regular practice of my spiritual workout."

As the regular accountability that Faithwalking provided came to an end, Toni became less consistent with her spiritual workout. Over time, her workout almost disappeared. One day, desperate to get back on track, she called her Faithwalking coach and told him what had happened.

In the Faithwalking experience, all participants in phase two of the training are assigned a coach. Each week the Faithwalking participant has assigned homework, and at the end of the week there is a coaching call. The coach checks in with the participant to ask if all the homework has been done. If it has all been done, the coach asks the participant to reflect on her experience and learning. If the homework has not been done, the coach helps the participant explore the obstacles that stood in the way of completing the assignments.

Toni called her coach and said she hadn't realized how dependent she had been on the accountability.

"Would you be willing to hold me accountable for my spiritual workout again?"

Her coach reminded Toni that in Faithwalking, the accountability was a built-in part of the process.

"But now that Faithwalking is over, it seems to me that you need to provide the accountability," her coach told Toni.

"But it's clear that I can't do that."

Her coach paused for a moment.

"When you were in Faithwalking, I called you every week and asked if you did your spiritual workout. What if I agree to hold you accountable now, but you take responsibility for the call?"

For about four months, Toni took the initiative to call her coach to check in. She missed a few weeks and when she did, her coach would check in with her. But, mostly Toni initiated the accountability.

One day at about four months later, Toni said to her coach, "I think I have more confidence that I can stay the course now. I'd like to be able to call you if I get stuck, but I'd like to try this on my own again."

I saw Toni at about the eight-month mark and asked how it was going.

"It's going really well. I've never had so much consistency in my spiritual workout, and this experience has grown my confidence that God can trust me with other assignments now. As I look back, I had a lot of power that came to me from my spiritual workout, but I had failed to take seriously the impact of accountability. When I lost my way and went back to my coach, he was so wise in not taking responsibility for me but in helping me take responsibility for myself. Without him as an accountability partner, I do not think I would have made it."

Honoring My Word

In the Ridder Church Renewal, we have learned and are practicing a way of growing our capacity to manage ourselves in the midst of an anxious system so that we can hear the voice of God's Spirit and obey—even in moments of high anxiety. In Chapter 4, we describe a powerful process that we call honoring your word. To be transformed we must give our word to being and doing what God calls us to be and do. We *must* give our word, and when we do, we empower the accountability process. All of us will have gaps between what we give our word to and our actual practice.

Honoring my word is what I do when I can't keep my word. I honor my word (1) by acknowledging I didn't keep my word; (2) by getting present to the impact of not keeping my word; (3) by offering a heartfelt apology; and (4) by repromising. This four-step structure of honoring my word gives me a framework for healthy, life-giving accountability.

When you and the person to whom you are being accountable share this integrity framework, accountability can begin by giving your word to yourself, to God, and to your accountability partner for the change God is trying to bring in your life. Then in a relationship of trust and openness, any time you don't keep your word, you confess that to your accountability partner. He or she then holds you accountable for getting into action to faithfully honor your word.

Finding a good accountability partner is essential. Making a good match may be a little like dating—you keep looking until you find the right partner. How do you know if you've found the right accountability partner? I would suggest the following.

First, choose someone who will take the relationship seriously but not too seriously. For accountability to work, your partner must have a vested interest in your spiritual growth and development. They care enough to serve you, to establish some of the parameters described below, and they follow through faithfully. They serve you but they are not in charge of accountability. That is always your role. In the early stages you may relinquish that role to your partner, as Toni did to her coach. But you can take the responsibility back because you are in charge. Trisha Taylor has said to me on more than one occasion, "When I care more about someone's growth and development than they do, something is out of balance." So you want your accountability partner to care, but not too much. You'll know you have a good partner when that person can find this balance.

Second, determine how you want accountability to be expressed. Accountability is a very personal thing. I tend to be a very direct person in my communication style. I want my accountability partner to be really direct also. I know others who are put off by really direct communication. They like the message delivered more gently. Neither directness nor gentleness is "right." They are right for a given person in a given context.

Sit down with your accountability partner and have a conversation. If your partner is not familiar with the content in Chapter 4 on integrity and particularly the part of the chapter related to honoring one's word, share that information with her. Are there specific questions you want your partner to ask you? What do you need from your partner when you have not done what you said you would do? Are there certain words or phrases that trigger shame in you? Ask your partner for what you need. The right partner will take the job seriously in terms that meet your self-expressed needs for accountability.

Third, set a beginning and end time for the duration of this relationship. I've had the same accountability partner for nearly two years. However, every six months we have a specific conversation about the relationship and whether my partner is willing to continue serving in this manner. That provides a place to assess how things are working and to make any adjustments needed.

Here's one final word: I distinguish between a coach and an accountability partner. A coach has a specific kind of training that an accountability partner does not have. For a while now I have had both a coach and an accountability partner. While I often talk to each about some of the same things, the nature of the conversations is different. The accountability relationship is peer-to-peer and I establish the framework within which the accountability takes place. In the coaching relationship,

I have given authority to the coach to take me outside of my comfort zone, to push me, to challenge me—in a way that doesn't happen in a well-defined accountability relationship.

Personal transformation precedes congregational transformation, and personal accountability is a key tool that grows your capacity to hear God's voice and obey God's voice in all of life's circumstances.

Practice and Reflect

Set this reading aside for a few minutes and get your journal. Reflect on something about yourself that you would like to see changed—something where there is a gap between your current practice and God's intended design for you. Maybe you'd like more patience. Or perhaps you would like to be more joyful or to express more courage. Maybe you are confused about your calling and would like to get more clarity. Choose something that, if you saw dramatic improvement in your ability to live into that change, doing so would make a big difference in your relationships and in your impact in the world.

Once you've gotten the change identified, think of a person in your life who seems to have a strong of mastery of that trait. Now, in your prayer life, imagine what it would be like to go to that person and ask them to hold you accountable for developing the character trait that you see in them and that you want in you. As you imagine that, what do you experience? What do you feel? Where do you find resistance? What do you fear? Hold all of that before God and ask God to speak to you.

Now, make a call and initiate the process of engaging an accountability partner who will support you as you seek this change in your life.

Congregational Accountability

Congregations face similar challenges with integrity gaps. They have given their word to be on mission with God as God seeks to reconcile the world to himself. Yet congregations are often internally focused, self-absorbed, and/or in conflict with each other. They have big gaps between what God intends and what they actually practice. Congregations need accountability for many of the same reasons that individuals do, because left to their own devices, they don't seem to be able to close the gap between what they have given their word to and their actual practice.

In Ridder Church Renewal, participants are taught to use four tools that guide the congregational accountability process: (1) a clear, shared, and compelling narrative of current reality; (2) a clear, shared, and compelling narrative of God's emerging future; (3) clear metrics about how they will gauge progress; and (4) a coach who helps ask good accountability questions.

In Chapter 10, Nate Pyle wrote about how to develop the narratives of current reality and God's emerging future. In the context of accountability, you might go back and reread that chapter. Congregations should develop these narratives in a way that they are clear, shared, and compelling, and if they cannot do this on their own, they need the accountability and the support of a coach.

Once these narratives are in place, the congregation should develop metrics—what they will measure—to help them assess whether they are making progress toward their emerging future. Every congregation that is represented by the pastors writing this book has made significant progress in this journey, so I could tell many stories to illustrate what I'm trying to communicate. For the sake of brevity, I will tell a part of the story of Midland Reformed Church in Midland, Michigan where Mike DeRuyter serves as the pastor.

Midland Reformed Church's Story

Mike and his Ridder Church Renewal Team took what they learned about generating and sustaining creative tension and worked over a two-year period of time to come to a missional focus for the church. In doing their work about current reality they discovered that their county had a very high percentage of single parents who lived at or below the poverty level. Over time, they began to sense God calling them to garner the resources of their congregation to make a measurable impact on this group of people. On their web site, midlandreformed.org, they describe their mission: "Our Missional Focus is to bring hope and wholeness in Christ to distressed single parent families of Midland County."

Recently, I asked Mike about the metrics for this mission and he responded, "Our congregational missional focus is measured by: (1) tracking the number of collaborative partnerships we form with other congregations, agencies, businesses, and organizations, (2) counting the number of mentoring relationships we form with single parents or children of single parents, (3) and tracking the physical resource assistance we provide for single parent families."

Many congregations develop the narratives about current reality and God's emerging future but then fail to agree on metrics. Often the by-product is a set of well-discerned documents that end up sitting on the shelf because they fail to give the congregation a sense of progress being made and obstacles that must be overcome. The metrics component of the accountability process adds that dimension. Midland Reformed models accountability well.

Practice and Reflect

What is the narrative in your congregation regarding current reality and God's emerging future? If you know this narrative, what are the metrics that the congregation uses to track progress? If you don't know the answer to these questions, ponder the reasons why. Is this something to which your congregation has not given rigorous attention? If not, what are some of the obstacles that may be standing in the way?

Part 4—Equipping Ourselves for More Effective Leadership

Resistance to Accountability

Often congregations resist the work of getting the components of accountability in place. I see three common reasons why:

Some congregations resist because of unresolved past experiences. One pastor who was doing this work called me about two months into the process and said, "We are stuck. I am finding a lot of resistance." As I asked a series of questions to more fully understand, I learned that the congregation had a leadership crisis ten years earlier. A youth pastor had been asked to leave. Some said the decision was made because of insubordination and poor job performance. Others said the senior pastor used the youth pastor as a scapegoat to cover her own poor job performance. There was a fair amount of conflict that was handled poorly during this time and then, two years after firing the youth pastor, the senior pastor resigned and moved to another congregation.

After a long interim, the church called a new pastor. About two years after becoming a part of the church, the new pastor asked them to do the work of developing the current reality narrative. As I talked with the pastor, it became clear that this past conflict was looming in the space of the current conversations. Five years later, unresolved feelings were still present. Trust of leadership had been impacted and not addressed. While no one was saying, "We don't want to do this work because it means we will have to dredge up the pain of that past unresolved experience," that was in fact where the resistance was.

The pastor convened three of his wisest elders and suggested that before they could work on the current reality narrative, they needed to name this problem and do some work to help bring healing and closure. This is exactly what they did. They went to the congregation's consistory and had a crucial conversation about the impact of the previous experience. They developed and carried out a plan that allowed congregational members to share their experience, to grieve the losses, and to put the experience in their past. The pastor reported that this experience provided the impetus to begin making real progress toward developing a clear, shared and compelling narrative of the congregation's current reality.

Some congregations resist because of painful past experiences with getting clear about God's emerging future. The idea that congregations should discern God's leadership and make plans based on that leadership is nothing new in congregational life. In the '70s and '80s, we called this long-range planning. In the '90s and well into the 2000s, most major denominations called it strategic planning. More often these days, we call these processes congregational discernment. Whatever name we give it, virtually every congregation comes to this process with a history of planning, and for many, there are two kinds of pain in that history.

The first kind of pain is the pain of spending hundreds of hours, sacrificing time and energy, and then seeing nothing change. Elaborate strategic planning documents get put on a shelf and the changes fail to be implemented. No one intends that to happen. There is not a big hoax where leaders deliberately mislead the members of the congregation. Often these plans fail because the goals that are contained within the plans fail to take seriously the underlying, and very normal, resistance to change. They fail to take seriously that for the plans to be implemented, congregational leaders will be required to be transformed (personal transformation precedes congregation transformation). They fail because of past pain that is unresolved. They fail because of a lack of clear metrics to measure progress. Whatever the reason, the plans do not get implemented, and congregational members are resigned and cynical about any real change taking place; therefore, energy for this work is virtually nonexistent.

In the very first congregation I served in Monroe, Louisiana, the new pastor suggested that the congregation develop a long-range plan. After he suggested this, the very candid, practical, and outspoken chairman of the deacons said, "Why would we do that? We have two previous plans that we spent hundreds of hours developing and they are still sitting on the shelf. Nothing changed as a result of those plans. Why would we waste our time working on another plan?"

The second kind of pain relates to congregations' past difficulties with learning to overcome obstacles. Plans get made and good metrics are established, and in every congregation, there will be obstacles to achieving the goals. Failure to overcome these obstacles can affect a congregation's sense of worth. Sometimes, the result is that leaders look for someone to blame—"If we just changed the worship style, then the obstacles would go away"; "If we could just start this new program, then our problems would be solved." Sometimes the blaming becomes personal and focuses on the leadership of the pastor or a staff member. No matter who or what is blamed, the result is that obstacles don't get overcome, people get hurt, and a layer of resistance to doing more planning emerges. Rather than taking a systems approach and asking, "What is each of us doing or not doing that keeps this current obstacle in place?"—we look for a scapegoat. Rather than saying, "This obstacle means that there is something to learn here. What can we learn and how would we go about learning it?"—we simply work harder at what we have been doing.

Congregational leadership must take the presence of this pain seriously. Pretending that past pain is not present is a formula for disaster. Talking openly about the pain is a place to begin. Leaders must acknowledge that this work is going to be costly and that it is essential. Leaders must tell the truth about the deep changes that the culture has endured and the challenges congregations across the country have and are facing as they learn how to respond effectively.

Some congregations resist because they fear that if they get clear about God's emerging future, they might lose members. I have a pastor friend who frequently repeats the saying, "Clear vision both unites and divides." He is expressing the reality that congregations can amass a wide collection of people with varying opinions about the mission and vision of the church, and as long as the church doesn't try to get clear about its focus, all can more or less peacefully coexist.

In these congregations, there is often a lot of motion but no clear direction. Anyone can start a ministry. One member hears about a program that another congregation is using successfully and gets permission from the congregation's leadership to start that ministry in her congregation. Another has a particular passion that he wants expressed through the congregation's common life, and he starts a program that garners congregational resources. This becomes a pattern as the congregation allocates resources. The result is a collection of people with an eclectic set of programs that mostly serve the existing members. Over time there is no clear vision—just a collection of good activities that take the congregation in a variety of competing directions. So, while there is a lot of motion, there is no clear direction.

In these congregations, there is resistance to getting a clear, shared, and compelling narrative of God's emerging future because when the congregation says "yes" to a direction, it will mean saying "no" to the things that do not contribute to moving in that direction. Whenever this becomes clear, the congregational leadership will face resistance. For some people, it is more important to keep everyone together than it is to get clear about the future to which God is calling them.

Accountability Case Study

Several years ago I served as a consultant to a congregation in Miami with a lot of motion but no clear direction. It was a congregation of about eight hundred active worshipers on any given Sunday morning. The congregation had been built largely around the winsome personality, excellent preaching, and terrific work ethic of the senior pastor. Over several years, the pastor had quietly but persistently been asking himself the question, "Is our congregation making an impact in the community? If we fell off the map tomorrow, would our neighborhood or our city miss us?" Those questions led to a crisis of faith for the pastor, and that crisis led to him register for a congregational leadership course that I was teaching. We developed a good working relationship, and he asked me to serve as a coach to him as he began to help his congregation get a clear sense of how they would make real impact in their neighborhood and city.

He convened his leadership team, an existing group that had been elected by the congregation to develop strategy around the congregation's mission and vision. The pastor had shared his questions about the congregation's impact on the community. He had engaged this team by expressing concerns about the lack of impact and letting them know what he was learning at every point along the way. So, when he told the team that he wanted to bring me in to assist with their work, they were not surprised. The team had a growing sense that the pastor was going to ask them to help him lead in some kind of change. In the face of that understanding, the team was ready to start asking the question, "What must change in order for us to have more impact in our community?"

I worked with the pastor and his team to establish a process and a timetable for developing two narratives—one of current reality and one of God's emerging future—and of establishing metrics that would help the congregation know when progress was being made. The team was divided into subgroups to do research on current reality. Some looked at key measures of success within the congregation—attendance, giving, new members, mission involvement. Some looked at the community. They got information on the demographics and psychographics within a five-mile radius. They interviewed key community leaders to learn about community assets and needs.

After working for a month in their subgroups, each group wrote a report on their findings. These reports were compiled into a notebook and distributed to the entire team. Team members agreed to become familiar with all the content in preparation for a weekend retreat. Over the weekend each group presented their findings to the team and the findings were discussed. After the retreat, the findings were summarized in a document they called "Here's What's Happening Now in Our Church and Community."

The document was mailed to every member of the congregation. Over a six-week period, the congregation interacted with this narrative. The pastor preached on it four times, focusing on different findings and exploring those findings in light of his understanding of biblical mission. The team conducted small group listening sessions to share their findings and ask for feedback. One town hall meeting was conducted where the entire congregation was asked to come together for a congregational dialogue about the impact of the findings.

Based on feedback that they got in these various settings, the team developed a revised draft of the findings. They distributed this to the congregation and invited all the elected leaders of the congregation—elders, deacons, Sunday School teachers, program leaders, and staff to attend a weekend retreat in which they would use the "Here's What's Happening Now in Our Church and Community, 2.0" to begin focusing on a vision for the future in which the congregation would have more impact on its community.

Out of this weekend retreat, a clear vision began to emerge. The leadership team nurtured the development of this second narrative to completion. Though I will not describe the visioning process for writing the narrative about God's emerging future in the detail that I just described the manner in which they came to a current reality narrative, I wanted you to see the care and patience that was taken in getting broad engagement in this work.

The visioning process unfolded over an eighteen-month period of time with several new directions emerging. One of the major shifts occurred when the leadership team determined that they needed to move away from content-oriented Sunday morning Bible study classes to missional small groups that met in homes or workplaces. The team established the following metrics: "We will measure success by the number of missional small groups that we launch, by the presence of a clear missional focus in the community for each group, and by the stories of life change that we hear as these missional communities do their work. Our goal is to establish 10 missional communities in the first year and to have 100 missional communities in five years."

It was a significant shift and a bold goal, and the leaders knew that they needed to go slow and develop clear understanding within the congregation for why they thought this change was needed.

They held a congregational meeting where they told the congregation they were considering this change and announced a series of small group meetings where they would share more details about their reasoning, answer questions, and listen to feedback. Immediately following the congregational meeting, one very vocal church member said to the pastor, "I'm opposed to this. If we go in this direction, what will happen to the class that Jack teaches?"

Jack had been a part of the church for ten years. He moved to Miami from Birmingham, Alabama and as he was visiting the church, he asked about the opportunity to teach a Bible class. Jack was a skilled communicator who had a seminary degree. Early in his adult life, he left his work in the local church to go to work in business, but he loved to teach and wanted to attend a church that would provide the opportunity for him to do so.

Within a year of joining, Jack was asked to teach a class and the class grew quickly. Eventually the only space that would contain the seventy-five people who wanted to hear his weekly lecture was the church's worship center. Before the leadership team announced its plans to move in this new direction, two of the team members had actually gone to Jack to have a personal conversation about what they were about to propose. They acknowledged that this change would have a big impact on him, and they were concerned about that. They also stated that they were convinced that God had spoken clearly to them as a team and this move was an important one for the church. They hoped he would find a way to be supportive.

For several weeks following the announcement by the leadership team, the anxiety in the congregation was fairly high. It was not just concern for Jack that drove this anxiety. This shift was a significant change, and many had questions and concerns. The leadership team succeeded in remaining mostly calm and carried out their work in the town hall meetings. Over several weeks, the anxiety began to calm down, and it looked like the shift was going to be easier than the leadership team had anticipated.

Then the bombshell was dropped. Jack asked for an appointment to see the pastor. When the designated hour came, Jack showed up with two other members who were active in his Sunday morning Bible class. They announced to the pastor that they did not want to be a disruptive force in the church, but they could not support the direction the leadership team was going. After a couple of meetings with members of the class, a group of them had decided that they were simply going to quietly join another church in the community who had a commitment to Sunday morning Bible study classes.

When the dust had settled, thirty-five members left the church. To their credit, the pastor and leadership team remained mostly calm. They had a clear sense of God's leadership in the direction they were taking and this helped immensely. There was a season of time where the anxiety remained high but manageable, and over time the congregation made this transition successfully.

Coaching

Throughout this book we have stressed the importance of understanding systems as a force that is at work in the life of any congregation. One thing about systems is that when I am a part of the system, it is often really difficult to see how the system is impacting me and how I am impacting the system. In working on my own personal transformation and in working on congregational transformation, there is great power in the accountability of a coach who stands outside the system.

In the Faithwalking community, we discovered that having a personal coach to support a person in the personal transformation process increased positive results dramatically—so much so that now, every person who comes through the Faithwalking experience is assigned a coach.

Having a coach for the congregational process also increases positive results dramatically. In general, there are two kinds of coaching experiences available in the marketplace today. Content-neutral coaching is coaching in which the coach listens thoughtfully, asks good open-ended questions, and helps the one being coached to choose actions she will take between calls to achieve her goals. Content-specific coaching is all of that, and the coach's questions are guided by the specific content of a book or a training experience. Ridder Church Renewal offers content-specific coaching that is built around the ten core components of our training.

The Reformed Church in America and the Christian Reformed Church (the two partner denominations in Ridder Church Renewal) place an extremely high value on coaching and provide an extensive network of content neutral coaches for pastors and local congregations. Especially in the early stages of the process, and for many, throughout the process, having a coach is an essential part of getting a successful outcome.

If you are reading this book and are not a part of Ridder Church Renewal, I encourage you to check with your local denominational entity to ascertain what coaching resources are available. I just completed a quick Google search for pastoral coaches and numerous entities and individuals came up. If the coach is not attached to a denomination or a reputable group, be sure to determine if they have any certification and ask for references. The time it takes to find a good coach will be good time spent.

Going Deeper

In this chapter I have held up for you the core conviction that accountability is essential in the transformation journey. Personal transformation and congregational transformation are not possible apart from an intentional and empowering relationship with accountability. While personal transformation precedes congregational transformation, they also occur side by side. As you begin to get accountability for your own personal transformation, you will be more effective in engaging in the work of congregational transformation. And, as the congregation begins to be transformed, you will be required to grow as a leader.

My colleague Trisha Taylor often says, "It's like walking with two feet—first one and then the other. It is the rhythm that keeps you balanced and moving ahead." So, where is accountability being expressed in your life and in the life of your congregation? What steps do you need to take to overcome obstacles that stand in the way of an empowering relationship with accountability? What personal goals is God calling you to in your own journey of transformation and who will hold you accountable? What is God's emerging future, and what are the metrics in place that help the congregation know about progress and obstacles?

Giving clear, focused attention to these questions and getting the needed accountability for progress will contribute significantly to faithful and fruitful missional living.

References and Additional Resources

Collins, Jim. *Good to Great and the Social Sectors: A Monograph to Accompany Good to Great.* New York: HarperCollins, 2005.

Conclusion
From a Program-Driven Institution to a Learning Community

Jim Herrington

There is no final destination on this journey toward missional living and church renewal. There truly are no quick fixes or one-size-fits-all templates. Our highest hope was that we could go farther and faster in our learning together than we ever could alone.

The best part of this journey began when we realized that we really had become a learning community. We saw that we were going deep in challenging ourselves in new ways and we were consistently sharing our learning with each other. We told the stories about our successes and our failures, and we celebrated both as we moved together toward real transformation.

*T*hroughout this book we have been attempting to hold up a picture of the local congregation as a learning community. In this final chapter we want to define a learning community as clearly and explicitly as we can: *a learning community is a small group of people who are deeply committed to continuously improving their capacity to achieve results that truly matter to them,* a definition adapted from the work of Peter Senge.

I first heard the words *learning community* in 1990 when I read Senge's *The Fifth Discipline: The Art and Practice of the Learning Organization.* Senge asserted that in the post-modern information age, the pace of change was so rapid that the only organizations that would thrive were those that *learned how to learn* more rapidly. He then proposed five disciplines that leaders of organizations like local congregations could master in order to accelerate their capacity to learn.

I was so inspired by these ideas that my colleagues, Mike Bonem and James Furr, and I wrote *Leading Congregational Change.* One of our goals in writing was to make learning organization ideas available to local congregations. Since *Leading Congregational Change* was published in 2000, we have been experimenting with developing learning communities in a variety of congregational settings.

Ridder Church Renewal is the best and most successful working example of a learning community that I've experienced. One of the memorable moments of transformation in this experience occurred in the first Ridder pastors' retreat at Camp Tejas near Austin, Texas. Trisha and I were standing at the front of the room as we were gathering for the first meeting. The pastors were sitting around the edge of the room, and Trisha and I noticed and commented to each other that their body language seemed at best distant, and at worst hostile.

Authenticity is a core value of the Ridder Church Renewal process, so Trisha and I each began by authentically telling a part of our story. We told the real version, not the cleaned-up Sunday School version. There was a noticeable shift in the group's posture, and with each passing moment, the pastors opened up. By the time the retreat was over, a significant bond had been formed within the group, and between the group and Trisha and me. One of the pastors told me on the final day, "I came because one of our synod leaders asked me to come, and I wanted to respect him. And, it was three days in Texas in the midst of a brutal Michigan winter," he said with a smile on his face. "But, my internal dialogue was resigned and cynical. A lot of money and time was being spent on another program that was not going to change anything for me or my church." He paused and then he said, "I've never had an experience quite like this. The conversations were so authentic—so real and at times even raw. This experience has changed me."

That was the beginning of our shared journey into building the Ridder Church Renewal learning community. In this chapter, I want to share some practices that you can use as you seek to develop a learning community in your own context.

A learning community is *a small group of people* who are deeply committed to continuously improving their capacity to achieve results that truly matter to them. In my experience, five to nine people who are working together within a congregation can make a huge difference. Rather than attempting to legislate change through the congregation's governing processes, a learning community functions like yeast. The small group gets clear about results and then works to achieve those results. As they make progress, others in the congregation are drawn to and impacted by the learning that is taking place and the results that are being achieved.

In a learning community, the small group of people shares three common characteristics.

First, each person is growing in his or her capacity to live an emotionally mature life. Leaders who are part of congregations that are making an impact don't just know the right things to do. They have the capacity to do the right thing, even when doing the right thing stretches them way out of their comfort zone.

Second, as a part of the journey to emotional maturity, these leaders get clear about their negative vows, share them with their learning community, and ask to be held accountable for living into a set of positive vows that empower them to reach the goals they have for themselves and their congregation.

Third, these leaders are committed to a "systems view" of the world. In this book we have offered insights into understanding living systems and organizational systems. Learning to think systems and then to watch the process of anxiety at work in the system is one of the most powerful ways that learning communities avoid getting undermined or sabotaged.

Standale Reformed Church's Ridder Team has made great strides in becoming a learning community. In the early stages of their experience, they heard the call to *take responsibility for your learning.* After listening to presentations on the various core components of the Ridder curriculum made at our retreats, they would return home and work diligently at mastering what they had learned. As they sought to learn to live missionally, they began to care for a person from their community, and then the circle of care was extended to that person's family. This particular family was not functioning well at this season of their life and had a ton of needs. Pastor Jessica Shults is quick to point out that the Ridder Team did not generate this opportunity. It came to them, and when it did, they faithfully responded.

Mike, one of the Ridder team members, shared about this individual the team cared for: "She was not the kind of person who would normally come to our church, but in retrospect, it's clear that she represents a lot of people who live in our neighborhood." Step-by-step, and then day-by-day, the team reached out, ministered to and cared for this family. Of necessity, they involved other people in addressing the multiple challenges that this newcomer and her family faced.

As the new family came to Christ and was integrated in the congregation, the congregation was changed. At a Ridder gathering in the Spring of 2013, several members of the Standale Team told the story of how this experience was changing the congregation's mental model of ministry, challenging some of them out of their comfort zones, and drawing more people into the learning process. The most common word they used to refer to the experience was *hope.*

A learning community is a small group of people *who are deeply committed* to continuously improving their capacity to achieve results that truly matter to them. Learning communities only succeed when members of the community are deeply committed. Here, it is important to distinguish commitment from compliance. Far too often in local congregations, individuals agree to serve and participate on the basis of compliance. The pastor or a key leader asks for volunteers to teach a class or serve on a committee. Individuals often say yes, not because they are deeply committed to the task, but because they want to please the pastor or key leader. Learning communities cannot function with team members who operate at the level of compliance. Deep commitment is required.

For the learning community to succeed, team members must be committed to the renewal of the church as a vibrant force that courageously loves the people in their community. They are not attempting to recreate the past. They have a clear-eyed view of how much the world has changed and are committed to being a force for love in the real world that surrounds their home, their workplace, and their congregation.

Because the journey of congregational transformation is so daunting, learning communities must ask the question, "How do we sustain commitment over time?" This work is much more like a marathon than a sprint.

How do you sustain commitment over a long period of time? We've attempted to communicate the relationship between personal transformation and congregational transformation. Commitment is sustained as each team member is being encouraged, held accountable, and challenged to keep his or her own transformation journey alive. There is a rhythm to planning and praying, to meeting and retreating, to problem-solving and story-telling. There is no magic formula for sustaining commitment over time. Teams must ask and answer this question for themselves and periodically assess the level of commitment that is present.

One big obstacle to sustaining this effort is what happens when you get stuck. You've been to the retreat and gotten some new information. You've been given homework to do back in your context. Then, as you start working, something doesn't make sense or you can't figure out how to move ahead. The first group of pastors who went through Ridder Church Renewal responded to this concern in a creative way. One way they took responsibility for their learning was by forming a Facebook group. A pastor and his or her Ridder Team would get stuck or face an obstacle. That pastor would then describe the issue and ask the rest of the group to say what they were learning. The responses were rich and instructive—not just for the person posing the question but for all of us, and that practice continues today, five years later.

A learning community is a small group of people who are deeply committed *to continuously improving their capacity* to achieve results that truly matter to them. We say it often and with some fervor because we believe it to be profoundly true. Personal transformation precedes congregational transformation.

A commitment to personal transformation is an essential component of a successful learning community. Each member should have clear goals for personal transformation that are shared with the rest of the learning community. These goals should include, but not be limited to, growing capacity to manage anxiety in the midst of change initiatives, closing gaps between espoused values (such as authenticity, integrity, courage and love), and making big personal contributions to achieving the community's goals.

Resistance and how you respond to resistance is a central component of work that learning communities face. When you seek to get different results than the ones you are currently getting, you will experience resistance. What is your automatic response to resistance? Is your response a self-protective one? Does your response help the community achieve its goals?

When Ridder Church Renewal was first launched, Drew Poppleton and I had an adversarial relationship. We each triggered vows that the other had. At almost every point along the way in the first two retreats, Drew was resistant. In fact at times he was combative. He would make fun of some of the learning exercises we asked him to do. He talked to others at his table while presentations were being made. In general, he was a disruptive force in the process.

I was resistant to his resistance. Pretty early on, I wrote him off as a troublemaker and as someone who I would have to overcome or overpower (my vows showing up). I avoided him during breaks and at meal times. I was always right on the verge of shaming him for his behavior.

Toward the end of the second retreat, I realized what was happening. I had a brief conversation with Trisha to get some coaching. Then, I went to Drew. I confessed that I was frustrated with his behavior and had written him off as a troublemaker. I asked him to tell me about the impact that my behavior had on him. He was really open and authentic with me. It was a messy, authentic, painful, and ultimately hopeful conversation. Something shifted!

Since those early days, Drew has become a good friend. He is a major contributor to my learning and to the learning of our Ridder Team on an ongoing basis. That would have been lost if each of us had not been willing to face our resistant behaviors and learn to behave in some new ways.

In the context of a Ridder learning community, one central way that we increase our capacity is by mastering the ten core components of our process—our core values, our skill sets, and our commitment to missional living—the subject matter of a large portion of this text.

The four core values that we seek to deepen are authenticity, integrity, courage, and love. While each person in your community might espouse these as values, there is likely a gap between the espoused value and the value in practice. Telling the truth about this gap and doing the work to begin closing the gap (a lifelong journey) is central to the learning community.

Five skill sets grow out of the new mental models we create. Each skill set represents a new way of thinking for most congregations and includes practices for:

- Reclaiming discipleship
- Growing emotional maturity
- Generating and sustaining creative tension
- Building high-performance teams
- Understanding your congregation as an organizational system

Finally, the tenth component is the end game. The endgame that we are after is faithful and fruitful missional living both personally and corporately. All of the first nine components contribute to getting to the end game.

A learning community is a small group of people who are deeply committed to continuously improving their capacity *to achieve results that truly matter to them*. It is not a new idea that churches must measure things. Historically we have measured attendance, offerings, and baptisms. Mostly these measures were developed from the attractional model of church, where church growth and the strength of the institution was what mattered most. It can be challenging for congregations to develop new measures that focus on mission and community impact. It is important that the learning community set big goals—contrary to traditional church leadership training that instructs you to set a goal that you know you can reach. God-sized goals empower learning communities because they have to learn and grow if the goal is going to be reached.

Learning communities can be a huge help here. They can dialogue about and experiment with the right metrics to track before asking the entire congregation to take those things on. In Ridder Church Renewal, we utilize the work of Jim Collins (2005) that is found in *Good to Great in the Social Sectors.* If your learning community has not read this short monograph together, I encourage you to read and discuss it.

Collins gives a helpful frame of reference for thinking about metrics when he distinguishes input, from outputs, from outcomes. Nate Pyle described these metrics in some detail in Chapter 12, but let me review them briefly here and give you some illustrations from a congregational learning community I'm consulting with.

Outcomes are the long range, systemic change that we hope to see. We begin with the end in mind so that our daily activities are more likely to contribute to those deep systemic changes. *Outputs* are the goals that we are seeking to reach over the next twelve to twenty-four months or more. Generally we have meetings, programs, experiences, and processes that are set up to help us achieve the goals. All of these are outputs. *Inputs* are the things we do to make the meetings, programs, experiences, and processes take place. Reading the *Good to Great* monograph and rereading Chapter 12 will give you a much richer understanding of each of these.

I worked with a congregation that formed a learning community that would serve as the yeast to help the congregation develop a growing number of learning communities focused on missional living. They started with one small group.

As this group explored the current reality of the neighborhood around the congregation, it became clear that education for children in pre-K to third grade was a critical issue that the community faced. After prayer and dialogue, and when it became clear that there was a lot of passion and commitment for this within the learning community, they agreed that they would focus their learning community's efforts around an attempt to make a big impact in this arena.

They wrote their *outcome* statement: "Over the next ten years, we will work and live in a manner that insures that every child in our community has a significant relationship with a trustworthy adult and completes the third grade, reading on grade level." Clearly this is a long-term goal that can be measured but that will have multiple causative factors. Getting clear about the outcome helped the learning community ask this question: "Of all the things we could do, what are the two or three things that we can do that *we believe* (this is always a faith proposition) will help us make a contribution to achieving our desired outcome?" This question provided their *output* statement that read: "In ten years, every child in our school district who needs a mentor will have one."

The learning community set one-, three-, and five-year goals that met both outcomes they were after. The goals they set were huge, and it was clear that apart from God's intervention and some serious learning on the part of the learning community, these goals would not be reached.

They then set out to reach their goals. They developed relationships with key principals in the neighborhood. They recruited mentors from

their own congregation and then from other congregations in the neighborhood. They planned training sessions for mentors. They published a
document that stated the need, shared the research on why mentoring was
so important, and told some stories from successful mentors in other settings. These are a few of the *inputs* they made. These inputs led to the outputs of children being mentored by a trustworthy adult. They do not yet
know if the outputs will lead to the outcome. There is always a faith element
in conducting outputs to outcomes because there is generally a big gap in
time from when you start working until the long-term results that you get.

Alert! This is an illustration, not a roadmap. We shared a part of a
story like this at one of the Ridder retreats. In the break after the session,
a small group of the participants came up to Trisha with some alarm and
anxiety in their voice. One of the group said, "We are not sure what to do.
We're afraid we can't be missional. We don't have a school with which we
can become involved." They had missed the point. This learning community took on the needs of pre-K to third grade because that was the need
they felt led to take on. They could just as easily have taken on a variety
of other things. The key is that they examined their community, found a
deep systemic need, discovered that their learning community was passionate about the need, and went to work setting big goals and measuring
progress at every step along the way. In your setting, the needs may be
different and that will determine your goals. The passions of the learning
community may be different and that will determine your goals.

Regardless of the need you set out to meet, understanding inputs, outputs, and outcomes is important because all learning communities must
increase their capacity to get *results* that matter to them.

I want to conclude this chapter where we started. The neighborhoods
and communities where our congregations exist cry out for the incarna-
tion and proclamation of the Good News of Jesus Christ. The endgame of
the Ridder Church Renewal is faithful and fruitful missional living, both
personally and corporately. There is an urgent need for congregational
leaders to dream really big dreams and then courageously learn how to
achieve those dreams.

In the opening chapter of this book, Brian Stone painted a powerful
picture of the dreams that God places in our hearts. I've worked with hundreds of congregations across North America in my lifetime, and every
time I get below the surface of their day-to-day routines, I've discovered
some dream that was waiting to be fulfilled. Often the dream is lost in the
day-to-day routine of the congregation's life, but it is still there. I believe
that understanding and mastering the practices of a learning community dramatically increases the likelihood of those dreams being fulfilled.
There is *no quick fix*, but a ton of possibility fueled by the hope that is illustrated in the stories of the pastors and congregations you've read about
in this book.

Along with Trisha and the pastors who have coauthored this book, I urge you to dream big again. Form a learning community in your congregation and take on the learning in the practice and reflection sections of this text. Begin your personal and corporate journey toward the epic life God designed you for. There are no quick fixes, but personal renewal can lead to congregational transformation. The journey is costly and liberating—and we urge you, if you have not already done so, to get started now. There's no time to waste.

References and Additional Resources

Collins, Jim. *Good to Great in the Social Sectors: A Monograph to Accompany* Good to Great. San Francisco: HarperCollins, 2005.

Herrington, Jim, Mike Bonem, and James H. Furr. *Leading Congregational Change: A Practical Guide for the Transformational Journey.* San Francisco: Jossey-Bass, 2000.

Senge, Peter M. *The Fifth Discipline: The Art & Practice of the Learning Organization.* New York: Doubleday, 1990.